THE "COUNTERFEIT" MAN

THE "COUNTERFEIT" MAN

The True Story of the
Boorn-Colvin Murder Case

GERALD W. McFARLAND

PANTHEON BOOKS   NEW YORK

Library of Congress Cataloging-in-Publication Data

McFarland, Gerald W., 1938–
The "counterfeit" man : the true story of the Boorn-Colvin murder case / Gerald McFarland.
p. cm.
Includes bibliographical references and index.
ISBN 0-394-58009-5
1. Murder—Vermont—Manchester—History—19th century—Case studies. I. Title. II. Title: Boorn-Colvin murder case.
HV6534.M28M34 1991
364.1'523'097438—dc20   90-52524

Grateful acknowledgment is made to the Vermont Historical Society for permission to reprint material from Judge Dudley Chase's papers, cataloged in the Vermont Historical Society as MSS 26-#49, Vermont-Biography-Boorn Trial.

To Dorothy, with love.

Contents

List of Illustrations

List of Illustrations

List of Illustrations

Preface

One question came up repeatedly when I told friends
about my work on the Boorn-Colvin case. How, they asked,
did I first learn about the case? The answer is simple, and
it serves to explain some of my thinking about the present
book. From a familiarity with the Lizzie Borden murder trial
I knew that a controversial crime could provide an excellent
starting point for studying a community and the social tensions that afflicted it at a given time. I therefore decided to
look for a murder case that interested me and, because of
health problems that made travel difficult, to restrict my
search to New England crimes. I took several anthologies
on New England murders out of the library and discovered
that cases that had been thoroughly explained lost a lot of
drama in the retelling, no matter how puzzling and engaging
the mystery had been prior to being solved. Then I came
across the Boorn-Colvin case in Richard Dempewolff's *Famous Old New England Murders*. I was immediately drawn
to the case because so many details had not been explained
satisfactorily, and I kept going on it because I felt that future

readers would share my enthusiasm for playing historical detective and trying to sort out these puzzles.

In the course of my work I benefited enormously from assistance provided by many individuals. I particularly want to acknowledge the help I received from the staffs of the American Antiquarian Society, the Manchester Town Clerk's Office, and the Vermont Historical Society, and from Mary H. Bort of the Manchester Historical Society, J. Kevin Graffagnino of the University of Vermont, the Reverend Steven P. Jewett of the First Baptist Church of Manchester Center, Helena Franklin and Wendy Wolf of Pantheon Books, Wilhelmina Van Ness of Leverett, Massachusetts, and my wife, Dorothy Tuck McFarland, also of Leverett.

THE "COUNTERFEIT" MAN

The
Feud

*When I returned from over the mountain, about five days
after the disappearance of my husband, I asked Lewis
where Russell was; he answered gone to hell.*

—SALLY COLVIN'S TRIAL TESTIMONY (1819)

ON the morning of May 10, 1812, Thomas
Johnson, a young farmer of Manchester, Vermont,
had business to conduct with a neighbor named
Mattison. Instead of walking to Mattison's place by the
longer route of the town road, Johnson took a shortcut directly across his neighbors' farm lots. The nearest of these,
immediately adjacent to Johnson's own farm, was a field
belonging to Barney Boorn. Johnson's path along the edge
of Boorn's field took him close to the line where the cleared

farm lots of the valley ended and the wooded lower slopes of the Green Mountains began.

Nearby, Boorn Brook* tumbled down the mountainside, ran through the East Manchester district where Johnson lived, and, less than a mile to the west, joined the major local stream, the Battenkill (or Batten Kill). Like Johnson, most of Manchester's fifteen hundred residents occupied farms scattered throughout the valley. However, just over two hundred townspeople lived in two small crossroads communities, both located on the Battenkill's west bank, the larger known today as Manchester Village and the other as Manchester Center. Farther west, rising on the town's western border, the imposing profile of Equinox Mountain loomed over the valley below.

After a quick visit with Mattison, Johnson headed back home along the route by which he had come. It was not yet ten o'clock when he crossed a corner of Barney Boorn's lot and started to clamber over a fence. Hearing loud voices nearby, he turned and saw four figures below in Boorn's field. He recognized all four of them. Two were Barney Boorn's younger sons, Stephen and Jesse. The third was their brother-in-law, Russell Colvin, who, Johnson noticed, was wearing a felt slouch hat; and the fourth was Colvin's ten-year-old son Lewis. The men were engaged in a familiar ritual of New England farm life, clearing stones from a field. They were also having a heated argument.

Johnson strained to hear what was being said, but could not quite make out the topic under dispute. He continued on to his house and went inside. Soon, however, curiosity got the better of him and he opened the door to listen again. The argument was still in progress. Johnson walked to a vantage point in the woods from which he could see the Boorn field without himself being seen. He watched and listened until it seemed to him that the fracas was dying down.

*Now spelled "Bourn."

4

Johnson was wrong. The quarrel had not ended. As Russell's son Lewis told a packed courtroom seven years later, the dispute continued through the rest of the morning. Stephen was venting a long-standing resentment at the fact that Russell, his wife (Stephen's sister Sally), and their children lived with and were supported by Stephen's parents. Stephen accused Russell of not earning his keep and contended that the cost of helping the Colvins was ruinous to Barney Boorn's finances. Russell countered by boasting that his work around the Boorn place was money in the bank for Stephen's father. With growing vehemence Stephen hurled insults at his brother-in-law, calling him a "damned fool" and a "little tory."[1] (For men whose parents had supported the patriot cause during the American Revolution, "Tory" remained a stinging epithet, even though the revolutionary war had ended twenty-nine years earlier.)

At last, after the men had been quarreling for hours, their verbal exchanges exploded into physical violence. According to Lewis Colvin's story, first told seven years later, his father hit Stephen with a stick the size of a rider's whip. Stephen then picked up a short section of a tree limb and struck Russell, who fell to the ground. As Russell tried to rise, Stephen knocked him down again. Lewis, frightened when he saw his father lying motionless, ran away.

Precisely what happened next is shrouded in mystery, the full truth impossible to extract from the available sources. These include a number of self-serving accounts supplied by the Boorns, who were there, and numerous reconstructions from circumstantial evidence put together by people who were not. All the versions, however, follow one of three general lines. In the first, Russell, mortally wounded by Stephen's blow (or finished off later by the Boorns), never left the field alive. In the second, Russell survived the clubbing and ran off, only to die of his wounds soon after. In the third, Russell, dazed and perhaps damaged in wits that had never been too strong to begin with, survived and wandered off, leaving Manchester behind.

The only thing that can be said for certain regarding Russell Colvin in the years between the fight in Barney Boorn's field (May 1812) and the trial of Stephen and Jesse Boorn for murder (October 1819) is that Colvin was not seen again in Manchester. During these years, however, public opinion concerning his absence went through several distinct phases. From 1812 to early 1819 most Manchester residents who knew of Colvin assumed that he had simply wandered off. Even neighbors who were aware of the feud between Russell and his brothers-in-law were very slow to suspect that foul play might have caused his disappearance. In 1819, however, public opinion swung radically over to the view that the Boorn brothers had killed Russell Colvin. Jury selection proved difficult because by the fall of 1819 few local men eligible for jury duty could be found who were still willing to presume the Boorns innocent.

The simplest explanation for this dramatic shift in public opinion, and the one adopted in traditional accounts of the Boorn case, is that new information came to light. Although there is considerable merit to this explanation, it is not entirely satisfactory because what often mattered most in the Boorn case was not the available evidence but how that evidence was perceived. From the earliest days after Russell's disappearance, several of his neighbors were in possession of information that by 1819 would be seen as clearly indicating Stephen and Jesse's guilt. Yet it was not until 1816, at the earliest, that the brothers were suspected of murder. To understand why so many neighbors believed the Boorns innocent for so long, and why seven years passed before town authorities launched an investigation of Colvin's disappearance, it is, of course, important to learn what facts were known, when, and by whom. However, it is equally important to ascertain how these facts were interpreted, and why they were interpreted as they were. What, in other words, was it about Russell Colvin, the Boorns, and the town of Manchester that shaped the public's response in such a way that an official inquiry into Colvin's disappearance was delayed until 1819?

Colvin's absence would undoubtedly have caused more of a stir if the story that he had wandered off had not been so perfectly consistent with the behavior Manchester residents had come to expect of him. A man then in his early thirties, Colvin had grown up in Manchester, to which he had been brought by his parents around 1790 when he was about twelve years old. Contemporaries described him variously as "a weak man in mind" and "very simple and ignorant," and it was also said that he was "at times insane" or "deranged." Reportedly, he did well enough at simple manual labor but was not capable of effectively managing a farm and family finances. On at least one occasion between 1801 and 1810—it is not clear just when—he ran afoul of the law. Town authorities jailed him for a night or two because he had threatened to burn down a house. But the thing that most stuck in people's minds as an example of odd behavior was his habit of seemingly aimless wandering. He not only roamed around Manchester—as a long-time resident put it, he "was running round town often"—but he sometimes left Manchester altogether for varying periods of time, a day or two, a week, even a month, and on one occasion for nearly nine months. Such behavior made it easy for neighbors to dismiss Colvin's absence in 1812 as just another example of his peculiar wanderlust. No one except his sister, Clarissa Ferguson, the only one of his four brothers and sisters who still lived in Manchester, seems to have become worried. He had never, she said, gone off before without advance notice nor failed to stay in touch while away.[2]

Russell Colvin was also a marginal man whose low economic and social standing increased the likelihood that he would be written off by Manchester residents. His parents, Richard and Rosanna Colvin, had owned a small farm in town, but had never managed to get ahead. Moreover, Richard Colvin had been known for his own wandering ways, and memories of the elder Colvin may have reinforced a "like father, like son" dismissal of Russell's disappearance in 1812. Approximately fourteen years earlier, in 1798 or 1799, the father had abandoned his family and gone off to Rhode Island, leaving his wife and the town officials uncertain whether he was dead or alive. The matter was of some legal consequence. Russell had just come of age, having achieved freeman or voting status in 1799. A year or two later, he married Barney Boorn's daughter Sally. In his father's absence, Russell became responsible for running the Colvin farm. The situation worried town authorities, since they were obligated to protect the rights of widows, and if Rosanna Colvin had indeed become one, they were duty-bound to make sure that her son's mental limitations did not result in a mismanagement of the family's farm that would cause Rosanna to become a ward of the town. Not trusting Russell's ability to run the farm, the town took control of the Colvin place in late 1801 or early 1802. Russell was not only humiliated but was deprived of his patrimony, and subsequently was unable to provide adequately for his young wife and their rapidly growing brood of little Colvins. By 1812 he, Sally, and their six children had been forced to move in with Sally's parents, the very situation that gave rise to the animosity of Sally's brothers, Stephen and Jesse, toward the Colvins.

Once Russell's in-laws and neighbors had pigeonholed him as a weak-minded, no-count man from a no-count family, they interpreted everything he did accordingly. Traditional histories of the Boorn mystery have done little more than echo this bias. Yet even such one-sided sources provide facts upon which to construct an alternative description of Russell's life, one in which his behavior need not be simply dismissed as "odd" or "deranged" but can be understood as an outgrowth of the adverse circumstances he faced.

The Feud

In order to tell the other side of the Russell Colvin story, it helps to divide his life into pre-1802 and post-1802 phases. In the period before 1802, he seemed to be making modest headway in the face of considerable odds. Here was a man of limited means from a family that, measured by the assessed value of its property, ranked in the bottom quarter of Manchester households. The father's desertion of the family suggests that Russell did not have a very happy or stable home as a child, and such conditions were scarcely conducive to the development of self-esteem, particularly in a boy who was told all along that he was weak-minded. Nevertheless, despite the negative factors in his background, Russell managed, in the three years from 1799 to 1801, to accomplish a number of things for which he could justifiably take pride. He came of age and joined the militia. He was accepted by the town as a freeman with a vote in town affairs. He married a young woman from one of the town's middling prosperous pioneer families. Sally was either seventeen or eighteen and very likely pregnant, a not uncommon situation in an era when fully one-third of rural New England brides were pregnant on their wedding day. The Colvins' first child, a son they named Lewis (Sally's mother's maiden name), was born in January 1802. Moreover, in the 1799–1801 period, when Russell became responsible for running his parents' farm, he very likely assumed that it would pass to him in whole or in part on his mother's death. For a few years prior to 1802, therefore, Russell's worldly prospects seemed to be growing brighter.

An unhappier phase of Russell's life began in 1802. It was at about that date that town authorities intervened, taking management of the Colvin farm out of Russell's hands. Only one source on the Boorn mystery, a pamphlet published in 1820, refers to the devastating impact this event had on Colvin, and even this source interprets Colvin's reaction as a further example of his supposed mental instability. "Finding the little patrimony he had by his father, taken from him by the town, and his expenses increasing beyond his ability to meet, he became quite frantic, and became partially deranged."[3] But what was perceived here as "deranged" behavior may well have been an expression of unendurable anger and frustration at the town's treatment of him. This anger, dampened with time but still smouldering, may have flared up again in the threat he made to burn down a house and, much later, in his belligerent response to Stephen Boorn's taunt that he was a fool, and worthless to boot.

Even Russell's habit of wandering, which contemporaries saw at best as peculiar and at worst as a sign of derangement, may have been prompted by anxiety over his personal and financial troubles. His oft-cited eight- or nine-month trip to Rhode Island involved an attempt to claim his patrimony and to reestablish himself on a firm financial footing, for he made the trip in hope of either finding his father or gaining certain knowledge of his death. Either result, he believed, would enable him to obtain a deed to the Colvin farm in Manchester. Russell's departures were never unannounced— he always let someone know that he was leaving—and were not totally whimsical or irrational. His going off usually occurred after his wife had already left town on one of the unaccompanied trips or visits that she was in the habit of making—trips that in their freedom and frequency were unusual for a married woman of her time. The absence of a wife at home, or impotent anger at her free and easy behavior, might well have contributed to restlessness and dissatisfaction on his part. However, whatever his feelings toward Sally, his wanderings did not represent a total rejection of family, since he often took his favorite son along, carrying little Rufus on his shoulders.

To sum up: had Colvin's neighbors and Manchester town officials thought of Colvin as a man who generally had good reasons for whatever he did, they might well have taken his disappearance more seriously in 1812. However, they did not take it seriously. Moreover, Sally Colvin could have forced town authorities into action had she registered an official complaint about her husband's absence, but she did not. The question remains, therefore, why Sally did not ask that something be done.

The most succinct judgment of Sally comes from her brother Stephen, who said that she was "one of the devil's unaccountables." Certainly there were many times when she seemed to do just as she pleased without regard for what her family and neighbors thought, but it might well be a mistake to ascribe her behavior to simple willfulness. More likely it was a product of an ongoing struggle to hold her own under sometimes hostile circumstances. Born in Manchester in 1783, she found herself in a world in which it was imperative to attach herself to a man—father, brother, or husband—for protection. When she married Russell Colvin in 1800 or 1801, she probably felt that she had solved the problem of who would support her. But Russell soon proved to be a poor provider, and Sally the survivor quickly turned to her parents for help. Meanwhile she developed her own independent network of friendships and sustained these through frequent out-of-town trips. Her destinations varied; she often went "over the mountain," a local phrase for going east across the Green Mountains toward the Connecticut River valley; on another occasion she was said to be visiting friends in Bennington, a town twenty-four miles south of Manchester; at least once she reportedly went visiting out of state, probably in New York. Two illegitimate daughters that she bore after Russell disappeared were in all likelihood products of out-of-town liaisons. Her unsuccessful attempt to extract support from the father of one of these children is another example of her readiness to apply for help wherever it might be obtained.[4]

A well-developed instinct for self-preservation may also explain Sally's failure to register an official complaint regarding Russell's absence. If her testimony at her brothers' trial in 1819 may be taken at face value, her efforts to ascertain her husband's whereabouts were, at best, feeble. She reported that she had been out of town when Russell was first missed. About five days after he disappeared she returned to Manchester, and at that time she said, "I asked Lewis where Russell was; he answered gone to hell." Sally seems not to have pressed Lewis for more details. Possibly she did not much care, given her husband's inadequacy as a provider. On the other hand, if she suspected that her brothers might be responsible for Russell's disappearance, she probably would not have wanted to trigger an investigation that might expose their guilt. Even more to the point is the question of what her parents knew and what Sally knew they knew. In her trial testimony she went out of her way to say, "I heard nothing at my father's [of] what had become of my husband." By 1819, when Sally made this statement, her parents had come under suspicion because they had defended their sons and had offered alibis for them, and her testimony may have been intended to exonerate the elder Boorns. Similarly, in 1812, she would have been reluctant to stir up trouble that might involve her parents, on whom she and her children were dependent.[5]

Stephen and Jesse Boorn had even less cause to encourage questions regarding Russell Colvin's whereabouts. If foul play had taken place, the Boorn boys were the most likely suspects. Fortunately for them, community perceptions of the Boorn family in general encouraged the belief that Stephen and Jesse were innocent of any serious crime. The Boorns' deep roots and generally respected position in the community led most of their neighbors to assume that the family was not likely to produce murderers.

Stephen and Jesse's grandparents, Nathaniel and Freelove Boorn, emigrated to Manchester from Swansea, in southeastern Massachusetts, before the American Revolution. Nathaniel shared in the second (1766) and third (1771) divisions of town land and almost certainly occupied his property by 1771, if not earlier. The town's first settlers had arrived only a few years before, in 1764 and 1765, and Nathaniel soon took his place in their ranks as a solid contributor to the settlement's early history. He supported the patriot cause as a militiaman during the Revolution and served four consecutive terms (1778–81) on the town's Board of Selectmen. Although himself not one of pioneer Manchester's major power brokers, he fought and worked side by side with the men who were: Martin Powel, Gideon Ormsby, Timothy Mead, Christopher Rogers, and Jeremiah Whelpley. When the time came to organize religious societies in Manchester, Nathaniel again stood ready to help. His and Freelove's names appear as signers of the original Baptist church covenant in 1781. In the records of the congregation's early and often embattled years, Nathaniel's name appears on page after page. He was clearly a mainstay of

FOUR GENERATIONS OF MANCHESTER BOORNS

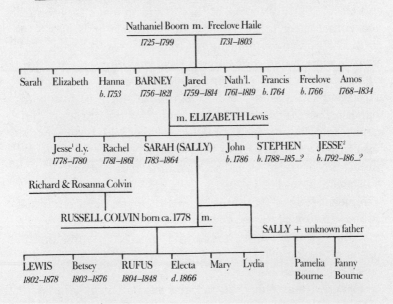

Nathaniel Boorn m. Freelove Haile
1725–1799   *1731–1803*

Sarah   Elizabeth   Hanna   BARNEY   Jared   Nath'l.   Francis   Freelove   Amos
                    b. 1753   *1756–1821*   *1759–1814*   *1761–1819*   *b. 1764*   *b. 1766*   *1768–1834*

m. ELIZABETH Lewis

Jesse¹ d.y.   Rachel   SARAH (SALLY)   John   STEPHEN   JESSE²
1778–1780   *1781–1861*   *1783–1864*   *b. 1786*   *b. 1788–185_?*   *b. 1792–186_?*

Richard & Rosanna Colvin

RUSSELL COLVIN born ca. 1778   m.

SALLY + unknown father

LEWIS   Betsey   RUFUS   Electa   Mary   Lydia   Pamelia   Fanny
1802–1878   *1803–1876*   *1804–1848*   *d. 1866*   Bourne   Bourne

the fledgling organization, serving on its building committee, various visiting committees, and the like.

Nathaniel was also a town proprietor, which put him in
an advantageous financial position. Although the specific
form of the proprietary system varied over time and from
place to place in colonial New England, in general it was a
system under which a township's original purchasers or
grantees obtained so-called proprietary rights from the tribe
or colony that held title to the land. Holders of proprietary
rights gained control over the distribution of town land and
also over such important decisions as the location of town
lots, church lots, burying grounds, and roads. The usual practice was for proprietors to distribute only some town lands
to themselves initially, with large sections of land held back
for subsequent divisions that the proprietors voted as
needed. In Manchester the first division (1764) was of one
hundred acres to each proprietor, and the second (1766) and
third (1771) were for fifty acres per proprietor. Most of the
best agricultural land was distributed in this way by the
end of 1771, but divisions of less desirable back lots continued periodically until the seventh and last in 1803. Non-
proprietors who wanted land in town could either buy
already distributed land (a purchase that carried with it no
right to participate in subsequent divisions) or negotiate
with the proprietors to obtain rights to share in future divisions. The lands that proprietors received through divisions could be retained by themselves, sold to others, or
handed over to one's heirs. The latter point was especially
important to pioneers such as Nathaniel and Freelove Boorn,
who had a large brood—nine children—to provide for.

At least four of Nathaniel and Freelove's sons remained
in Manchester the rest of their lives. Nathaniel Jr., whose
occupation was given as "mechanic," probably made his living as a blacksmith, the trade his oldest son also entered.
Jared and Amos both stuck mainly to farming, although
Amos appears on the 1820 tax list as the owner of a small

mill or distillery. Barney started out as a farmer, but in his mature years he supplemented his income as a butcher. Contemporaries described the Boorns of this generation as "persons of respectability" who lived in "comfortable circumstances."[6]

Nathaniel Boorn's sons did not equal their father's accomplishments. An examination of the town tax lists for 1803, 1811, and 1820 indicates that Nathaniel's sons were all in the middle range of taxpayers. Although that status was, broadly speaking, much the same as their father's, three of Nathaniel's four sons slipped slightly in relative rank between 1803 and 1820. The younger Boorns also played a somewhat smaller role than their parents in religious affairs. In early nineteenth-century Vermont a person's relationship to local religious institutions was often defined by membership in one of two organizations known respectively as the "church" and the "society." Members of the church, who were relatively few in number, were fully converted and confessed Christians, and it was this group that controlled the internal religious affairs of local congregations. The society was composed of a much larger group of people who supported the church financially, but were not full communicants and did not participate in the church's internal governance. In states where some churches were tax-supported institutions, all town residents were nominally members of the society, but in Vermont after 1777 support for the local society was essentially voluntary. It is instructive that most of the younger Boorns, like their parents, supported the Baptist Church at Manchester through its society, but unlike Nathaniel and Freelove, none of the sons except for Jared became members, and as a result the Boorn family's influence in internal church matters gradually diminished. Similarly, none of the four sons matched their father's political achievements. Nathaniel Jr. came closest, serving one term (1807) as a selectman. Amos and Jared held minor posts only—hayward and surveyor—and then on only a few occasions. Barney, so far as can be determined, was never chosen for a town-wide office.

Barney (whose name was also spelled Barna, Barnard, Barned, and Barnet) was Nathaniel and Freelove's oldest son. Born in Massachusetts in 1756, he came to Vermont with his parents, and married Elizabeth Lewis in the late 1770s. Elizabeth became a member of the Baptist Church at Manchester Center. Barney, meanwhile, supported the work of the congregation through the Baptist Society. Five of Barney and Elizabeth's children surived to maturity: Rachel (b. 1781), Sarah/Sally (b. 1783), John (b. 1786), Stephen (b. 1788), and Jesse (b. 1792). Most histories of the Boorn-Colvin case suggest that the children were not as respectable as their parents, and that judgment seems generally true, though there is some evidence to the contrary. For example, in 1788 the children's mother, Elizabeth Lewis Boorn, came under scrutiny by her Baptist coreligionists and had to defend herself against charges of unspecified moral lapses. By contrast, her eldest daughter, Rachel, married into the Richardson family, a puritanical Congregationalist

Barney and Elizabeth Boorn's house.

16

clan whose reputation for moral starchiness was virtually unrivaled during Manchester's sometimes wild and woolly pioneer period. Similarly, Barney and Elizabeth's eldest son, John, a farmer, was a dutiful fellow who served faithfully in a variety of minor town offices and whose private life was untainted by scandal.

Then there were the other Boorn children: Sally, Stephen, and Jesse. Sally, as noted earlier, was tough, spirited, and disrespectful of convention, traits that led many neighbors to think poorly of her. Stephen and Jesse's reputations, like their sister's, lay under a shadow, even before their fight with Russell Colvin. According to one contemporary who knew them, the younger Boorn boys were "rather wild and reckless." Jesse, the youngest, seems often to have followed Stephen's lead. Detailed examples of their alleged bad conduct are largely lacking in early accounts, but threatening and quarrelsome behavior and "imprudent and profane language" were among the specific misdeeds ascribed to them. One source offered more information about Stephen's temperament, describing him as "malicious, passionate, and when angry, blind to consequences." This characterization seems to fit quite accurately Stephen's behavior during his feud with Russell Colvin. However, in fairness to Stephen and Jesse, it should be noted that their feud with Russell had other origins besides pure malice. In early 1812 Stephen was twenty-three and Jesse nineteen. Neither man yet had land of his own. Both had to hire out as laborers and live in rented quarters. Finding themselves at the bottom of local society, with little immediate prospect of significant improvement, they were threatened by the fact that Sally and Russell Colvin seemed to have the inside track in the competition for their parents' limited resources.[7]

Despite their reputations, Stephen and Jesse were shielded from close public scrutiny of their possible responsibility for Russell's disappearance by at least three factors besides the relative respectability of their family. First, as

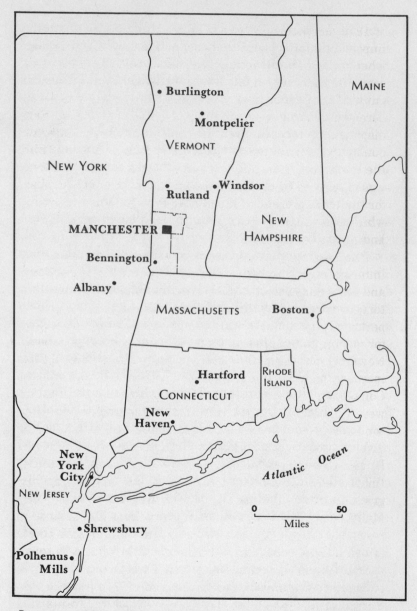

Location of Manchester and other towns and cities that figure in the Boorn-Colvin case.

of 1812, neighborhood gossips were still not privy to many important details about the feud, and only the Boorns knew whether Russell had actually been killed. Second, as we have seen, the then known facts were explained away as consistent with the participants' idiosyncrasies—Colvin was a wanderer, the Boorns were roughnecks—and the fact that Sally displayed no concern about her husband's absence also undoubtedly contributed to the general lack of alarm. Third, the community's casual acceptance of the Boorns' behavior was influenced by the social conditions of the time and place, for the 1810s were not far removed from a pioneer period in which bad language and brawling had been commonplace and even tolerated in town.

Prior to 1820, social disorder in Manchester was often immediately connected to a larger phenomenon, the political and economic turmoil that had characterized Vermont history during the first three decades (1761–91) of the pioneer period. Desire for land was the primary motive of settlers for moving to the area, but a jurisdictional dispute between New York and New Hampshire initially made all land titles insecure. New York insisted that its eastern border was the Connecticut River, while New Hampshire claimed that its western border extended to within twenty miles of the Hudson River. New Hampshire began to sell land grants in the disputed territory as early as 1749. However, in 1764 the British Crown ruled in favor of New York, and that colony threatened to invalidate the titles of the New Hampshire grantees if they did not pay substantial fees to New York. Many owners of the New Hampshire land titles chose to resist New York control. After appeals to colonial courts failed to bring relief, New Hampshire title holders in towns such as Manchester that were west of the Green Mountains took up arms to protect their claims. In 1771, a posse of New York sheriffs crossed into the New Hampshire Grants area only to be repulsed by Ethan Allen and his Green Mountain Boys, a band of armed settlers, who sent the New Yorkers on their way with a warning not to come back. Such incidents kept tensions high in the new settlements during the years before the outbreak of the American Revolution.

The tendency of Green Mountain pioneers to resort to force of arms when the force of law did not settle matters to their satisfaction persisted into the later 1770s. News of Lexington and Concord in April 1775 sent war parties of settlers on a raid that succeeded in capturing British outposts at Ticonderoga and Crown Point. Meanwhile, in the absence of any other established civil authority, settlers organized citizens' associations, the so-called Committees of Safety, to manage local affairs, and in July 1777 a convention at Windsor drew up a constitution for the new state of Vermont. Since the Continental Congress did not recognize the fledgling state's existence, in effect Vermont was now an independent republic. However, its independence was soon threatened by a large British army under General John Burgoyne's command that advanced southward through the Champlain Valley. Again Vermonters took up arms, sharing in important victories at Bennington (August 16, 1777) and Saratoga, where Burgoyne surrendered in October.

Although the threat of direct military attack abated after Saratoga, civil peace did not come to the Green Mountain settlements. Vermont's independent political status, under which it was neither part of the British empire nor a state with membership in the American Continental Congress, made the young republic's political prospects exceedingly uncertain. Moreover, Vermont had incurred significant war costs, and the confiscation of Tory property, the expedient chosen to pay for these debts, intensified rather than reduced civil turmoil. In many localities, including Manchester, some of the town's largest landowners were stripped of their property, and those who did not yield peacefully were forced to submit.

Decades of social and political disruption contributed to producing a Vermont character that was at once liberal and libertine. The 1777 state constitution was notable for its enlightened prohibition of slavery, protection of freedoms of religion, speech, and the press, and grant of suffrage to all adult males. However, Vermonters also gained a reputation for being rough, undisciplined, contentious, and irreligious—and for being as free with their fists as they were fervent about their freedoms.

Conservative men who came from settled parts of southern New England were shocked by the irreligion, hedonism, drunkenness, and violence they observed among Vermonters. Vermont towns west of the Green Mountains became known as refuges for religious liberals: freethinkers, deists, and universalists. The Reverend Nathan Perkins of West Hartford, Connecticut, concluded after a 1789 visit that no more than half the inhabitants of Vermont supported public worship. "The rest," he lamented, "would have no Sabbath, no minister, no religion, no heaven, no hell, no morality." Widespread indifference to religion and the relative weakness of most Vermont churches produced widespread disregard for an orderly sabbath. As one evangelist complained:

> The sabbath, instead of being observed as a day of holy rest, was improved as a reason of relaxation from ordinary business, only for the purpose of amusement, convivial entertainments, public houses, or shops, sleigh-riding, trading, or gambling.

A close connection between irreligion, disregard for the sabbath, and heavy drinking was also made by the Reverend Timothy Dwight, another pious traveler who spent one Saturday night in 1798 in a town near Manchester. Much to his disgust, he observed that the local practice of "tavern-haunting" commenced on Saturday evening, continued until "near two o'clock in the morning," and resumed "early the next morning [when] these wretches assembled again, for their Sunday morning dram." Ever the moralist, Dwight said nothing about the economic reasons for the presence of one or more distilleries in many small Vermont towns. The primitive transportation system of the pioneer period encouraged the practice of converting hard-to-ship bulk grains into distilled liquids, mainly grain whiskey, that could readily be carried to distant markets. Nevertheless, a lot of Vermont distillery production went down the throats of the natives. Taverns encouraged consumption by offering a wide array of mixed drinks, with eggnog, rum flip, toddy, and assorted punches among the favorite concoctions. Many Vermonters overindulged in distilled spirits, and drunkenness was a major cause of the disorderly conduct found among Vermont pioneers. As John Clark, a Connecticut native who migrated to Clarendon, Vermont, wrote in his diary in the mid-1780s, the rule rather than the exception among his neighbors seemed to be "profanity, debauchery, drunkenness, quarreling, by words and blows, and parting with broken heads and bloody noses."[8]

The residents of Manchester, one of the oldest settlements west of the Green Mountains, were every bit as disorderly as Vermont pioneers elsewhere. When Reverend Perkins passed through town on his 1789 tour, he described Manchester as follows: "a half shire town hemmed in by lofty mountains. A number of houses in the center, a small meeting house, half Baptist, *a loose Town*." A visitor in the 1790s, John A. Graham, who did not himself criticize the morals of Manchester's citizens, nevertheless noticed some things about their holiday activities—"they run horses, go on shooting parties, and play at bowls"—that would not have passed muster with a pious observer like Reverend Perkins.[9]

Horse racing, associated as it was with drinking, gambling, and general pleasure-seeking, would doubtless have struck the good reverend as particularly noxious. Horse racing and horse breeding were extremely popular in Vermont, which during the early national period was said to be rivaled in those activities only by Kentucky. Vermont races usually

*A two-horse race,
about 1800.*

took the form of two-horse matches run over a quarter-mile
course on town roads, preferably with both the start and the
finish line near taverns. A route of this sort in Manchester
followed the old Bennington Road north from Eliakim Weller's tavern to one of the taverns, Allis's or Munson's, near
the village center. Plenty of bragging, drinking, and betting
preceded the contest's start, with onlookers weighing the
relative merits, say, of Christopher Roberts's bay champion
and Timothy Mead's black challenger. Then, at the drop of
a hat, the two horses and their riders would charge off, urged
on by shouts from all sides. At the finish line the boisterous
atmosphere would not die down until long after the race was
over. There were bets to collect, toasts to drink, and, if tempers got out of hand, as they often did, fights to be fought.
It was enough to leave a man of Reverend Perkins's persuasion red-faced with indignation.

The best account of rowdy times in early Manchester came
from the pen of the Boorn brothers' contemporary, John S.
Pettibone, a lawyer, judge, and longtime resident of the
town. Although a few Manchesterites from the 1860s onward
were aware of the manuscript version of his memoirs, a
project he never completed, Pettibone's recollections were

not available to a general readership until the Vermont Historical Society published them in 1930. Born in Manchester in 1786, Pettibone was able to speak from firsthand knowledge of the customs and events of his childhood years. He was convinced that the disorderly conduct he observed as a boy in the 1790s had had its origins in the Revolution, which, he wrote, had "a bad influence on the minds of the people," since "the leading men in Town had formed habits of drinking" and "the habit of assembling at taverns," practices that endured long after the war itself ended. Since Manchester was located on both the main north-south and a major east-west stagecoach line, there were many taverns to choose from, at least eight in all, four of them in Manchester Village, a small community populated by fewer than two hundred souls. Prior to the mid-1790s, none of the local tavern keepers felt it his duty to maintain "an orderly house where no drunkenness or gambling was allowed," and unregulated drinking led to a great deal of intoxication. On holidays there were additional reasons for proposing and downing toast after toast. For example, on August 16, 1798, the town celebrated the anniversary of the Battle of Bennington with a brief ceremony at the court house, after which everyone adjourned to Pierce's Tavern for refreshments. Pettibone, then a boy of twelve, was an interested observer. Many years later he shared his recollections of the event with Loveland Munson, a mid-nineteenth-century historian of the town. Of this exchange, Munson, a very proper Victorian, would say only that he gathered that "rather a lively and boisterous time" was had by all. Pettibone's own description of Manchester Village's moral climate in the 1790s was much pithier. It was, he wrote, "an immoral place. Drinking, gambling, and whoring were common."[10]

In a community where disorderly conduct had such a long history, the feuding between the Boorn brothers and Russell Colvin might go almost without notice. After all, the Boorn boys and many of their neighbors were descendants of pi-

A rural tavern interior.

oneers who had temperaments suited to surviving in a very
unstable and dangerous place. As one historian said of the
first generation of Vermonters, "only adventurous, reckless
people are likely to migrate into an area where both the title
to the land and the authority of the government are being
debated by armed men."[11] The fact that Stephen and Jesse
Boorn's grandparents, father, and uncles had joined this migration does not prove that the older Boorns personally subscribed to the permissive moral code of pioneer times or that
they were themselves "reckless" men. But the word "reckless" was certainly applied to Stephen and Jesse, who, in
common with many inhabitants of turn-of-the-nineteenth-
century Manchester, still displayed an attachment to the
rough-and-tumble ways of an earlier era.

Times were changing, however, and any general movement toward a less permissive atmosphere was apt to affect
people's attitudes toward the Boorn brothers. According to
John S. Pettibone, the first significant challenge to the
easygoing habits of the pioneer period came from "a new

set of merchants and professional men," many of them college educated, who began to arrive in town in the late 1790s. Over the next several decades, these young respectables brought about, in Pettibone's words, "a great moral change" in Manchester. The new men included several tavern owners who, unlike their predecessors, refused to allow customers to gamble or drink to excess on the premises. The young newcomers also supported organized religion, and even if they did not join a church, they supported one financially, usually the Congregational Church in Manchester Village, and approved of the evangelical revivals that swept Manchester in the late 1810s. Also, as the political leaders of the pioneer era—Martin Powel, Gideon Ormsby, and Timothy Mead—died off early in the new century, Pettibone's young respectables took control of town affairs.[12]

David Claypool Johnston's 1819 watercolor, "A Militia Muster."

The triumph of the new order over the old did not come immediately, however. At first, the number of young respectables in town was quite small. Moreover, some of the institutions that ought to have been vehicles for moral change did not immediately serve that end. The town's churches, for example, were logical allies in opposing moral laxity, but for many years their actual impact was slight. The problem was that only a tiny minority of townspeople were members of the three churches (Baptist, Congregational, and Episcopal) that were organized locally. As a result, through most of the 1790s, no local congregation was able to support a permanent minister. Another local institution, the militia, was a bastion of the old frontier morality, and membership in its ranks was generally regarded as a license for misbehavior. As one former Manchester resident complained, the oldtime militiaman knew only three commands: "Mount! Drink! Fall Off!"[13]

The staying power of older customs was further illustrated by the fact that criminals were still subjected to traditional punishments—flogging, mutilation, and branding—well into the first decade of the nineteenth century. Not a sight for the fainthearted, flogging consisted of a specified number of lashes delivered to the criminal's bare back with a whip made of knotted cords. The last public flogging in Manchester took place in 1806 or 1807. And only a few years earlier, in 1803, a crowd had gathered in front of the Allis Tavern to watch as another form of frontier justice, mutilation and branding, was meted out to a convicted horse thief. According to one account:

> The victim was placed standing on the horse-block, and his head tied to the sign-post. Then the sheriff cut off the lower portion of his ears, and threw the pieces under his feet. Meanwhile an assistant had been leaning over a kettle of coals, blowing its contents into life, and heating the iron brand. This the sheriff now took, and branded the culprit on the forehead.[14]

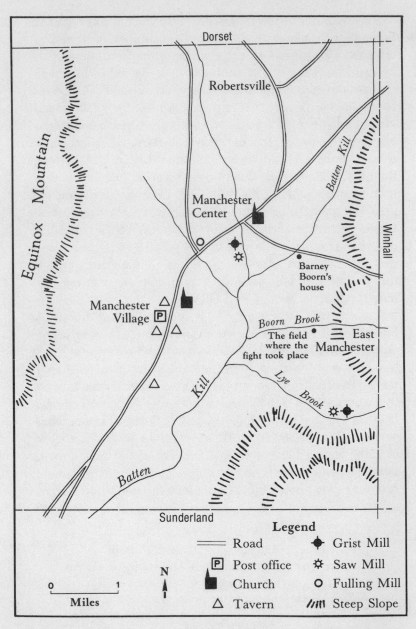

Manchester, Vermont, in 1812.

The goal may have been law and order, but the method was brute retribution, an old-fashioned approach that the new elite felt had no place in the criminal justice system of the 1800s.

Another circumstance that retarded the new elite's rise to power was the lack of overall cohesiveness in the town's residential pattern. To speak of Manchester prior to 1820 as one unified entity is rather misleading. There was, of course, a six-mile-square township of that name, but its fifteen hundred residents were dispersed into many scattered communities, each somewhat isolated from the other.

Of Manchester's various subdivisions, the most populous was Manchester Village, a cluster of thirty to forty stores, taverns, and residences that was located near the town's geographic center. Manchester Village was also the site of many of the town's most important public buildings: the aforementioned taverns, the court house, the post office, the jail, and the Congregational meeting house. In addition, Manchester Village was home to most of the town's new elite and the place where their moral revolution first took hold. Across the Battenkill to the east was a district known as East Manchester, and most of the Boorns lived there, along the banks of Boorn Brook. However, Barney Boorn's house was about half a mile north of Boorn Brook on the road to Manchester Center, a location that facilitated his butchering business.* Manchester Center itself was a small settlement consisting of perhaps twenty buildings. Although these included the Baptist meeting house, a store, a distillery, and three mills, one knowledgeable observer of town life asserted that as late as 1812 Manchester Center had so few residents that "it could scarcely be called a

---

*After the railroad's arrival in the 1850s, the part of town where Barney Boorn's house was located became known as Manchester Depot. Today's Manchester Center was called Factory Point by the United States Post Office from 1828 to 1886, and "Factory Point" was commonly used locally long after the Post Office officially abandoned the name.

village."[15] Farther north on the road to Dorset was an even smaller community known as Robertsville. Like other locales in the town's outlying districts where a handful of houses clustered in close proximity—Rootville, Hicksville, Barnumville—Robertsville was named after the chief family residing in the vicinity. Although none of these settlements was more than four and a half miles from Manchester Village, each neighborhood had its own independent character in such important aspects of life as the flow of gossip, the enforcement of social values, and the influence of institutions.

As the crow flies, it is only a mile and a half from Barney Boorn's field in East Manchester to Manchester Village, but the social gulf and lack of communication between the two communities made them worlds apart. A simple but telling illustration of East Manchester's remoteness from Manchester Village can be derived from a review of the witnesses

Two views of Manchester, Vermont, from the part of town in which Barney Boorn's house was located.

who testified at the trial of Stephen and Jesse Boorn in 1819. Twelve can be clearly identified as residents of East Manchester. Ten others are known to have lived in Manchester Village. Testimony by the East Manchester residents revealed an intimate knowledge of the Boorns and their feud with Russell Colvin. By contrast, no witness from Manchester Village had been party to the rumors about the Boorns that had kept East Manchester gossips buzzing for the better part of seven years.

That the two groups of witnesses were so insulated from each other will seem less surprising when two other group characteristics are brought to light. First, the East Manchester and Manchester Village groups had different religious affiliations. The East Manchester witnesses were associated with the Baptist Church at Manchester Center, while the Manchester Village witnesses were, with one notable exception, affiliated with the Congregational Church. Second, the two groups of witnesses were from opposite ends of the economic ladder. All but one of the East Manchester

residents were from the bottom half of the town's tax-payers as measured by the assessed value of their real and personal property, and six of ten for whom extensive details are available fell into the bottom third. The reverse was true of the Manchester Village witnesses. All were members of the new elite and most were quite wealthy, six of ten ranking in the top twelve percent of the town's taxpayers.

Although for a time the several factors described above shielded Stephen and Jesse Boorn from suspicion that they were responsible for Russell's absence, the efficacy of those factors gradually eroded between May 1812 and March 1819. Eventually, explanations of Russell's absence that had at first seemed adequate came to seem less persuasive.

Initially, the Boorn brothers had two basic ready answers when asked about Russell. Stephen's typical reply, "Russell ran away," was sufficient to satisfy most questioners. Jesse, on the other hand, told an elderly acquaintance in 1813 that Russell was "an enlisted soldier in the service."[16] This also seemed plausible, the War of 1812 having begun in June 1812, about the time Russell's disappearance would have been first noticed. Never mind that the war with Britain was not particularly popular in Vermont, largely because its ostensible cause, a defense of American maritime rights, had little connection, except in a negative way, with the economic interests of inland towns like Manchester. The prewar and wartime trade restrictions imposed by the Jefferson and Madison administrations in retaliation against infringements of American rights had very harmful effects in northern Vermont counties that had extensive trade with Canada. The resultant depression spread to other parts of Vermont and caused the near bankruptcy of at least one merchant in Manchester, James Whelpley, who ran a small store where the Boorns sometimes traded and who was later to figure prominently in the Boorn mystery. Still, a combination of partisan devotion to Jeffersonian Republicanism and nationalistic fervor for defending the young republic inspired thirty-eight Manchester men—Whelpley among them—to volunteer for military service during the war. If Russell Colvin, a man who had failed at everything else, had gone off to try his luck at being a soldier, no one would have been surprised.

The explanations that Stephen and Jesse initially offered neighbors for Russell's absence might satisfy inquisitive outsiders, but what was to be done about Lewis, Russell's ten-year-old son? Surely he needed special handling. He had been picking up stones with his father and uncles while the quarrel was in progress, and he had seen his father and Stephen exchange blows. After his father was clubbed to the ground, the boy ran off to his grandparents' house, about two-thirds of a mile away, where he was living at the time. Lewis saw his Uncle John, Stephen and Jesse's brother, working with a team in the yard, but did not mention the fight to him. He went inside and told his grandmother, Elizabeth Boorn. She then sent the boy to town on an errand from which he did not return until evening. Stephen and Jesse were waiting for him when he got back.

Just what transpired that evening between Lewis and his uncles is difficult to reconstruct, since the available sources contain apparent contradictions. Seven years later Lewis at first told court officers, "I have never heard Stephen say anything about what became of Russell, nor has Jesse said any thing about it." Of his encounter with his uncles at the Boorn house later on the day of the quarrel, Lewis stated that he "heard nothing from them about Russell's absence," adding that it was a year before he heard his father's name mentioned by either uncle. Yet something was almost certainly said about Russell's absence that first day or soon thereafter. Stephen himself told people that on the day Russell disappeared, Lewis had asked his uncles where Russell was and they had answered, "one of them, that he had gone to hell, and the other that they had put him where potatoes would not freeze." Strengthening the case for this version's authenticity is Sally Colvin's statement that when she returned to town about five days after Russell was first missed, she asked Lewis where his father was, and the boy replied, "gone to hell." Here Lewis is described as repeating verbatim words that his uncle said he had used to him five days earlier. Lewis's ready acceptance of this dismissive way of speaking about his father is perhaps explained in part by the boy's resentment of Russell for his favoritism toward a younger son, Rufus. However, Lewis had another reason for parroting his uncle's words: fear. By the time of the exchange with his mother, the boy was frightened out of his wits. According to Lewis's later testimony, a day or two after the fight Stephen had stopped by his parents' house, taken Lewis aside, and threatened him, saying that, in Lewis's words, "he would kill me if I told of his striking Russell." Lewis promised not to tell anyone.[17]

Lewis was not the only individual who could connect the Boorns, however circumstantially, with Russell's disappearance. At least three other neighbors possessed damaging information about the Boorns' feud with their brother-in-law: Thomas Johnson, William Boorn (a cousin of Stephen and Jesse), and William Wyman. Johnson and Boorn were apparently loath to use what they knew against Stephen and Jesse, but Wyman was ready and willing to tell all.

Of the tight-lipped pair, Thomas Johnson was in possession of the most incriminating evidence, since he had overheard the brothers quarreling with Russell Colvin on May 10 and knew that he had not seen Russell since. Johnson, however, had watched the argument from a hiding place and may have been embarrassed to admit to snooping. In addition, the Boorns were old friends and neighbors. For whatever reason, he was slow to share what he knew with others.

William Boorn was not only a relative of the Boorn brothers, but about their age and apparently on good terms with both. His knowledge of the family feud came from an angry remark Stephen had once made in his presence. Although William could not remember precisely when the remark had been made, its contents were unforgettable. They were also pure Stephen Boorn: careless, profane, and violent. Stephen had told William that "he wished that Russell and Sal were both dead, and that he would kick them into hell if he burnt his legs off."[18]

William Wyman was a neighbor of the Boorns in the Boorn Brook section of East Manchester. He not only knew about Stephen's anger toward Russell and Sally, but had also heard Stephen swear that he intended to take some sort of action against the Colvins. In April 1812, three or four weeks before Russell's disappearance, Stephen had complained to Wyman about his obnoxious sister, her incompetent husband, and their many children, who since they were living with his parents were draining off money that might have gone to more deserving Boorn offspring, such as himself. According to Wyman, Stephen wanted to know whether his father "was obliged to support Colvin's young ones." Wyman replied that in his opinion Barney Boorn had no choice but to do so. At that point, Wyman recalled, Stephen asked if there was not some way that he could "prevent the intercourse between Russell and Sally." Wyman replied that nothing could be done, since the Colvins were lawfully married. Stephen's anger boiled over, and with an oath he vowed to take matters into his own hands. "If there was no other way to put a stop to it," Wyman reported Stephen saying "he would put a stop to it himself."[19]

Although Stephen's pent-up wrath was ultimately directed against Russell, Stephen's statements to William Wyman and William Boorn plainly indicate that Sally was no less an object of his ire. What infuriated Stephen was Russell and Sally together, the two of them unable to support themselves but nevertheless continuing to produce children whom Barney and Elizabeth Boorn had to house and feed. Just how he intended to "put a stop" to this process is unknown, and it is possible that he had nothing more in mind than to confront Russell and demand that he stop having sexual relations with Sally. As Wyman tried to suggest, this was hardly realistic, and the absurdity of the idea that Russell would forego sex with his wife out of consideration for Stephen's wishes has tended to make most writers who have dealt with the Boorn-Colvin case portray Stephen as foolish as well as reckless. In addition, traditional accounts of the case, which mention only two Colvin children, Lewis and Rufus, make Stephen's sense of grievance seem wholly out of proportion to the supposed provocation. However, a recently-discovered probate record for Rufus Colvin, who died unmarried in 1848 without a will, lists all his potential heirs, including five siblings, a brother and four sisters, born before 1812. The fact that Russell and Sally had at least six children in eleven years makes Stephen's anxiety that his sister and her husband would continue to have children seem more understandable.[20]

If Stephen had any hopes that Russell's absence would keep Sally from getting pregnant, he was soon disappointed. In June 1813, eleven months after Russell disappeared, Sally, who had been the only one of Barney and Elizabeth's five children to join the Manchester Baptist Church, was dismissed from membership. The church minutes recorded the reasons for her excommunication in general terms only, simply saying that the assembled members "were satisfied that her walk for a number of years past was irregular and contrary to the rules of the gospel."[21] Although this wording suggests that church worthies felt Sally had been transgressing against the church covenant for a long time, the immediate cause of her dismissal in 1813 was almost certainly that she was obviously pregnant and that the child's father could not have been her long-absent husband.

Although the church's action was not surprising, the abrupt way that it was taken was most unusual. In the early 1800s, excommunication was the penalty that Manchester

Baptists invariably applied when an erring member showed no remorse for his or her sins. However, the handling of Sally's case did not conform to the New Testament prescription for dealing with a fallen sister, a prescription the congregation followed in case after case during this period. Under the formula found in Matthew 18:15–17, the offending party was first to be confronted privately by a fellow member, then visited by two or three elders appointed by the congregation, and finally, if neither of the first two steps produced satisfactory signs of remorse in the accused, the case would be aired at a congregational meeting to which the offender was invited. Only after all these steps were complete, and then only if the offending party failed to confess and beg forgiveness, was the wayward member excommunicated. In the Manchester Baptist Church it typically took a year or more to complete all of the prescribed stages, but in Sally's case the usual process was bypassed and the vote for dismissal came at the first and only meeting (June 5, 1813) devoted to her offense. The explanation given in the church minutes for bypassing normal procedures—that Sally had "left the town and state"—seems inadequate, since the church had often sent letters to accused persons before excommunicating them.[22] The unseemly haste to bring Sally's case to closure perhaps indicates that the church worthies were annoyed because Sally had managed to escape public humiliation by skipping town.

During Sally's frequent absences, her parents were left to care for her children. Reading between the lines, it sounds as though Barney Boorn was not at all happy about the situation. The upkeep of Sally's children was a financial burden. Also, he and Elizabeth, now in their late fifties, had only recently finished the task of raising their own five children and were probably something less than overjoyed to be responsible for an even larger brood of grandchildren.

Manchester town officials also kept a not-disinterested eye on the situation. Should Barney Boorn prove unable to provide for the Colvin children, they might well become indigents, and under the laws of the time the town's taxpayers would then have to assume responsibility for the children. It was in the town's interest, therefore, to help Barney Boorn do the job, and in 1814 the Town Meeting took steps to do precisely that. Russell Colvin's mother, Rosanna Colvin, had recently died, leaving the family's farm unoccupied except for a tenant. The tenant had been farming the place and paying rent, which the town had been collecting and using to assist old Mrs. Colvin. Her death meant that the rent money could now be diverted to help Barney Boorn care for his Colvin grandchildren. This ingenious solution, typical of the resourceful way that towns fulfilled their social responsibilities in the era, was voted by the February 1814 Town Meeting, which determined that "the money already arisen for the rent of the Colvin place be paid over to Barney Boorn for the support of the children of Russell Colvin."[23] In 1816 Manchester's selectmen voted to continue the arrangement with only minor modifications.

Although Manchester Baptists in 1813 and the Town Meeting in 1814 made decisions based on an awareness of Russell Colvin's absence, neither the Baptists nor town officials yet suspected Stephen and Jesse Boorn of being responsible for their brother-in-law's disappearance. By early 1815, however, the brothers' initial explanations for Russell's missing-person status—that he had run off or had enlisted in the military—seemed less plausible. News of the Treaty of Ghent, which ended the War of 1812, reached the United States in February 1815. If Russell had gone off to fight, why did he not return once the war had ended? The other explanation of his absence, that he simply had wandered off again, also seemed less convincing as time passed. Russell's longest previous trip had lasted only nine months, and he had kept in touch with his family while he was away. By early 1815 it was nearly three years since he had last been seen in town, and not one word had been heard from him.

With the old explanations losing credibility, anything that drew attention to the feud that preceded his disappearance was bad news for Stephen and Jesse Boorn. Unfortunately for them, in 1815 the troublesome Sally triggered an incident that got them in hot water. She was pregnant again, and she hoped to take advantage of a Vermont law under which the mother of an illegitimate child could "swear the child," as the phrase for naming its father went, and ask the town to compel him to provide child support. Town officials sometimes took the initiative in the process of determining the father's name, their interest arising from the fact that a child who had no acknowledged father and whose mother's family could not support it might become a ward of the town. Thus, if an unmarried woman did not identify her lover, town officials would press her for his name, the favored time for such interrogations being while she was in labor. Sally, however, was not reluctant to swear her child. She needed financial help and this was one way to get it. She went to see a Manchester lawyer named Hitchcock and asked him to help her start legal proceedings to obtain child support from the man by whom she was pregnant. Hitchcock, however, explained that the law gave some protection to unmarried women, but none to a married woman bearing an illegitimate child. As Sally later put it, "I could not swear my child on any person if my husband was living," and as far as anyone knew, Russell Colvin was still alive.[24]

But was he? Sally had her doubts, and at that moment, for all practical purposes, it probably seemed that she would have been better off with him dead. Following her disappointing interview with Hitchcock, Sally went to her parents' house. Stephen and Jesse were there. In a first-person account given more than four years later, Sally recalled that

Stephen, upon hearing what Hitchcock had told her, said straight out that she "could swear the child, for Russell was dead and he knew it." According to Sally, Jesse confirmed what Stephen said, although he was more cautious. He told her that she "could swear it, but would not," meaning apparently that if she had her brothers' best interests at heart she would not do it.[25] No great harm would have been done had the substance of this exchange remained known to the Boorns only. But Stephen, who at times could be his own worst enemy, was so upset by the defeat of Sally's plan to find outside support for the latest fruits of her promiscuity that he could not let the matter rest. He subsequently told at least two people outside the Boorn household that Colvin was dead, and some local gossip-mongers began to wonder how he could be so sure.

Still, Thomas Johnson, who had more reason than most to wonder about the Boorns, did not yet suspect them of foul play, even though, in addition to having witnessed the May 1812 quarrel in Barney Boorn's field, he also knew of three odd occurences that took place in 1815 involving the same field. Johnson had, in fact, become the field's owner in December 1814, having approached Barney Boorn about buying the land earlier that year. At first, Barney was reluctant to sell, perhaps because the parcel was one of the first he had owned and the site on which a house that the Boorn family had occupied for many years prior to 1800 had once stood. Bargaining dragged on through the summer, but in the end Barney's head won out over his heart. The practical fact was that he needed cash more than he needed land. In recent years he had done almost no farming, concentrating instead on his butchering business. Moreover, he knew that his sons, all three of whom were now of age, were worried about their legacies. John, the oldest and steadiest of the three, had the least to fear, since he expected that he would one day take title to the best piece of Barney's property, a sixty-two-acre parcel. But Jesse and Stephen, particularly Stephen, were perennially complaining that their father would have nothing left for his younger sons. It was about this time, probably in response to these entreaties, that Barney promised to give Stephen one hundred dollars, twenty-five of which was to be turned over to Jesse, and it was not much later, perhaps just after the sale went through, that he made good on his promise. In any event, by fall of 1814 Barney had decided to sell the old field and gave Johnson permission to plough it in preparation for planting the next spring. In December 1814 the two men completed the deal and Johnson paid Barney Boorn $128.00 for the land.

What Johnson received for his money was an eight-acre parcel, at least four acres of which were cleared for farming. The site of the Boorn family's former residence was located near the center of the open section. The house itself had been torn down around 1800, exposing the stone root cellar below. The cellar's small size—it was not more than three and a half by four feet—gave mute testimony to the minimal housing standards of Vermont's pioneer era. In the first decades of settlement, when the Boorns and other East Manchester pioneers had been clearing their land, few had either the time or energy to build fine frame houses with large foundations and deep cellars. However, small root cellars were a virtual necessity because indoor temperatures during Vermont's winters sank so low that everything froze unless buried below the frost line. The remnants of the Boorns' cellar were still clearly visible in the middle of the field.

The field also contained a barn that had been built to protect the Boorns' small flock of sheep. Free-roaming sheep were easy targets for wolves, which were still common in southern Vermont in the late eighteenth century. As late as 1797 in Dorset, the town just north of Manchester, residents complained that entire flocks of sheep had been wiped out by wolf packs in a single night's raid. Barney Boorn's field, located near the edge of the well-timbered slopes of the Green Mountains, was vulnerable to similar attacks, which made the barn necessary.

Despite the predator problem, most Vermont farmers felt they had to have at least a few sheep. It was the age of homespun, when, as one historian has written, "every farmhouse was a miniature textile factory." The main raw materials were wool and flax, the latter spun into linen thread. Nearly all home production was done by women. "Mother and daughter power" turned out woolen and linen goods, as well as numerous other necessities—soap, candles, baskets, and cheese, to name but a few. Looms and spinning wheels were essential tools for textile production, and the eight looms and two spinning wheels that appear on the list of household effects inventoried in 1819 with the estate of Nathaniel Boorn, Jr. (Barney's brother) were typical of what one would have found in the homes of most East Manchester families.[26]

In March of 1815 the sheep barn on Johnson's newly purchased property burned down. Lewis Colvin, now thirteen years old, walked across town to tell his Uncle Stephen, who was living at the foot of Equinox Mountain, about the fire. A day or two later Stephen visited his father in East Manchester and made a point of stopping to see the ruins of Johnson's barn. The mystery of how the fire started was not solved until 1819 when Rufus Colvin, Lewis's younger brother, confessed to having set it.

Later in the spring of 1815 Thomas Johnson's children came home one day carrying an old slouch hat they had found. Johnson recognized it as the very hat Russell Colvin had been wearing while picking up stones in Barney Boorn's field in 1812. Having lain in the elements for nearly three years, the hat was in bad shape, "very mouldy and rotten," but Johnson was sure of its identity. When Russell's sister, Clarissa Ferguson, heard that Russell's hat had been found, she was very worried. "Russell did not," she asserted, ". . . go about the country without a hat, but was careful of his hat."[27]

Also in the spring of 1815 Johnson planted his new field for the first time. He hired Jesse Boorn to help him with some of the planting, but on another occasion, when he was working with a man named Vaughn, he noticed that there was a three-foot-high volunteer apple tree growing in the cellar hole of the old Boorn house. He and Vaughn pruned the young tree. In trying to date the precise time of year when this had taken place, Johnson's son Michael, who had also been present, remembered that the tree had not yet leafed out, it being too early in the season for that. Both Johnsons were more than a little puzzled when, later in the year, they found that the young apple tree had disappeared and that, as Thomas Johnson recalled, "the ground about the cellar hole appeared to have been moved."[28]

Four years later these three incidents from 1815—the barn burning, the discovery of the hat, and the disappearance of the apple tree—would be offered as some of the circumstantial evidence that pointed to the conclusion that the Boorn brothers killed Russell Colvin. However, Thomas Johnson insisted that neither in 1815 nor for three years thereafter did he suspect that Russell's disappearance might have been the result of foul play. Perhaps Johnson was too trusting, but he had known the Boorns for a long time, both as neighbors and as members of an East Manchester family that, like his own, attended the Baptist Church in Manchester Center. Barney Boorn had sold him land. Jesse had, on occasion, worked for him, and Stephen and he had served in the militia together, which, given the reputation that the era's militiamen had for rowdiness, probably meant that they had shared some youthful moments of raising Cain.

Not all the Boorns' neighbors were so reluctant to entertain questions about Stephen's innocence. Russell had been missing too long. Now his hat had been found, and Stephen was known by some to have said that he knew Russell was dead. As of late 1815 and early 1816, the questions about

43

Russell were still being asked more out of curiosity than otherwise, but the pressure for answers was beginning to tell, especially on Stephen.

Jesse tried to keep a low profile. When asked about Russell's disappearance, he would reply that Russell had run off, and "nobody knew where he had gone to."[29] In December 1815 Jesse paid $19.50 for a six-and-a-half-acre lot in a part of East Manchester where the soil quality was quite poor. As far as anyone could see, he seemed content to stay in town.

Stephen was evidently less comfortable in Manchester. Having been the one to assert that he knew Russell was dead, he had more to explain. In September 1815 Stephen turned twenty-seven. By that date he was either married or about to be, for only three and a half years later he and his wife had three children. Earlier, between September 1812 and July 1814, he had briefly owned a small farm in Manchester, but he had not been able to earn an adequate living from it. He sold out at a slight loss and returned to tenant and hired-hand status. Nevertheless, in August 1815, Stephen scraped together two hundred dollars, some of which was probably from the seventy-five dollars his father had given him, and purchased a twelve-and-a-quarter-acre farm and a house in Dorset, the next town north of Manchester.

Stephen ruined his chance for a fresh start in a new place by failing to keep his mouth shut. He was soon complaining about his sister to two Dorset acquaintances named Daniel and Eunice Baldwin. Daniel, never having heard of Sally Colvin before, innocently asked where her husband was. Too ready to say too much, Stephen replied that "he did not know but some thought that he had killed Colvin." Not true, he added. Russell had been acting "very strangely" and had simply wandered off into the woods, never to be seen again. Unwilling or unable to drop the topic, Stephen went on to say that he and Jesse, on being asked by Lewis Colvin where his father was, had told the boy that "they had put him where potatoes would not freeze." Perhaps Baldwin's eyebrows shot up, because Stephen immediately tried to explain away these seemingly incriminating words. Surely, he argued, he and his brother would never have said such a thing if they had killed Russell.[30]

Stephen may have made trouble for himself, but he was also dogged by bad luck. During the first year he owned his Dorset farm, Vermont suffered one of the worst growing seasons in the state's history. A hard freeze struck on June 8, 1816, killing crops that were already in the ground. Farmers replanted, but the weather remained cold and dry, and several more frosts hit during the summer months. In the fall there was very little to harvest. Even such hardy crops as cabbage and turnips were undersized. With nearly empty barns and larders, Vermonters had to get through the winter on very sparse diets that included such usually disdained foods as boiled nettles and porcupines. It was enough to make one leave the state, which is exactly what Stephen and his wife chose to do. They sold their Dorset place in January 1817 and moved to Denmark, in northern New York's Lewis County, approximately two hundred miles from Manchester.

Although Stephen's specific motives for migrating are unknown, some facts about his decision are nevertheless worthy of comment. Stephen moved at least five times between 1812 and 1817. Some unidentified former neighbors of Stephen's later said that his frequent moves were efforts to escape "the ghost of the murdered Colvin," whose "supernatural appearances" had given Stephen nightmares.[31] If bad dreams were a stimulus for moving, they were a reason that was unique to Stephen, but in every other respect the story of the Boorns' migration was similar to those of thousands of Vermonters in the period. The year-long winter of 1816 was an economic disaster that uprooted numerous Green Mountain residents, making 1816 and 1817 the peak years for migration out of Vermont between 1809 and 1820. As a twenty-eight-year-old, Stephen was typical of the departing Vermonters, three-fourths of whom were not yet thirty years old. Like Stephen, many migrants were children or grandchildren of pioneers whose old family farms could no longer provide adequately for the younger generation. With Vermont's topsoil already showing wear or washed away, the West's more fertile lands beckoned. Most migrants headed west on the now nearly completed Erie Canal route. Their most popular destinations were the Genesee Valley in western New York and the Western Reserve region in northeastern Ohio. But Stephen's chosen route (almost certainly the recently completed St. Lawrence Turnpike between Plattsburg and Carthage in New York), and his ultimate destination, Lewis County, were also shared by thousands of Vermonters seeking new homes in these years.

In March 1819, two years after he moved to New York, Stephen returned for a visit to Manchester and Dorset. The visit turned out badly. Stephen encountered tough questions and even taunts from former neighbors who had begun to suspect that he had killed Russell Colvin. Stephen made matters worse by overreacting. While talking with Johnson Marsh outside Marsh's East Manchester home, Stephen was challenged by a girl who called out, "They are going to dig up Colvin for you, ain't they?" Furious and frightened, Stephen replied, "Damn Wyman" (a reference to William Wyman, whom Stephen believed was turning people against him by saying that Stephen had been out to get Russell in the weeks before Russell disappeared). Stephen swore that he would go to Wyman and "thump him." Marsh tried with some success to calm Stephen, who nevertheless headed for Wyman's soon thereafter. Once there, Stephen said that he wanted to clear the air of rumors and demanded that Wyman help by not circulating stories implying that he, Stephen, had killed Russell. He went on to deny that he and Russell had ever picked up stones together or even worked together, as he put it, "to the amount of one hour." Moreover, he insisted that on the day Russell disappeared, he, Stephen, had been ploughing a field on the Hammond farm, a place some distance from the field where Russell had last been seen.[32]

Here, for the first time, Stephen was offering an alibi for himself. No longer was it sufficient simply to explain Colvin's absence. Stephen now felt that he had to prove that he could not have been responsible for Russell's disappearance.

On the defensive now, Stephen and Jesse, backed by their parents, both tried to show that they could not have been in Barney Boorn's field on May 10, 1812. Barney and Elizabeth Boorn loyally tried to help by telling all who would listen that their sons had not lived at home at the time when Russell disappeared. This was true enough. However, it did not prove that the boys had not worked with Russell in Barney Boorn's field, although that was the conclusion the parents wanted listeners to draw. Meanwhile, both Stephen and Jesse went about giving inconsistent accounts of where they had been on the day Russell was last seen. Jesse told one person that he had been out of town that day, and told another that he had been working at David Briggs's blacksmith shop in Manchester Center. Stephen repeated his story about ploughing at Hammond's to several people, including his cousin William Boorn and Benjamin Deming, a Dorset acquaintance. But in conversation with Johnson Marsh, Stephen maintained that he had been in a neighboring town, Sandgate, when Russell left. He even tried to convince his old friend Thomas Johnson that he had not been to his father's field the day that Russell and Lewis had been picking up stones there. When Johnson replied that he knew better, Stephen grudgingly conceded that he might have briefly stopped "to see the boys," but he insisted that he had worked the rest of the day at Hammond's and another neighbor's.[33]

A measure of Stephen's growing desperation was the tall tale he now concocted to explain to Thomas Johnson why Russell had left town. Stephen said that, while mending fence on the Hammond place, he had killed a woodchuck.

His nephew Lewis Colvin, on an errand for Barney Boorn, stopped to chat. Stephen gave the boy the woodchuck to take home to Sally. Sally then cooked the woodchuck and served it to Russell for dinner, after which Russell got up and stormed out the door, saying that "it was the last dinner he should ever eat there." The story may have seemed plausible to Johnson, for whom the terrible winter of 1816–17 was still a vivid memory. Having been forced to subsist on such unpalatable foods as woodchuck meat—which, as one nineteenth-century Vermonter wrote, "is sometimes eaten, but is not much esteemed"—Johnson could sympathize with Russell's reaction. The woodchuck story, however, was pure fabrication. Lewis Colvin later said that he did not remember anything about a woodchuck dinner, and Sally, the supposed cook, testified that she had not even been home the day her husband disappeared.[34]

By the end of March 1819, when Stephen returned from Manchester to his New York home, he must have felt enormously relieved to get away. Still, for all the growing suspicion regarding his role in Russell's disappearance, no official investigation had been launched, in part because no one yet had any hard evidence that Stephen had killed his brother-in-law. Another obstacle to official intervention was that the men who would have to take the lead in any formal legal proceedings, the young respectables of Manchester Village, were not part of the gossip circuit in East Manchester and other rustic farm districts where the stories about Stephen Boorn were being circulated. But even these remaining barriers to official intervention were about to crumble. What happened next can best be described in terms more suitable to the mentality of East Manchester in 1819 than to that of the present century: with Stephen's departure from Manchester, Russell Colvin's ghost was evidently deprived of the chief object of its nocturnal wanderings, and the restless shade, in search of another victim to torment, chose to visit Stephen's uncle, Amos Boorn.

Colvin's Ghost

*It seems as if the age of ghosts and hobgoblins had re-
vived; and that every house was haunted by the ghost of
Colvin.*

— SAMUEL PUTNAM WALDO,
A BRIEF SKETCH . . . (1820)

IN April 1819, not long after his nephew
Stephen had gone back to New York State, Amos
Boorn had a dream. So urgent was the dream's
message that the dream was repeated: three times in all,
Russell Colvin's ghost came and stood beside the slumbering
Amos. The ghost said that it had been murdered and that
it wanted to show Amos the place where its body lay buried.
Amos followed the ghost to the grave site, the old cellar hole
in the field Thomas Johnson had bought from Barney Boorn.

Amos Boorn, the recipient of the ghost's message, was
Barney's youngest brother. Born in 1768, he was twelve

Amos Boorn homestead with Boorn Brook in the foreground.

years Barney's junior. Between 1799, when their father died, and 1819, when Barney's sons were tried for murder, Amos gradually edged ahead of Barney in economic status, thus beating the odds that almost always favored the eldest son over younger siblings. Although the difference between the two men's economic position was not extreme, it was large enough to be significant. Both men spent their entire lives in the broad middle section of the community's social ladder, but Amos managed to climb slightly in rank, while his brother Barney slipped a little. Amos achieved his small step up in spite of having eleven children to support. Barney had only five, although, thanks to Sally, he ended up with six or more dependent grandchildren as well. By 1819, Amos had a house that was valued at nearly twice as much as Barney's. He had also held several town-wide offices, while Barney had held none. Contemporaries considered Amos, in the words of the local Congregational minister, "a gentleman of respectability, whose character is unimpeachable."[1]

Reported as it was by such a solid citizen, the ghost's tale of murder gained instant plausibility. Whether or not the ghost explicitly named Stephen and Jesse Boorn as its murderers (many secondary sources have it so, but the most reliable contemporary account, one written by a Manchester resident in 1819, recounts the dream without mentioning the brothers), local opinion immediately supplied their names as the perpetrators of the alleged crime. Had this been Amos Boorn's intention all along? A few contemporaries thought so, going so far as to express doubt that Amos had ever had the dream at all, and suggesting that he had disguised his personal suspicions as a dream in order to avoid seeming to accuse his nephews of murder.

In any event, Amos certainly had many reasons to think long and hard about what might have happened between his nephews and Russell Colvin in 1812. Not only did he have close family ties with the feud's participants, but the site of their quarrel was almost literally in Amos's back yard, just up the hill from his house. Amos was also well aware that the past use of the old cellar hole fit perfectly with his nephew's indiscreet statement that they had put Colvin "where potatoes would not freeze." Moreover, it must have bothered him that William Wyman, a neighbor whose children were friendly with his own, was convinced that Stephen had killed Russell. Finally, in mid-March 1819 Amos was the recipient of a death-bed statement made to him by his brother Nathaniel. Although no particulars are known, the subject of Nathaniel's declaration was "what he knew had taken place" on the day Colvin disappeared.[2] Less than a month after Amos received these confidences, he reported having his troubling dreams.

As news of Amos Boorn's dream spread, "other good people of Manchester" began to have "strange dreams and unaccountable visions." No detailed descriptions of these incidents survive. The country folk involved in them left no written record, while the editors, lawyers, and clergymen who wrote the earliest accounts of the Boorn mystery either ridiculed or suppressed the ghost stories out of a feeling that they were the products of ignorance and superstition. Undeterred by the opinions of these enlightened worthies, witnesses in East Manchester and other remote parts of town reported numerous sightings of Colvin's shade. According to one summary, the ghost was usually seen either "flitting across the declivities of the mountains, or walking with solemn step around the fields." Early in 1820, Samuel Putnam Waldo, a sober-minded lawyer from Hartford, Connecticut, studied the Boorn-Colvin case with the help of a close friend in Manchester. Waldo was dismayed to find that people of his day and age could be subject to such delusions, but he had to admit that stories about the specter's visits had caused a sensation in Manchester. "The ghost of Colvin," Waldo wrote, "seemed to have had, if possible, a more serious effect upon the minds of the people, than that of the King of Denmark upon Hamlet."[3]

What Waldo almost certainly did not realize was that folk traditions regarding supernatural and occult powers had a long history in Manchester. Once, only about twenty-five years earlier, there had been a terrific public furor over a case of alleged vampiric activity. Broadly speaking, both the vampire incident of 1793 and the ghost sightings in 1819 illustrate how even in the 1790s and early 1800s some Americans tended to resort to folk beliefs about sorcery, witchcraft, satanism, apparitions, and the like in an effort to understand and deal with unexplained events, such as the mysterious illnesses and deaths involved in the 1793 incident and, later, the unexplained disappearance of Russell Colvin. In addition, these two events were linked in more specific ways. Both had a particularly significant impact on the lives of people in the Manchester Center part of town. Also, there were family and personal connections among participants in the two incidents: many of the leading players in the 1793 drama were from families—Mead, Powel, and Whelpley—that had numerous ties to the Boorns.

The history of the 1793 incident was as follows. In March 1789 Captain Isaac Burton married Rachel Harris, whose mother was a Whelpley. Rachel was said to be "a fine, healthy, beautiful girl," but shortly after her marriage she became ill with consumption. She died in February 1790, less than a year after the wedding. To put her story into a broader perspective, it should be added that consumption, as pulmonary tuberculosis was then known, was one of the great killers of the time. It has been estimated that "no single disease accounted for more deaths [in the United States] before the Civil War." Moreover, since consumption "often struck young women and gave them a languorous air and the flush of low fever," the hectic beauty with which it endowed its victims made the disease seem all the more mysterious and tragic.[4]

In January 1791, less than a year after his first wife's death, Captain Burton married Hulda Powel. Hulda was described as "a very healthy, good-looking girl," although she was thought to be "not as handsome as his first wife." She, too, soon fell ill with consumption, and by February 1793 her desperate relatives were ready to try anything to save her. Someone suggested that a vampire that had killed the first wife was now afflicting the second, and that it might help to make, as an old account put it, a "sacrifice to the Demon Vampire who it was believed was still sucking the blood of the then living wife of Captain Burton." The first wife's body was dug up and what was left of her heart, liver, and lungs were removed. Then, in a ceremony presided over by Timothy Mead, a close personal and political friend of the sick woman's father, Martin Powel, the first wife's organs were burned in a blacksmith's forge that was made to do duty as an "altar," in hopes that this would propitiate the Demon and "effect a cure of the sick second wife." The ceremony aroused such avid curiosity that, according to one source, it was attended by "from five hundred to one thousand people" (perhaps half or more of the town's inhabitants, since the 1791 census put Manchester's population at 1,276). Despite the efforts on her behalf, Hulda Burton died less than six months later, on September 6, 1793.[5]

The survival of the sort of folk beliefs that inspired Timothy Mead's "sacrifice to the Demon Vampire" in 1793, and the East Manchester ghost sightings of 1819, was not a phenomenon limited to southern Vermont. According to a modern authority on the topic, "as a matter of individual and collective preoccupation, and even of informal *action,* witchcraft was part of New England life well into the nineteenth century." For a Vermont example contemporary to the Boorn-Colvin case, one need look no farther than the writings of the Vermont novelist Daniel Pierce Thompson (1795–1868), who produced many works, including the popular novel *The Green Mountain Boys* (1839) and a story "The Rangers, or, The Tory's Daughter," whose heroine was from Manchester, Vermont. As a young man of twenty, Thompson spent the winter of 1815–16 teaching school in a rural northern Vermont district, and his novel *Locke Amsden: or, The Schoolmaster* (1847) was a thinly disguised account of his experience. In the course of the winter term, many of Amsden's (i.e., Thompson's) young charges became "melancholy, drooping, and sickly," and parents noticed that several of the most severely afflicted had been urged, with some success, by their teacher to improve in arithmetic. Eventually, a number of angry parents accused Amsden/Thompson of resorting to an "unlawful art or power" to lead his pupils into such "forbidden paths" as the "black art" of numbers. Everyone knew, as one of the accusers told a special town meeting, that "strange things could be done with figures." Happily for Amsden/Thompson, a few stubborn skeptics defended him, and he was finally vindicated by a tough-minded physician who proved that a lack of fresh air in an overcrowded schoolhouse had caused the children's declining health.[6]

Thompson made several cogent observations about where and among what sorts of people beliefs in magic and witchcraft persisted in the United States in the early 1800s. He had found such notions prevalent among what he called "the common classes of people" in New England and other northern states. He had often, he wrote, come across "isolated neighborhoods, even in the heart of intelligent communities," where belief in "witchcraft, sorcery, divination, and the like" was still entertained.[7] Thompson's phrase "isolated neighborhoods . . . in the heart of intelligent communities" seems an apt description of East Manchester, where dreams and visions of Russell Colvin's ghost were proliferating.

Despite their relative isolation socially from the town's elite, East Manchester residents were not entirely without influence on town officials in Manchester Village. Amos Boorn was neither well-to-do nor particularly well educated, and he was certainly not one of the Village elite, but he was a respected citizen whose statements carried sufficient weight to lead town officers to arrest Jesse Boorn and set up a court of inquiry to investigate whether a crime had taken place. The only thing, at that moment, that prevented the arrest of Stephen Boorn was that he was living two hundred miles away in New York State.

The court of inquiry, which functioned much as an initial police investigation might today, opened on Tuesday, April 27. Squire Joel Pratt, the town clerk and also a justice of the peace (Esquire or Squire being the title of respect commonly conferred on rural JPs in this period), and Truman Hill, the town's grand juror for the 1819 term, took charge. The prisoner, Jesse Boorn, was housed in a log jail that had been constructed during the American Revolution as a prison for Tories and had undergone few physical improvements during its subsequent forty-year history. Ordinarily, Jesse would have been brought from the jail across the street to the upper-floor rooms of the court house, a two-story clap-board structure whose lower floor was occupied by a tavern. The normal procedure had to be abandoned, however, because the number of spectators clamoring to attend the court of inquiry was much too large to fit in the regular court rooms. As a result, the proceedings were moved to the Congregational meeting house, an unpainted wooden building "without steeple or ornament" that was located on the east, or jail, side of the street, just north of the jail.[8]

The rather primitive physical conditions of the town's jail, court house, and meeting house in no way inhibited the efforts of the court officers to conduct a solemn proceeding and to build the case on evidence rather than prejudice. An initial interrogation of Jesse Boorn produced little beyond denials of wrongdoing. The next day, therefore, Wednesday, April 28, the court of inquiry began field work in search of evidence. Guided by Amos Boorn, the court and a crowd of inquisitive hangers-on went to Thomas Johnson's field to examine the old cellar hole that the ghost had said was the site of Colvin's grave. It was a cramped space, not more than three and a half feet by four feet, and Abel Pettibone was selected as the court's designated digger. Before long his shovel turned up a variety of artifacts: a few pieces of crockery, a coat button, and two knives, one "an old fashioned long jack-knife," the other a small pen knife.[9] There were also some bones, but they proved not to be human remains. As each item was discovered, Pettibone handed it to Squire Pratt for safekeeping.

The court of inquiry delegated two respected Manchester Village men to take the artifacts to Sally Colvin for possible identification. Squire Pratt was joined by Richard Skinner, a wealthy lawyer who was also the Town Meeting's moderator for 1819. Sally provided a positive identification of the jackknife as her husband's. Pratt and Skinner asked her about the design of the buttons on the coat Russell had been wearing when last seen, and she gave a brief description.

Then, in Skinner's words, "we in her presence rubbed the button [and] discovered the colour and flower in the centre."[10] It was precisely the color and design that Sally had told them had been on the buttons of Russell's coat.

The court of inquiry continued in session through Friday, April 30. The key witnesses, Lewis Colvin and Jesse himself, did not provide the court with any facts that were immediately damaging to Jesse's claims of innocence. Lewis testified that he and his father had been picking up stones by themselves on the day of the alleged fight. Russell, he said, began to behave in a deranged way, "throwing [fence] rails about," at which point Lewis had run off to his grandparents' house. He had never seen his father thereafter. Jesse, in his testimony, continued to deny responsibility for his brother-in-law's disappearance. To the large audience, the accused seemed a very cool customer as he stood in one of the meeting-house pews and scarcely blinked when shown the battered hat Thomas Johnson's children had found in 1815 and the old jackknife court members had unearthed earlier in the week. His only gesture was to lean forward and grasp the back of the pew in front of him as if to get a better view. His only comment about the jackknife was a seemingly casual aside to his Uncle Amos, whom he asked "if it was not the knife of Peperell Skinner."[11]

By Saturday morning, May 1, the court of inquiry had run out of leads, and its members were inclined to call off the investigation and release Jesse. They did not have much to show for their efforts. Private appeals to Jesse to "confess the facts" had produced neither a confession nor any information.[12] Public testimony had yielded little except highly circumstantial evidence, and neither the rumors nor the artifacts that had been collected were sufficient to prove that Colvin had been murdered or, if so, by whom. There were, of course, the stories of dreams and visions of Colvin's ghost that were being circulated, but the enlightened gentlemen of Manchester Village were insistent on keeping all such spectral evidence out of the record, lest they and the whole legal process be discredited.

One member of the court, Truman Hill, was not quite ready to give up, as he still had a trick left up his sleeve. On Saturday morning about ten o'clock, having gotten the keys to the jail from the town constable, Hill let Thomas Johnson in to speak with Jesse. What Johnson said to Jesse is not known, but whatever was said, it accomplished Hill's purpose.

When Johnson came out, Hill entered Jesse's cell and found the prisoner "much agitated." Jesse confessed that, contrary to his statements earlier in the week, he had recognized the jackknife shown him in court as Russell's. He also admitted that when the knife had been produced, "his feelings were such as to oblige him to take hold of the pew to steady himself." Hill asked, "What was the matter?" to which Jesse replied, "There was matter enough." Hill urged him to go on, and Jesse proceeded to tell how during Stephen's recent visit to Manchester, he and his brother and their cousin William Boorn had been talking at William's blacksmith shop. According to Jesse, Stephen said that he had given "Russel [*sic*] a blow, and laid him aside, where no one would find him." The occasion of this conversation, Jesse insisted, was the first time that he had believed that his brother had killed Russell. Hill added that Jesse, having now had a chance to mull things over, "thought he knew within a few rods where Colvin was buried."[13]

News of the breakthrough in the investigation and of Jesse's statement that Russell lay buried in East Manchester set off a wild rush to find Russell's bones on Sunday, May 2. Showing little or no regard for the sanctity of the sabbath, "nearly all the people for miles around" joined the search, or so one old-timer recalled. During the course of the day "stumps were overturned, cellar-holes examined, and the side of the mountain back of the premises carefully searched." Despite these exertions, the diggers who tried to follow Jesse's directions returned empty-handed.[14]

A separate party of diggers who followed a lead provided by an East Manchester boy and his dog enjoyed greater success. The previous day the boy had been walking with his pet spaniel along an old road that ran from the Battenkill past Barney Boorn's house to the field that Barney had sold to Thomas Johnson. At a point near the east bank of the Battenkill, the dog ran over to a roadside birch stump. It dashed about, whined, and pawed at the ground, thereby drawing its master's attention to a hollow in the stump. On close examination the boy found what appeared to be a cache of bones in the opening. This discovery was reported to town authorities later in the day, and on Sunday Squire Pratt, Amos Boorn, and Josiah Burton, a wealthy merchant and mill owner, showed up to excavate the site. The hollow stump was overturned, revealing a pile of bones, many of which had been damaged by fire. Picking through the contents of the pile, Josiah Burton found what appeared to be a human thumb- or toenail. Subsequently another such nail, or part of one, was discovered.

Speculation about the charred bones led to the development of an elaborate theory that explained how they had been deposited in the hollow stump. According to this popular reconstruction, Russell's first resting place had been the old cellar hole where his coat button and jackknife had been found. However, based on the fact that Thomas Johnson had noticed that the ground around the cellar had been disturbed the first spring he owned the field, it was assumed that Russell's remains had been removed and placed under the floor of the nearby sheep barn. When the barn burned down, the bones were exposed. The murderer or murderers then recovered the remaining charred bones and deposited them in the hollow stump down the road from the field.

This was an intriguing, even elegant, thesis, but not without flaws. Four physicians were called in to examine the charred bones. What followed resembled at times an *opéra bouffe* in which the limited anatomical training of the era's medical men was all too painfully evident. At first, the four doctors agreed that the bones were remnants of a human foot. However, one member of the panel, who was from the neighboring town of Arlington, owned a skeleton. When he got home, he consulted his skeleton and concluded that the Manchester relics were not human. The next day he returned to Manchester, but was unable to budge his colleagues from their conviction that the bones were human. After much debate, the panel of physicians decided to settle the issue in an empirical way. It seems that a man named Salisbury who lived about four or five miles from Manchester Village had lost a leg through amputation. A delegation was sent to the neighboring town where Salisbury's leg was buried, the remains of the limb were exhumed, and the bones were compared with those found in East Manchester. All four doctors now agreed that the East Manchester bones were not of human origin. Of course there were still the toe- or thumbnails, but one-and-a-half toenails that could not be proven to be Russell's did not make a very satisfactory *corpus delicti*.

Although the gentlemen conducting the court of inquiry would have preferred to have physical evidence of Russell's decease, it was not necessary to have the victim's corpse or skeleton in order to prosecute a homicide case successfully. Had the rule been otherwise, many a murderer could have escaped the gallows simply by being sufficiently thorough in disposing of the victim's body. However, what the court of inquiry now had was Jesse's statement that his brother Stephen had admitted murdering Russell Colvin. Also, subsequent to Jesse's revelations, two members of the court had grilled Lewis Colvin, and he had broken down and admitted that he had witnessed a fight between his father and uncle. These statements from Jesse and Lewis were more than enough to cause the court to issue a warrant for Stephen's arrest.

A three-man posse was immediately dispatched to Denmark, New York, to take Stephen into custody. Truman Hill and Samuel Raymond were accompanied by Robert Anderson, a substantial farmer, who, like Hill, was a veteran of the War of 1812. Their trip covered a distance of one hundred ninety-eight miles, and according to a contemporary, they reached Denmark after only three days on the road. Their average pace of sixty-six miles per day meant that the three men pushed themselves and their mounts hard. This pace also serves as a reminder that Manchester Village's elite was not composed of soft-handed aristocrats and men of leisure. Whether they were relatively rich—Anderson and Burton ranked in the top twenty-five percent of the town's taxpayers—or only middling in status, as was the case with Truman Hill, Manchester's political leaders were generally well-conditioned, hard-bodied men able to stand up to demanding physical tasks.

Fearful that their quarry might escape, the three Manchester men enlisted the aid of several local residents, including an innkeeper, Eleazer Sylvester, and two other Denmark men named Clark and Hooper. That night Sylvester guided them to Stephen Boorn's house, and while Clark went in to keep Stephen occupied with small talk, the five remaining men surrounded the house. When they moved in for the arrest, they encountered no resistance. Stephen was stoical, but his wife became extremely upset, especially when she learned that the posse was going to take Stephen away for an indefinite period. How, she asked, was she supposed to support herself and her small children? Moved by her distress, the three Manchester men dipped into their pockets and gave her some money to tide her over. The next morning, with Stephen manacled, the posse started back for Manchester, arriving at their destination on Saturday, May 15.

Immediately, the court of inquiry was reopened and many witnesses reexamined. Throughout the trip to Vermont, the posse members, particularly Hill and Raymond, had urged Stephen to confess, but, as an old account reports, "he peremptorily asserted innocence, and declared he knew nothing about the murder of his brother-in-law." Once back in Manchester, Stephen was kept in a separate cell from his brother Jesse. Calvin Sheldon, the state prosecuting attorney, joined the chorus of voices urging the Boorns to come clean, but to no avail. Finally, in hopes that bringing the brothers together would loosen their tongues, court officers had the two men placed in the same cell. The end result, however, was that Jesse, after a tongue-lashing from Stephen, retracted his earlier statement that Stephen had killed Russell. The court of inquiry nevertheless voted to hold the brothers in jail pending a grand jury hearing and possible formal indictment in September. Convinced that this predicament could have been avoided if Jesse had not come undone and talked to Hill, Stephen bitterly commented to a friend, "if Jesse had kept his guts in [we] should have done well enough."[15]

On Sunday, May 16, the day after the posse returned with Stephen in tow, the Manchester Baptist Church met to consider a disciplinary case involving Stephen's mother, Elizabeth Boorn. She was accused of "un-Christian conduct," by which was meant, apparently, her supposed dishonesty in trying to provide her sons with alibis. Opinion ran so strongly against her that, in the words of the church records, it took only "a few minutes" to decide to excommunicate her. Then, following the afternoon service, a public announcement was read (probably from the meeting house's steps), denouncing Elizabeth Boorn as "unfit" for fellowship with the Baptists.[16]

The church's handling of Elizabeth Boorn's case was unusual in several respects. Elizabeth was dismissed from membership, as her daughter Sally had been four years earlier, without the congregation taking any of the procedural steps that were supposed to precede dismissal under the New Testament formula that governed such cases. Moreover, the public nature of the rebuke, the fact that it was announced to the community at large, was both unusual and revealing. By mid-May 1819 a consensus had emerged in town that the Boorn brothers were guilty, a view shared by most of the Baptists. Elizabeth Boorn was the only member of the Boorn family closely connected with the murder case who was a member of the church. In rushing to excommunicate her, and in giving that decision immediate publicity, the good Baptists sent a clear signal that they not only endorsed the growing anti-Boorn sentiment but disavowed any responsibility for the Boorns' conduct.

With the tide of public opinion swinging strongly against the Boorns, Barney Boorn also came under scrutiny. Soon after Stephen was brought back to Manchester, his father was arrested as a possible accessory in the murder of Russell Colvin. Like Elizabeth Boorn, Barney had tried to provide his sons with an alibi by suggesting that they would not have been working in his field at the time of Russell's disappearance because they were not living at home in May 1812.

Barney was fortunate to draw John S. Pettibone as the examining magistrate for his case—the same Pettibone who later wrote a loving memoir of Manchester's pioneer era. In 1819, he was a thirty-three-year-old lawyer, a justice of the peace, and a member of the Manchester Village elite, but he retained his boyhood sympathy for older members of certain pioneer families like the Boorns. He also had the independence of mind to resist popular prejudices; after giving Barney Boorn "a severe examination, [Pettibone] discharged him, much to the indignation of the public."[17]

Stephen and Jesse Boorn were, of course, the main targets of public indignation. The former widespread assumption that they were innocent of any wrongdoing had been replaced by an even more intensely held conviction that they were guilty. From mid-May onward, the brothers were incarcerated in the town's ancient log jail. Days and weeks passed with little to break the monotony except visits from friends and frequent interrogations by town officials. The officials' persistence was founded on the hope that confessions might yet be extracted from the brothers. Astute magistrates such as Joel Pratt and Calvin Sheldon were all too aware that the case against the Boorn brothers was far from airtight. It was rankling to the grand jury's chairman, Truman Hill, who had successfully gotten Jesse to accuse Stephen, that Jesse had retracted his statement. Samuel Raymond, who had been a member of the posse that arrested Stephen, and Raymond's business partner, Josiah Burton, badgered both brothers by insisting that they were sure to be convicted. Still, no one was able to shake any admissions from the Boorns.

By early June it was obvious to the official inquisitors that they were making no headway with the Boorns. Since the direct approach was not bearing fruit, they turned to subterfuge, enlisting the aid of another prisoner to act as a stool pigeon. About this time, Stephen and Jesse, who had been sharing a cell, were separated. Stephen was now moved to a dark, windowless room and placed in triple chains; that is, he had shackles on his hands and feet, and was also chained to the floor. Jesse was put in another cell with Silas Merrill, who was being held on charges of perjury.* Merrill and town officials never admitted it directly, but circumstantial evidence indicates that Merrill had been promised lenient treatment if he could provide significant information about Colvin's murder.

---

*Perjury was the crime attributed to Merrill by a member of the court of inquiry in a letter to Samuel Putnam Waldo in 1820. However, a New York City newspaper (*National Advocate*, December 17, 1819) reported that Merrill was accused of forgery, a description adopted by many subsequent writers, including Leonard Sargeant, the Boorns' defense attorney, whose pamphlet on the case was published in 1873.

Before June was over, Merrill claimed to be the recipient of stunning revelations from his cellmate. One Sunday, Merrill said, after having received a visit from Barney Boorn, Jesse seemed upset and nervous. Just what transpired between Jesse and his father to cause the son's distress is not known, but it may have concerned a plan that Jesse allegedly concocted about this time to save himself and Stephen. According to a letter written by an unnamed Bennington lawyer six months after the fact, Jesse had asked his father to confess to having killed Russell, believing that this would secure his and Stephen's release from jail and that the authorities would pardon Barney, "he being an old man." It is possible that Jesse's anxiety after talking with his father that Sunday was the result of his just having received Barney's categorical refusal. In any case, as Merrill told it, Jesse was very wrought up that evening. Later, after Merrill had fallen asleep, Jesse awakened him and said "he was frightened about something that had come into the window, and was on the bed behind him." This incident, the only example of spectral activity to make it into official records of the Boorn-Colvin case, apparently loosened Jesse's tongue in a big way.[18]

Merrill's version of Jesse's confidences began with what had happened in Barney Boorn's field on May 10, 1812. According to Merrill, Jesse said that he, Stephen, Russell, and Lewis were picking up stones when a fight broke out between Stephen and Russell. Stephen clubbed Russell to the ground, and Lewis ran off. Then Stephen struck Russell again and "broke his skull" so that "blood gushed out." After a while Barney Boorn arrived and asked whether Russell was dead. Stephen and Jesse said he was not. Barney went away, returning twice more, only to receive the same answer each time. On his third visit to the field, according to Jesse, "the old man said *damn him*," and directed Jesse to grab Russell's legs and Stephen his shoulders. Together the three men carried Russell to the cellar hole, where Barney used Stephen's penknife to cut Russell's throat. By the time they buried Russell in the old foundation it was nearly dark.[19]

Later, Merrill went on, the Boorn brothers dug up Russell's remains (this would have been in 1814 or 1815) and hid them under the floor of the nearby sheep barn. When the barn burned down in 1815, Jesse and Stephen went back and retrieved Russell's bones, pounded them into small bits, and dumped them into the Battenkill. The skull was so badly burned that it crumbled into small pieces. Finally, a few leftover bone fragments were gathered up by Barney Boorn and stuffed into "a hollow birch stump near the road."[20]

At his earliest opportunity, Merrill passed on his news about Jesse's middle-of-the-night confession to Squire Pratt. Pratt and his colleagues immediately tried to use Merrill's story as a lever to extract definitive confessions from the Boorn brothers, but Jesse denied that he had shared any such confidences with his cellmate, and Stephen rejected Merrill's allegations out of hand. The court officers found themselves still short of an airtight case, since Merrill, as an accused perjurer, was not an unimpeachable source. Thus, as June became July, the investigators continued to press the brothers, particularly Stephen, for full confessions.

The motives and conduct of the Boorns' principal inquisitors—Josiah Burton, Truman Hill, Joel Pratt, Samuel Raymond, and Calvin Sheldon—during the critical summer of 1819 deserve much more attention than they have received. At first glance it might seem that there is little to say about these pillars of Manchester society except that they were conscientious men, possibly a bit overzealous in their methods at times, but nevertheless doing their best to solve a difficult case. However, such a view does not take into account a great deal of what was going on in Manchester in 1819. A more complete understanding of events requires some inquiry into social context, into how conflicts in the community might have influenced the conduct of the leading participants.

Both the investigation conducted by Squire Pratt and his colleagues and the subsequent court trial were, of course, devoted to establishing the Boorns' guilt or innocence, and neither the inquiry nor the trial was concerned with documenting the pressures that town officials were under at the time. Nevertheless, such pressures existed and were germane both to the conduct of the trial and its outcome. A careful combing of the sources reveals three distinct yet related types of pressure to which Pratt and his associates were reacting during the summer of 1819: first, there was an insistent public outcry that they solve the case; second, there was a perceived need to bring the town's unruly outlying districts into line and under the control of the Manchester Village elite; and third, there was tension among the court officials themselves, mostly due to a bitter controversy that was threatening to tear apart the Congregational Church, to which nearly all of them had close ties.

The pressure of public opinion against the Boorns was intense. Richard Skinner, who had helped Squire Pratt interview Sally Colvin about her husband's jackknife, later told a young friend that "it would have been as easy to resist the cataract of Niagara as to arrest [the] torrent of passion and prejudice" unleashed by the Boorn case. Beginning at the time Amos Boorn's dream became public, and throughout the summer months the Boorn brothers spent in jail, public opinion was overwhelmingly against them. News of the dream's content was taken, according to one old source, as "confirmation strong as proof of holy writ" that Colvin had been murdered. Another early account, Samuel Waldo's, put the point even more dramatically. "All, all was consternation!" Waldo wrote. "Every mouth was ready to exclaim, *murder! murder!*" Then, after the discovery of several of Colvin's artifacts precisely at the spot where the ghost said Colvin's body would be, "many of the good people of Manchester and its vicinity," in the words of a pamphlet published in 1820, regarded both the dream and the subsequent discoveries as "supernatural truths. 'Murder most foul' had been committed. No doubt remained that Stephen and Jesse Boorn were the murderers." Jesse's assertion, at the end of the first week of the court of inquiry, that Stephen had killed Russell simply clinched things. As noted earlier, even Jesse and Stephen's parents were tarred with their son's guilt.[21]

Squire Pratt and his colleagues were in a tight spot. Things had reached a point at which nothing short of incontrovertible evidence of the Boorns' innocence would overcome the public's conviction of their guilt. Theoretically, one way of proving their innocence was to show that Colvin was still alive, but lacking any evidence to support that thesis, Pratt and his associates were left with having to prove the brothers' guilt. The trouble there, however, was that the officials closest to the inquiry knew that the case against the Boorns was weak, cobbled together from scraps of circumstantial information that might not persuade a jury to render a guilty verdict.

In response to the perceived need to strengthen the case against the Boorns, a faction of court officers led by Samuel Raymond took a very hard line in interrogating the brothers, particularly Stephen. Raymond told Stephen that he had "no doubt of his guilt," and Raymond's business partner Josiah Burton at once chimed in that Stephen was "a gone goose."[22] According to Raymond and Burton, Stephen's only hope for escaping the hangman's noose was to confess to having killed Colvin, in exchange for which they would support a move to get him a reduced sentence. Here Raymond and the men who followed his lead were playing a risky game, since their vague, unauthorized promises might later be challenged as a form of pressure on Stephen that invalidated any confession thus elicited. But Raymond and his allies apparently felt the risks were justified, inasmuch as the public outcry likely to follow a failure to convict Stephen and Jesse would make the public indignation over the release of Barney Boorn seem slight by comparison.

Much of the demand for a clear-cut solution to the Boorn-Colvin case came from East Manchester residents who had lived with the uncertainty created by Russell Colvin's disappearance for fully seven years. Seven years of rumors and gossip had created suspicion and ill will of the sort exemplified by the girl who hurled taunts at Stephen and by the Baptists who moved so precipitously to dismiss Elizabeth Boorn from their ranks. Pent-up tension also found expression in the talk about ghosts and ghost-sightings that became widespread in East Manchester and the town's back districts in the late 1810s. Like the gossip about Stephen Boorn, some of these stories may have been circulating prior to the critical year of 1819. There are vague reports of unnamed individuals who claimed that before Stephen left town in 1817 he had long been haunted by a specter-poltergeist who tormented him with "horrid dreams" and awakened him from "his sleep at midnight, by the thundering of stones upon his house top." A better-known instance of spectral activity, Amos Boorn's dream, seems to be a product of the unconscious of an honest man who had not been able to bring himself to speak directly of his secret suspicions. The subsequent outbreak of sightings of Colvin's apparition as it wandered the hills and fields of East Manchester suggests that many other local residents also harbored uncomfortable feelings about Colvin's disappearance. "Every house," one contemporary wrote, "was haunted by the ghost of Colvin." It was an apt description. Everyone knew that Russell had disappeared, but almost no one had previously faced up to the probable cause, his murder. Nothing, of course, would not put the irksome shade to rest except the conviction and execution of Colvin's murderers.[23]

The widespread attention given to ghost sightings was doubly annoying to town officials, since it intensified the pressure on them to convict the Boorns at the same time that it demonstrated the public's faith in spectral evidence. Like most early nineteenth-century New Englanders of above-average wealth and education, Manchester Village's leaders had nothing but scorn for occult beliefs. Such notions, the elite contended, had no place in a progressive community in an enlightened age. Pratt and his colleagues were determined to emerge as victors in a struggle over which standard was going to prevail in 1819: the elite's concept of an orderly universe governed by natural causes, or the East Manchester residents' belief in ghosts and the supernatural. Resisting what seemed tantamount to a demand that they take a ghost's word as decisive proof that Colvin had been murdered, the court's officers made every effort to prevent ghost stories from figuring in official proceedings. In addition, they launched a counterattack by derisively dismissing the East Manchester ghost sightings as products of "a state of infatuation" suffered by "disturbed imaginations." As for Amos Boorn's now-famous dream, one member of the Manchester Village elite flatly declared that "there was nothing miraculous in the matter." Another contemporary spelled out the point: the dream's contents, he wrote, had entirely natural origins, since after years of talk locally about the Boorn-Colvin feud, "Mr. Boorn was greatly exercised about the matter, and had probably conjectured such things in his waking hours."[24]

The 1819 tussle between East Manchester ghost watchers and Manchester Village skeptics was but the latest skirmish in a cultural war of long duration. As noted earlier, from the mid-1790s onward there had been an influx of new settlers in town, many of them well educated and fairly wealthy, nearly all of whom had settled in the crossroads community of Manchester Village. Among the recent arrivals who later played prominent roles in the Boorn-Colvin case, Joel Pratt (arrived 1798), Richard Skinner (1800), Leonard Sargeant (1800), and Calvin Sheldon (1809) joined with representatives of older Manchester Village families— John Pettibone, Samuel Raymond, and Josiah Burton—to spearhead a movement to improve the town's reputation. In general, they sought to curb the pioneer era practices—horse racing, gambling, drinking, brawling, sexual irregularities, and disregard for the sabbath—that had given the town a reputation as a disorderly place, and to build a more sober and respectable community. By 1819, they had made considerable progress toward establishing the new ethic in the small community of Manchester Village. However, as the Boorn-Colvin case demonstrated, Manchester's older ways still held sway in East Manchester and the town's other outlying districts.

The Boorn-Colvin case was in certain respects the perfect vehicle for the village elite's renewed assault on the vestiges of the old ethic in Manchester. Jesse and Stephen Boorn represented some of the less savory aspects of the town's rough-and-tumble past. The Boorn brothers were reckless men—profane of speech, too ready to turn to physical violence, and very possibly murderers to boot. Moreover, their close friends and associates were no less discreditable. Stephen's sister Sally, whose notorious sexual promiscuity had led to her dismissal from the Baptist Church, could be pointed to as proof that moral laxity led to socially disruptive results. Similarly, William Farnsworth, a friend of Stephen's who often visited him in jail during the summer of 1819, was known to be a drunkard. He could be held up as an example of how "inveterate habits of intemperance," tavern-haunting of the sort that had prevailed in Manchester's early days, led a man to drink "so much ardent spirits as to render him often unfit properly to attend to his regular business."[25] Given these background facts, Squire Pratt and his colleagues had a reasonable basis for hoping that if they could prosecute the Boorn-Colvin case successfully, it would contribute to establishing the superiority of an ethic of rationality, respectability, and self-control. However, the higher the stakes, the greater the potential for significant losses, and as of mid-summer 1819, town officials could not be confident of their ability to control the outcome of the trial.

As if Squire Pratt and his colleagues were not already experiencing enough pressure due to the public outcry that they solve the case and their own desire to defend enlightened standards of law and morality, they also were subject to a third type of pressure in the summer of 1819. At first glance this third source of tension, divisions among themselves, may seem to have little direct bearing on the Boorn-Colvin case. But strains within the community of Manchester Village had a significant impact on the case, as was evident in a dispute that arose among the leading court officers. Disagreements over pre-trial strategy exposed a fairly serious split between hard-line conservatives such as Sheldon, Burton, and Raymond and moderates such as Pettibone, Pratt, and Hill. Moreover, these divisions within the Manchester Village elite were by no means new. They had their origin, in part, in a bitter controversy that had been raging for more than a year within the Congregational Church at Manchester Village.

Although the First Congregational Church of Manchester was founded in 1784, many decades passed before the organization achieved anything remotely resembling stability. At a low point in the church's history, during the early 1790s, the congregation had no minister and fewer than ten members. Not until 1805 could the tiny church support its first resident minister, Abel Farley; till then it had depended on visiting and borrowed preachers. Ten new members joined during Reverend Farley's first year of ministry, but even with these additions, a very important church meeting in 1806 mustered only twenty members. However, a significant increase in new memberships dated from the second year of the War of 1812. After adding no new members in 1812, the church recruited six new communicants in 1813, including Truman Hill and John Pettibone; eleven in 1814, including Calvin Sheldon; five more in 1815, and a huge harvest of twenty in 1816–17. Seven more new members were welcomed in 1818, the year that the congregation reorganized itself by establishing a Congregational Society to draw moral and financial assistance from local residents who were not full communicants. Forty-one individuals made financial subscriptions to the society, among them three men who played important roles in the Boorn-Colvin case of 1819 and who, though not themselves church members, had wives who were: Josiah Burton, Samuel Raymond, and Richard Skinner.

The increased institutional strength of Manchester's First Congregational Church was also part and parcel of broader trends in Vermont's religious history. According to a modern student of the subject, David M. Ludlum, in the early 1800s there was a "Puritan Counter-Reformation" in which evangelical Protestants who were either educated at or influenced by Yale launched an all-out attack on the mix of irreligion and liberal religion that had dominated much of Vermont, including Manchester, in the eighteenth century. The new revivalists espoused Calvinism's traditional tenets (among them, the doctrines of predestination, justification by faith, and the total depravity of human nature due to Adam's fall) and preached them with a crusading spirit that had begun to penetrate the citadels of infidelity and liberalism before the War of 1812. After the war, in 1816, a fresh phase of revivalism began in Manchester and elsewhere. The strict Calvinist emphasis on otherworldliness and on the inability of depraved humanity to save itself was gradually superseded by the so-called doctrine of benevolence that affirmed the human capacity for goodness and benevolent actions. As one Vermont theologian, Asa Burton, explained it in 1817, Christians were now believed, like their Maker, to be predisposed toward good, and were expected to exert themselves toward "the blessed objects of relieving human suffering, of dispelling human ignorance, of redeeming the human character from its corruption and guilt." In time, this doctrine provided the foundation upon which the Christian temperance and antislavery movements were built. But initially, at least in Manchester, the new evangelical mood led to a dramatic rise in the amount of time and energy that church members devoted to "watchfulness," that is, the use of disciplinary actions to insure the good conduct of members. From 1806 to 1816, on average, less than two pages per year were required to report disciplinary cases in the church minutes. However, with revival fires burning high in the late 1810s, the space devoted to the subject of watchfulness rose sharply to eleven pages in 1817, seven in 1818, and seventeen in 1819, a growth vastly out of proportion to the influx of new members.[26]

The charged religious atmosphere that led to numerous conversions and intensified watchfulness also had a significant and, unfortunately, a rather bruising impact on personal relations among certain members of the village elite. The most heated religious controversy of 1818 and 1819 involved the subject of infant baptism. Manchester had always been, as the Reverend Perkins observed in 1789, "half Baptist," and in the long period when the Congregationalists struggled without a settled minister, the town's Baptists enjoyed great stability under Elder Calvin Chamberlain, who occupied the Baptist pulpit from 1800 to 1824.[27] In an arrangement unusual for those nonecumenical times, Chamberlain sometimes preached at the Congregational meeting house in periods when Manchester Village had no other available minister. In 1817, the revival that reinvigorated the Congregationalists produced, if anything, an even greater outpouring of evangelical spirit among Chamberlain's Baptist flock at Manchester Center.

All was well until several Congregationalists started talking and acting like Baptists, a denomination that rejected the practice of infant baptism. In 1817 and early 1818 Truman Hill, soon to become a leading member of the court of inquiry into the Boorn-Colvin case, refused to present his children for baptism. This was a violation of the Congregational Church's convenant, which made infant baptism an article of faith and practice. Calvin Sheldon, the conservative lawyer who served as the prosecuting attorney in the Boorn murder trial, brought a complaint against Hill in March 1818. Hill responded a month later that children were not properly subject to baptism. The elders rejected this argument but struck a compromise which, as the poorly spelled minutes put it, allowed "Brother Hill an dispension of his obligation of giving up his children in Batism."[28]

Another strong-willed member of the Congregational Church, John S. Pettibone, was not willing to let Sheldon's attack go without further challenge. Pettibone had joined the church in 1813, but in so doing he had made it plain that he did not accept "the article relating to infant baptism." In the second half of 1818 he began to refuse to take communion, a neglect of one of his obligations under the church convenant. When asked to explain, he replied that he objected to the congregation having, as he put it, "received

John S. Pettibone
in later life.

Miss Flora Pierpont into their communion and fellowship without being baptized according to the rules and order of the gospel." The nub of his complaint was that Flora had offered no evidence of grace operating in her life and that her baptism as an infant was not, in Pettibone's view, either a correct way of administering the sacrament or a sufficient sign of faith, especially when one considered that Flora's father, Robert Pierpont, was not himself a church member. Not coincidentially, Flora was also related to Calvin Sheldon's wife.[29]

The fat was now in the fire. A panel of church elders initiated a disciplinary proceeding against Pettibone in February 1819. By April, they had called for a council of representatives from churches in neighboring towns to review the case. The council rendered its judgment on April 28, 1819 (the same day that the town court of inquiry recovered Russell Colvin's jackknife from the old cellar hole). Council members conceded that the evidence for Flora's "evangelical faith" was "slight," but they believed that her baptism was scripturally valid and that there was no sound basis for impugning the "credible piety" of her father. Moreover, "rebaptizing," something even the Baptists did not require of converts, was out of the question. The council, therefore, concluded that Pettibone had erred in withdrawing from communion. Sharing at the Lord's Table, they argued, "ought never to be considered an expression of approbation of every practice and of every article of faith either of the church or of individual members." The council closed with an appeal for a cease-fire in the Pettibone-Pierpont war: "We also exhort the Brethren to study the things which make for peace."[30]

It was too late. Peace through continued fellowship apparently did not appeal to either side in the controversy, although the recently appointed Congregational minister, Lemuel Haynes, proposed a belated compromise. He suggested that Pettibone refrain from judging Flora Pierpont's inner spiritual condition and return to the *status quo ante* under which he had been allowed his stated objections to infant baptism as long as he did not insist that they be subscribed to by everyone else. A majority of the church, however, had already shown itself to be less flexible and had voted on July 7 to admonish Pettibone, another step toward excommunication if he did not display contrition. Pettibone had no intention of doing so. Indeed, four days earlier, on July 3, 1819, he and Truman Hill had presented themselves before Elder Chamberlain and had been accepted as members of the Baptist Church. The Congregationalists, however, would not let the matter drop, lest others be encouraged to follow Pettibone's example. A letter mailed to him on July 24 contained an official notice of the July 7 vote to admonish. A second notice followed on September 6. Finally, on October 4, a congregational meeting voted to dismiss Pettibone from membership. By contrast, Hill was permitted to withdraw without disciplinary action because the 1818 case against him had been settled by a compromise.

The net result of the overlapping church and court controversies was to make the dog days of the summer of 1819 a very trying time for the village elite. Although some Manchester Village residents may have followed the Reverend Haynes's lead and tried to avoid taking sides, in the end, confrontation carried the day over compromise. The hard-liners gained an edge over the moderates in both the church and the court controversies. With the withdrawal of Truman Hill and John Pettibone to become Baptists, Calvin Sheldon and his conservative allies had purged the Congregational Church of its most articulate internal critics. At the same time, Sheldon, Samuel Raymond, and Josiah Burton, the hard-liners on the Boorn case, continued to put pressure on the Boorn brothers, despite the expressed reservations of Pettibone and other moderate magistrates. One cannot help wondering whether the intense pressure brought to bear on Stephen Boorn was not, in part, an outgrowth of the hard-liners' determination to win yet another skirmish with the moderates. But for them to succeed by removing all uncertainty about Stephen Boorn's guilt, they needed some help from the accused.

Stephen gave the magistrates his long sought confession on August 27, 1819. Just why he decided to confess in late August is unknown. He may simply have been worn down by more than three months in jail, during which time he had repeatedly been told by the Samuel Raymond–led hardliners that his only hope lay in confessing and asking for leniency. But it is also possible that Stephen's decision was another of his impulsive acts. Only two weeks after he had confessed, Stephen was already having second thoughts, according to William Farnsworth, who visited him in jail early in September. Farnsworth later claimed that in the course of this visit Stephen admitted that he had killed Colvin but regretted his written confession of the deed, saying that "he wished he had back that paper."[31] But for whatever reason, on August 27, Stephen had been in a very different mood, and he had asked one of his most persistent interrogators, Josiah Burton, to gather the court officials who were handling his case.

When the magistrates—Squire Pratt, Truman Hill, and Calvin Sheldon—arrived, they led Stephen from the jail, across the street, and into the court house. Pratt and Stephen went upstairs to the courtroom, where Stephen reportedly asked Pratt "about some small points."[32] Writing materials were brought to him. Pratt left the room, but Truman Hill went up to check on the prisoner. A short while later Burton traded places with Hill and was in the room when Stephen finished writing and got up from the table. Burton then escorted Stephen back to jail. Pratt and Hill signed the back of the confession as witnesses.

Stephen's confession covered most of the relevant facts about Russell Colvin's disappearance, although there were some significant omissions and a few places where he shaded the story in such a way as to put himself in the best possible light. In the first part of his confession, the core statement in which he admitted to having killed Russell, Stephen acknowledged that on the morning of May 10, 1812, he had visited the field where Russell and Lewis were working. According to Stephen, during a break in the work, he and Russell fell into an argument. When Russell boasted of "how many dollars benefit" he had been to Barney Boorn, Stephen ridiculed his claims.[33] In Stephen's version of the fight, which differed in small ways from Lewis's account as described earlier, Russell flew into a rage, picked up a beech limb, and struck Stephen a glancing blow. Then, Stephen said, he grabbed the club away from Russell and hit him twice. The second blow landed on the back of Russell's neck at the base of his skull and knocked him to the ground, and he died shortly thereafter.

The second section of Stephen's confession was a lengthy description of how he had disposed of Russell's body and, later, his bones. The night of the fight, Stephen wrote, he dug a grave, buried Russell, and, in his own awkward words, "went home crying along, but I want afraid as I know on."[34] A year or two later he went back, dug up Colvin's bones, and carried them to the sheep barn in the field, where he hid them in a hole he dug under the stable floor. In March 1815, after learning that the barn had burned down, he visited the site and recovered the bones that had survived the fire. The largest of these he carried down to the Battenkill and threw into a deep part of the stream. Shortly thereafter, he returned to the barn site again and scraped up a few smaller bits and pieces, which he stuffed into a hole in a stump beside the road near the river.

The vividness of the details and the naive awkwardness of the grammar make Stephen's confession, at first glance, seem both ingenuous and authentic. However, it was not without its artful aspects. By keeping his brother Jesse's name out of the story, Stephen was either attempting to protect Jesse or to eliminate any need on Jesse's part to defend himself by providing further evidence against Stephen. By making no mention of his father, Barney Boorn, Stephen also protected someone who might reciprocate by aiding him. Finally, by claiming that he had simply returned Russell's blow—that is, acted in an unpremeditated way and without murderous intent—he gave the court officers who had promised to get him a reduced sentence solid grounds for substituting a charge of manslaughter for murder. Significantly, Stephen did not contend that he had had to kill Russell to save his own life, an argument of self-defense that, if accepted, would have led a jury to declare him innocent of any crime in causing Russell's death.

The grand jury hearing on Stephen and Jesse Boorn's case was brief and undramatic, although not without some minor points of interest. Grand jury sessions were held in Manchester on the third Tuesday of September, and on September 26, 1819, the session opened with Judge Joel Doolittle, an associate justice of the Vermont Supreme Court, presiding. Calvin Sheldon, the State's Attorney, was responsible for presenting the prosecution's case. As far as can be determined, he did not choose to introduce Stephen Boorn's confession, most likely because it made no mention of Jesse's involvement, and Sheldon was seeking indictments against both Boorn brothers. Instead, he used Silas Merrill as the key prosecution witness. Merrill told the grand jury the story he claimed to have heard from Jesse in the middle of that June night when something had flown in the window and sat on Jesse's bed. Based on this and other testimony, the grand jury drew up indictments against Stephen and Jesse, charging that Stephen "feloniously, wilfully, and of his malice aforethought" struck and killed Russell Colvin, and that Jesse "then and there, feloniously, wilfully, and of his malice aforethought, was present aiding, helping, abetting, comforting, assisting and maintaining the said Stephen Boorn, [in] the felony and murder aforesaid." For good measure, a second indictment was prepared and voted "charging Jesse Boorn as principal and Stephen Boorn as aiding."[35]

The state obtained its indictments, but not without taking a few curious twists and turns. Since Stephen's confession was not introduced as evidence, the obvious contradictions between it and what Jesse supposedly had said did not become an issue. The Jesse-via-Merrill account was used very selectively, mainly to show that both brothers had been involved in killing Russell Colvin. It was also used to establish a few minor details such as the time of death. Had the whole Merrill account been accepted as true, an indictment of Barney Boorn would also have been forthcoming. However, a feeble attempt to indict the elder Boorn was quickly rejected, indicating that officials placed little faith in Merrill's report that Jesse said Barney Boorn had come to the field and cut Russell's throat.

Debates over these details were merely footnotes to the main result of the grand jury session, which was to bind Stephen and Jesse Boorn over for trial for the murder of Russell Colvin. Under then-current Vermont law, a capital crime had to be tried before an expanded panel of Supreme Court justices. The next such session in Manchester was scheduled for late October, at which time the Boorns' guilt or innocence would be decided by a jury of their peers. The Boorn family engaged the services of Richard Skinner, a skillful lawyer who felt that the case against the brothers was full of holes. However, realistically speaking, the odds against a jury's decision saving his clients from the gallows were very long indeed.

The
Trial

We think no man could doubt their guilt who heard the trial.

—GEORGE RICH AND OTHERS TO
JUDGE CHASE, 1819.[1]

PEOPLE started arriving for the Boorn trial early on the morning of Tuesday, October 27, 1819. On foot and on horseback, they made their way to Manchester Village from every part of Manchester and from the neighboring towns of Dorset, Arlington, Winhall, and Sunderland. The growing crowd compelled the court officers to move the murder trial proceedings, as they earlier had had to move the grand jury hearings, from the small upstairs room in the court house to the meeting house across the street. Even so, the meeting house, which measured thirty-six by forty feet, was not large enough. One keen observer, Lemuel Haynes, the Congregational minister who occupied the meeting house pulpit on Sundays, estimated that "six hundred people attended [the trial] each day."[2] If Haynes, who had many years of experience at sizing up crowds, was close to the mark with his estimate, the plain wooden meeting house surely could not have held all six hundred at once. Even with all the first-floor box pews jammed, every aisle crowded with standees, and the second-floor gallery filled to capacity, there would have been a significant overflow, leaving some people outside, perhaps clustered by open windows and straining to hear what was being said inside.

Eager onlookers who did manage to squeeze into the courtroom found themselves in the presence of an impressive group of judges and attorneys. The leading figure in the three-judge panel of Supreme Court justices was Chief Justice Dudley Chase.* Described by a successor as a "portly, dignified man of forty-eight," Chase was a 1791 graduate of Dartmouth College and a former United States Senator from Vermont.[3] (He was also the uncle of Salmon P. Chase, who would later serve in the U.S. Senate from Ohio before he became Abraham Lincoln's Secretary of the Treasury and then Chief Justice of the United States Supreme Court.) Second in seniority and seated to Chase's right was Associate Justice Joel Doolittle, who had presided at the grand jury hearings on the Boorn-Colvin case in September. He was forty-six years old and a Yale graduate, class of 1799. Seated to Chase's left was William Brayton, at age thirty-two much the youngest justice. He had attended Williams College but left without graduating. He made no known contribution to the Boorn-Colvin trial aside from his presence as the third

---

*Chief Justice is the modern title. In the 1800s the State Supreme Court's senior member was called Chief Judge and the associate justices bore the title Assistant Judge.

justice. Indeed, he left such a slight impression that only one of three eyewitness accounts even mentions his name.

Both the prosecution and the defense were ably represented. The State's Attorney was Calvin Sheldon. A thirty-four-year-old graduate of Middlebury College, he had been aggressively involved in the case almost from the first. Intelligent and tenacious, he was, nevertheless, young and relatively inexperienced, and perhaps for that reason at times a bit too eager to prove himself.

The Boorn family had hired Richard Skinner to conduct the defense, and in so doing they had also obtained the services of his twenty-six-year-old associate, Leonard Sargeant, who was studying law in Skinner's office. (A third member of the defense team, Daniel Wellman of Manchester, scarcely figured in the active defense, except through a very brief appearance as a witness.) Sargeant, a future Lieutenant Governor of Vermont (1846–48), was talented and energetic. He displayed a determination to save the Boorn brothers from the gallows that matched Sheldon's determination to

*Richard Skinner
(1778–1833).*

see them hang. Sargeant's mentor, Richard Skinner, although still a relatively young man of forty-one, already had
a distinguished political and legal career behind him. As a
friend put it, he had been "well educated in the profession
at the Litchfield school," an early Connecticut law school
with an excellent reputation. He was also active politically
as a Jeffersonian Republican, and his political fortunes had
risen and fallen with those of his party. Between 1800 and
1813, he had served as State's Attorney (1800–13) and probate judge (1806–13) in Bennington County. In 1812 he had
been elected to Congress, but the antiwar feeling that swept
large parts of Vermont during the War of 1812 prevented
him from winning reelection in 1814. The very next year he
was elected to the Vermont General Assembly and soon
thereafter served two year-long terms (1816 and 1817) as
Associate Justice of the Vermont Supreme Court. In 1818
he was chosen Speaker of the Vermont General Assembly,
and in 1820, the year after the Boorn-Colvin trial, he would
be elected to the first of three successive terms as governor
of Vermont. Admired by contemporaries for the "logical and
clear" way that he handled legal matters, Skinner was undoubtedly the best legal counsel the Boorn brothers could
have found.[4]

After a brief arraignment proceeding, during which both
Jesse and Stephen pleaded not guilty, their attorneys moved
that the brothers be tried separately, but this motion was
denied. The jury selection process began next. According to
Lemuel Haynes and Leonard Sargeant, the atmosphere at
the beginning of the trial was already poisoned against the
Boorn brothers. Of the jury selection process Haynes wrote,
"It was with much difficulty that a jury was obtained; but
few could be found who had not expressed their opinion
against the prisoners." A total of twenty-nine prospective
jurors were called before twelve were found to serve. Of the
seventeen who were dismissed, eleven, including all four
prospective jurors from Manchester, were challenged for

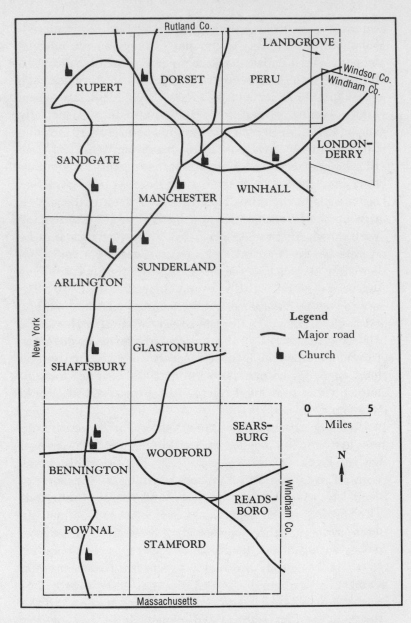

Towns of Bennington County, Vermont, 1812.

cause, that is, because their prior knowledge of the case had led them to form an opinion on it. The other six were dismissed after peremptory challenges, three each from the State's Attorney and the defense attorneys. A definite pattern can be seen in regard to the place of residence of those jurors who were dismissed as opposed to those who were empaneled. Prospective jurors were called from nine towns. The only towns from which no jurors were dismissed were Rupert and Landgrove, both of which were relatively remote from Manchester by the roads of that day. A total of four jurors were empaneled from those two towns. By contrast, all eight men called from Manchester and Sunderland (the town closest to Manchester Village by road) were dismissed. In other words, the closer one got to Manchester the harder it was to find people who, in Leonard Sargeant's words, "did not believe the prisoners guilty."[5]

In the final phase of trial preliminaries, the jurors were sworn in and the grand jury indictments against Stephen and Jesse were read. The persistence of legal formulas whose wording was derived from a medieval worldview that had long since ceased to have any practical significance for most American judges, lawyers, and juries is startlingly evident in two phrases from the indictments. In the first, it was said that the Boorn brothers, "not having the fear of God before their eyes, but being moved and seduced by the instigation of the devil," gave Russell Colvin a fatal wound on May 10, 1812. In the second, the murder weapon was described as "a certain beech club, of value of ten cents." The practice of assigning a value to the murder weapon dated back to the middle ages, when, as one authority reports, the object that was "the immediate cause of the death of a human being was deodand, that is, forfeited to the church, and applied to purchase masses for the repose of the soul of the victim." Later, the king replaced the church as the recipient of deodand, and it was under English common law that some deodands were declared and forfeited in the

American colonies prior to the Revolution. After independence, however, the custom of assigning a value to the murder weapon ceased to be anything but a formality in the United States.[6]

With these preliminaries out of the way, the presentation of evidence and the examination of witnesses began. The trial lasted from Tuesday, October 27, to Saturday, October 31. Over this five-day period, thirty-one witnesses were called, twenty-four of them by the prosecution. A number of individuals were called to the stand two or more times. Broadly speaking, the presentation of evidence can be divided into four stages, the first three of which were conducted by the State's Attorney. The fourth and final stage consisted of the defense's presentation of its witnesses.

In the first phase of his presentation, Sheldon called three witnesses: Richard Skinner, Amos Boorn, and Truman Hill. Since Russell Colvin's body had never been found, Sheldon needed to establish that Colvin was dead and that his death had not been due to natural causes. The State's Attorney chose his first three witnesses with an eye not simply to establishing these specific points, but to making them with a dramatic flourish. The selection of Richard Skinner, the leading defense attorney, served Sheldon's purpose well. Skinner told the court that Sally Colvin had in his presence identified the button and jackknife found in the cellar hole as her husband's. These facts could have been confirmed equally well by calling on Squire Pratt, who had shared responsibility with Skinner for interviewing Sally. But by questioning Skinner rather than Pratt, Sheldon showed the judges and the jury that even the Boorn brothers' attorney had to corroborate facts that indicated that Colvin was dead.

The choice of Amos Boorn as the second witness also served to convey a message that did not have to be stated explicitly. Like Skinner, Amos Boorn had little to say that could not have been told equally well by any one of several other prospective witnesses. Therefore, the main thrust of

Boorn's testimony, which consisted of his report that he had
been present when the knife and button were dug up and
when the toe- or thumbnails were found in the hollow stump,
could scarcely have been the primary reason for calling him
so early in the trial. But everyone familiar with the case
had heard about Amos Boorn's dream, and by placing the
dreamer on the stand Sheldon was reminding the onlookers
of the dream's content. To be sure, it did not serve the prosecutor's purposes to mention the dream itself or the apparition who was its chief character. However, it would
advance Sheldon's cause if having Amos as a witness implicitly reminded the jury that a close blood relative of the
Boorn brothers had, in essence, accused them of murdering
Russell Colvin. In an obvious attempt to reinforce this line
of thought, Sheldon brought up the subject of the deathbed
confidences regarding Russell Colvin's disappearance made
to Amos by his brother Nathaniel barely a month before
Amos dreamed his dream about the events of May 1812.
Though the defense objected to hearsay testimony, and
Judge Chase ruled it out of order, the subject of the confi-
dences had been raised.

Sheldon next recalled Richard Skinner to the stand.
Under questioning, Skinner testified that Jesse Boorn had
told him that Stephen had buried Colvin's body on the mountain slope where the extensive but unsuccessful search was
made in May 1819. Skinner also acknowledged that the jackknife found at the cellar hole had been identified as Russell's
by Jesse, who had said that he "had often seen old Mrs.
Colvin cut tobacco" with it.[7] Russell's mother had probably
been cutting a plug of cheap tobacco preparatory to smoking
it in a clay pipe, a fairly common practice among women of
her age and class in the early 1800s, but one that gradually
went out of fashion for women after 1820. In thus seeking
further confirmation of the knife's identity, Sheldon was
probably anticipating that the defense would argue, as it
later did, that knives and buttons were objects commonly

found in old foundations and that nothing was proved one way or the other about Colvin's fate by these discoveries.

Having drawn from Skinner the fact that Jesse Boorn had once said he thought he knew where his brother had hidden Colvin's body, Sheldon now called Truman Hill, the grand juryman who had first extracted this admission from Jesse. Hill reported how on May 1, 1819, Jesse had confessed to being very upset at the court of inquiry. In response to Hill's questions, Jesse had explained that the reason for his wrought-up state was that "he feared that Stephen had killed Colvin." Hill said that Jesse had added that "he thought he knew within a few rods where Colvin was buried," the assertion that had touched off the fruitless search for Colvin's remains the very next day.[8]

At this point Judge Chase interrupted Sheldon. Out of his zeal to demonstrate that Colvin was dead and that he had died of unnatural causes, Sheldon had started his presentation with events that took place in 1819, but this strategy left the judges and jurors who were from out of town confused about the background of these events. According to Judge Chase's trial notes, "the court suggested to Mr. Attorney the propriety of taking a different course in the examination of witnesses, and commence with the beginning of the transaction."[9]

Responding to Judge Chase's request, Sheldon now backed up and provided a history of the Boorn-Colvin case from 1812 onward. In this second phase of his presentation the prosecutor called fifteen witnesses. With one exception, they were the Boorn brothers' neighbors, friends, and relatives from East Manchester, Manchester Center, and Dorset. It was these ordinary folk, all of whom ranked in the bottom half of the town tax list and most of whom were in the bottom third, who were privy to the intimate history of the Boorn-Colvin affair during the seven-year period from 1812 to 1819.

Thomas Johnson led off with a description of the quarrel between the Boorns and Colvin in Barney Boorn's field on

May 10, 1812, which he had seen from a vantage point in the woods approximately four to five hundred feet away. A question arose whether Johnson, standing at such a distance, could be certain that he had identified the quarreling men correctly. Had he possibly confused Jesse Boorn with Jesse's older brother John? No, the witness stated, he did not think so. "John," he said, "is rather thicker and taller than Jesse."[10] (Jesse was 5'5" tall, a bit below the average height of 5'8" for men of his day.) The rest of Johnson's testimony covered such incidents as the discovery of Colvin's hat, the mysterious disappearance of the young apple tree, and the story of Sally having fed Russell woodchuck.

The next important witness was Lewis Colvin, now age seventeen, who told about two actions of Stephen's that badly undermined his uncle's claims of innocence. Lewis said he had seen his father fall to the ground after being struck by Stephen, and that Stephen had threatened to kill him, Lewis, if he told anyone about this incident. Lewis corroborated Stephen's claim that Russell struck the first blow, but the veracity of his testimony was not beyond challenge, since he had not always told the same story. As we have seen, in his initial testimony before the court of inquiry in late April 1819, Lewis had said that his uncles were not present the day that he and his father had been picking up stones in the field. However, on May 2, 1819, after Jesse's revelations had sent dozens of diggers to the mountainside in search of Russell's bones, Squire Pratt and State's Attorney Sheldon questioned Lewis again, and this time the boy admitted that his uncles had been present and that a fight had taken place between his father and Stephen.

Eager to show that nothing Lewis said could be trusted, Skinner for the first time rose to cross-examine a witness. The cross-examination exposed some of the contradictions in the rather confused account Lewis had just given regarding what had taken place after his father disappeared. For example, although Lewis had told the court that he had never heard Stephen say what happened to Russell, he had immediately contradicted himself by reporting that Stephen had told him that Russell had run off. Similarly, the youngster had testified that neither Stephen nor Jesse mentioned his father's name for a year; yet he had also stated that Stephen had threatened to kill him if he told anyone about the fight, and it sounded as though the threat had been delivered soon after the quarrel. Now Skinner tried to verify this impression by pinning Lewis down about the precise date the threat had been made. At first Lewis said it had been delivered the day after the fight, but he soon changed his mind and said it was two days later.

Sally Colvin was then called to the stand. The centerpiece of her brief testimony was her story about her unsuccessful attempt to swear her illegitimate child on its father. She described how Mr. Hitchcock had told her that she could not swear the child because as far as was known her husband was still living. She added that after her frustrating interview with Hitchcock she had gone to her father's to complain about her dilemma, and had been told by Stephen that she "could swear the child, for Russell was dead and he knew it."[11]

Eunice and Daniel Baldwin, a Dorset couple, followed with their recollections of Stephen's highly incriminating statement that he and his brother had put Russell "where potatoes would not freeze." Daniel added that Stephen immediately went on to deny that he and Jesse had killed their brother-in-law. But as far as Baldwin could tell, Stephen was not joking when he made his first statement. "This talk was serious as I understood it," Daniel reported.[12]

Of the ten witnesses who followed the Baldwins in the second phase of the prosecution's presentation, William Wyman was by far the most important. He described remarks that Stephen had made to him that seemingly provided evidence of a murder motive, namely, Stephen's anger at his sister and her husband for not being able to support their many children. Moreover, the fact that Stephen had made these hostile comments three or four weeks before the fight with Russell indicated that Stephen's striking Russell might have been premeditated and not a simple spur-of-the-moment act as he now contended.

The remaining nine individuals who testified in this phase of the trial were all chosen by Sheldon to support his case that the Boorn brothers had acted suspiciously, telling various and often contradictory stories after Colvin's disappearance. Even more incriminating, some of these stories appeared to be efforts to provide themselves with alibis.

Up to this point in his presentation Sheldon had established a possible motive for murder and introduced evidence indicating that a violent crime had taken place, but the success of his case was still far from assured. He could best clinch his argument against the Boorns by introducing their confessions. There were three in all: Jesse's alleged middle-of-the-night revelations to Silas Merrill, and two confessions of Stephen's, the one written in August 1819 and the other an oral statement he supposedly made to William Farnsworth in early September. The third and final phase of Sheldon's presentation was devoted to an attempt to get these confessions made part of the official trial record, an objective that led to a dramatic courtroom contest. Skinner and his associates fought to prevent the confessions from being admitted, not only because they contained very damaging statements, but because the Boorns' attorneys would not be able to counterattack by placing Stephen and Jesse on the stand to repudiate them. Under a Vermont law not repealed until 1866, the accused could not testify on his or her own behalf. As one twentieth-century critic explained it, the theory behind this rule was that the accused's "interest in the outcome was so great, and the incentive to falsify so strong, that his testimony would not be entitled to the credence of the jury. So, in order to remove the temptation to commit perjury, the unfortunate prisoner was prohibited from telling his story in court."[13]

Silas Merrill, the accused perjurer and sometime cellmate of Jesse Boorn, was called to testify. Before he could answer any of Sheldon's questions, he first had to respond to a challenge raised by Skinner, who asserted that anything Jesse might have revealed to Merrill was the result of questionable pressure exerted on him by town officers. Merrill admitted that on several occasions when Jesse had returned to his cell from an interrogation session, "he told me that *they* had encouraged him to confess the whole business with promise of pardon," which seemed to confirm Skinner's point.[14] But Merrill immediately denied that there was a connection between what had been said to Jesse by the magistrates and Jesse's decision to talk to him. Although Skinner objected to this line of reasoning and tried to block further disclosures by Merrill, the court ruled that the witness could proceed.

Merrill then once again told his story of what Jesse allegedly had revealed to him. He did not stop there, however. He went on to claim that in August he had also had a chance to talk with Stephen about Jesse's story. Merrill told the court, "I asked him if he did take the life of Colvin? He said he did not take the main life of Colvin."[15] This brief exchange became the principal basis for an elaborate theory about Stephen's confession that evolved after the trial. Stephen's reference to "the main life of Colvin" was taken to mean that he had not killed Colvin outright and that Colvin had run off into the woods, just as Stephen had originally said. When many years passed and Russell did not return, Stephen concluded that his blow had injured his brother-in-law so grievously that Russell had died of his wounds. Perhaps Stephen even felt remorse, and this, as well as promises of leniency, prompted him to confess. According to adherents of this theory, Stephen's later repudiation of his confession represented a reassertion of his belief that Colvin *might* be alive. In other words, Stephen honestly did not know whether Colvin was alive or dead.

Merrill also claimed to be the recipient of another revealing comment of Stephen's. Supposedly, not long after Stephen prepared his written confession, he and Merrill were taken to the court chambers and left alone. According to Merrill, "Stephen then said he had agreed with Jesse to take the whole business upon himself, and had made a confession which would only make manslaughter of it."[16]

Faced as he had been with a solid phalanx of authorities telling him that he was sure to hang, Stephen might well have decided to grasp at the possibility of getting the charge against him reduced from murder to manslaughter. The difference was of no small consequence. Conviction for homicide carried an automatic death penalty. Manslaughter, on the other hand, could result in one or all of the following three lesser punishments: whipping, "not exceeding one hundred stripes"; imprisonment, "not exceeding ten years"; and a fine, "not exceeding three thousand dollars."[17]

Having succeeded, despite Skinner's objections, in getting Merrill's version of Jesse's and Stephen's alleged confidences into the record, State's Attorney Sheldon moved to introduce Stephen Boorn's written confession of August 27, 1819. A preliminary issue that had to be settled was whether the confession was voluntary, that is, "made freely without the influence of threats or fear or promises of favor."[18] If involuntary, it would be excluded, both as unreliable and as contrary to the rule that the accused is protected against self-incrimination. Today, a ruling on the admissibility of the confession would be made by the trial judge, but in 1819 the issue had to be evaluated by the jury after hearing the evidence regarding the conditions under which the confession was made.

In rapid succession, Sheldon called as witnesses four members of the Manchester Village elite, all of them town officers who had been present at the time the confession was made: Josiah Burton, Joel Pratt, Truman Hill, and Samuel C. Raymond. In response to the prosecutor's questions about the circumstances under which Stephen had written his confession, Burton gave a very straightforward account of the events of the day without going into any discussion of what might have motivated the prisoner to confess. In his cross-examination, Skinner pressed for more information on the crucial point of Stephen's motivation. Did the witness, Skinner asked, know of the accused having been pressured to confess "by holding up to his view the hopes of pardon, or some other favor, by some officer, state's attorney, magistrate, grand juror, jailor, or deputy jailor?" Burton denied that such had been the case. Skinner persisted, asking, "Have you not heard some of the officers tell Stephen that his case was desperate, that he was gone if he did not confess?" Burton answered, "No."[19]

Joel Pratt was asked the same two questions by the defense attorney and replied to both in the negative. Skinner pressed on: "Do you know of any persuasion, and if any, what, tending to induce Stephen to make that confession?" Pratt sidestepped the question, answering that on August 27, Stephen had asked for his assistance in preparing a confession and he had given it. Skinner wryly observed that he had been asking for information about persuasion applied at "some previous time," but he let the matter drop there.[20]

Truman Hill, the grand jury chairman, was then asked to answer Skinner's question regarding whether town officers had promised Stephen a pardon in return for his cooperation. Hill, the maverick who had recently left the Congregational Church to become a Baptist, replied that "more than once" he had urged Stephen "to tell nothing but the truth, as the only way to pardon or favor." Of course, Silas Merrill had previously testified that Jesse's interrogators "had encouraged him to confess the whole business with promise of pardon," but Hill's statement was the first time an official had explicitly confirmed the use of such tactics with the Boorn brothers.[21]

Finally, Skinner called Samuel Raymond, an arresting officer and the leader of the faction of town officials who had advocated a high-pressure approach to get Stephen to confess. Not one to beat around the bush, Raymond did not try to dodge Skinner's questions. "I have heard," he said, "Mr. Pratt and Mr. Sheldon tell Jesse Boorn, that if he would confess, they would petition the legislature for him." Then, in an admission that gave Skinner the information he had been seeking, Raymond added, "I have made the same proposition to Stephen myself, and always told him I had no doubt of his guilt."[22]

Skinner clearly won this round. The jury ruled that Stephen's written confession was inadmissible as evidence.

Reading between the lines of Judge Chase's notes, it appears that State's Attorney Sheldon was momentarily at a loss as to how to handle this setback. His next three witnesses had little new to add. Sheldon's presentation did not regain momentum until the young prosecutor called the one remaining witness whose testimony might enable him to introduce a version of Stephen's confession: William Farnsworth, a friend who had frequently visited Stephen in jail.

No sooner had Sheldon begun by asking Farnsworth to describe the conversation he had with Stephen in early September, a few weeks after Stephen had prepared his written confession, than Skinner objected that these confidences should be excluded. Farnsworth's conversation with Stephen, he argued, had taken place after the activities of Raymond and his allies that had led the jury to rule Stephen's written confession inadmissable. The court nevertheless chose to conduct a preliminary examination of Farnsworth, who, as Jesse's confidant Merrill had done earlier, swore that he had not placed the prisoner under any pressure to tell all. As it had in Merrill's case, the jury voted to allow Farnsworth to continue his testimony.

This was a serious setback for the defense, and it soon prompted a major change of strategy by the Boorns' legal advisors. Farnsworth told the court about the conversation he had with Stephen in early September, during which Stephen allegedly admitted that he had murdered Russell Colvin, described many details of the crime (which Farnsworth proceeded to enumerate), and, finally, expressed regret at having given court officers a written confession.

At this juncture Skinner interrupted the proceedings. According to Chase's notes, "Here Mr. Skinner stated, that as Mr. Farnsworth had contrary to his expectations been allowed to testify, he now in behalf of the prisoner, called for the written confession, which was read as follows:"[23]

> May the tenth, 1812, I, about nine or ten o'clock, went down [to] David Glazier's bridge, and fished down below uncle Nathaniel Boorn's, and then went up across their farms, where Russell and Lewis was, being the nighest way, and sat down and began to talk, and Russell told me how many dollars benefit he had been to father, and I told him he was a damned fool, and he was mad and jumped up, and we sat close together, and I told him to set down, you little tory, and there was a piece of a beech limb about two feet long, and he catched it up and struck at my head as I sat down, and I jumpt up and it struck me on one shoulder, and I catched it out of his hand and struck him a back handed blow, I being on the north side of him, and there was a knot on it about one inch long. As I struck him I did think I hit him on his back, and he stooped down and that knot was broken off sharp, and it hit him on the back of the neck, close in his hair, and it went in about a half an inch on that great cord, and he fell down, and then I told the boy to go down and come up with his uncle John, and he asked me if I had killed Russell, and I told him no, but he must not tell that we struck one another. And I told him, when he got away down, Russell was gone away, and I went back and he was dead, and then I went and took him and put him in the corner of the fence by the cellar hole, and put briars

over him and went home and went down to the barn
and got some boards, and when it was dark I went down
and took a hoe and boards, and dug a grave as well as
I could, and took out of his pocket a little barlow knife,
with about a half of a blade, and cut some bushes and
put on his face and the boards, and put in the grave,
and put him in four boards, on the bottom, and on the
top, and t'other two on the sides, and then covered him
up, and went home crying along, but I want afraid as
I know on. And when I lived at William Boorn's I
planted some potatoes, and when I dug them I went
there and something I thought had been there, I took
up his bones and put them in a basket, and took the
boards and put on my potatoe hole, and then it was
night, took the basket and my hoe and went down and
pulled a plank in the stable floor, and then dug a hole,
and then covered him up, and went in the house and
told them I had done with the basket and took back the
shovel, and covered up my potatoes that evening, and
then when I lived under the west mountain, Lewis came
and told me that father's barn was burnt up, the next
day or the next day but one, I came down and went to
the barn and there was a few bones, and when they was
to dinner I told them I did not want my dinner, and
went and took them, and there want only a few of the
biggest of the bones, and throwed them in the river
above Wyman's, and then went back, and it was done
quick too, and then was hungry by that time, and then
went home, and the next Sunday I came down after
money to pay the boot that I gave to boot between oxens,
and went out there and scraped up them little things
that was under the stump there, and told them I was
going to fishing, and went, and there was a hole, and I
dropped them in and kicked over the stuff, and that is
the first any body knew it, either friends or foes, even
my wife. All these I acknowledge before the world.

STEPHEN BOORN.
Manchester, Aug. 27, 1819.

Some observers criticized Skinner's decision to have Stephen's confession included in the record, for in so doing he seemed to be abandoning ground that he had gained after a hard fight. In his defense it has been argued that, once Farnsworth had been allowed to give his version of Stephen's story, it would have done more harm than good to withhold the written document. The jury might well have suspected that the defense was trying to hide some particularly incriminating material found only in the written confession. In fact, it contained little that was not already part of the record. Admittedly, however, the complete success of the Farnsworth maneuver was a triumph for Sheldon. After the reading of the confession, the State's Attorney called only one more witness and then brought his presentation to a close.

Skinner and his associates made a much briefer presentation than the prosecution's. In all, the defense called fourteen individuals to the stand, half of whom had already testified. The points the defense attorneys tried to make on behalf of their clients can be grouped under four themes.

First, Sally Colvin, William Wyman, Joel Pratt, and Russell Colvin's sister Clarissa Ferguson were asked to confirm that Russell had frequently left town on previous occasions, in one case for a period of eight or nine months. Since the prosecution had been unable to produce a body, and the circumstantial evidence that Russell had been done away with was inconclusive, the defense was attempting to establish that Russell's disappearance might well be the result of his well-known predilection for wandering off.

Second, Squire Pratt was questioned about what Lewis Colvin, the only independent witness to a blow having been struck by Stephen, had said before the court of inquiry in April and May. Pratt replied that Lewis had first told the court that he and his father were alone in the field, that his father began "throwing rails about—act[ing] strangely," and that this so frightened the boy that he had run off to

his grandfather's.[24] In drawing attention to the fact that
Lewis's initial story was at odds with his subsequent statements, the defense once again attempted to discredit him as
a witness.

Third, Skinner and his associates sought to show that the
story of Colvin's body being buried in the cellar hole and
later removed and reburied under the sheep barn was possibly untrue. As noted earlier, the substantiation usually
offered for this story was the fact that a young apple tree
growing in the cellar hole had been dug up and the ground
beneath it disturbed, and that some time thereafter the
sheep barn had burned down and supposedly forced Stephen
to move Colvin's bones again. But Thomas Johnson, the
owner of the field, the barn, and the apple tree, was not only
vague as to when he had last seen the tree in question, but
had to admit that he believed he had seen it after the barn
burned. If the whole chronology of the alleged burial and
removal of Russell's bones was thrown into doubt, it raised
the possibility that Stephen had described these particular
actions in his confession not because they had occurred but
because they were what his interrogators wanted him to say.

The defense team's fourth goal was to discredit the various
confessions on which the prosecution's case relied so heavily.
Skinner tried to show that Silas Merrill's claim that Jesse
had confessed to him was a lie. Daniel Wellman, the third
and least active of the Boorns' attorneys, was called to the
stand. Wellman, who had probably been Merrill's attorney
either in the perjury case for which he was currently in jail
or in an earlier case, testified that when he had heard that
Jesse had confessed to Merrill, he asked Merrill if this was
true, and Merrill told him that Jesse "had not made a confession."[25]

Skinner then undertook to prove that the authorities gave
Merrill preferential treatment as a reward for testifying
against the Boorns before the grand jury. Cyrus Munson,
one of the town jailers, was questioned on this point and

admitted that "previous to [Merrill's] disclosure before the grand jury, [he] was confined in chains, and afterwards was freed from them."[26] Evidently, he was even let out of prison on several occasions, albeit only for the purpose of helping Munson with some farm work. Munson, however, contended that this change in jail routine had come about because the jail had fewer inmates after the grand jury sessions and that the reduced number of prisoners, not any special favors for Merrill, explained the more relaxed regime.

Skinner next attempted to document further his contention that the Boorns' confessions had not been voluntary, but were induced by pressures. Four witnesses testified on this point, all of them members of the Manchester Village elite. Once again, as in the earlier contest over whether Stephen's written confession was admissible evidence, divisions among the village's prominent citizens were openly on display. Samuel Raymond, the leader of the hard-line faction, and two of his allies defended the town officers' conduct. John Pettibone, however, the man who had taken an independent course in releasing Barney Boorn from custody the previous spring and in leaving the Congregational Church that summer, was more critical. Yes, he said, Jesse had been threatened by Squire Pratt and Josiah Burton, who had told him that unless he proved his innocence by providing a full description of what Stephen had done, he might "suffer with Stephen on his [Jesse's] former confession and denial." Here, Pettibone was referring to Jesse's admission, made on May 1 to Truman Hill, that "he feared that Stephen had killed Colvin," and to his subsequent retraction of that statement after Stephen was brought back to Manchester in mid-May. Meanwhile Stephen, according to Pettibone, was placed under pressure to confess by comments like Josiah Burton's "you are a gone goose," which implied that he would surely hang if he did not admit his guilt in hopes of receiving a pardon or a reduced sentence.[27]

The final statements of counsel were made on October 31, beginning with the prosecutor's summation. Sheldon began by asking, rhetorically, whether the crime under review in the Boorn trial was murder or manslaughter. His answer was that the malicious intent evident in Stephen's threats against the Colvins prior to May 1812 definitely made the killing of Russell Colvin an act of murder. The prosecutor next commented on the distinction between direct proof and circumstantial evidence and argued that the latter was an adequate basis for conviction when it could be shown that the accused and "no other person" was in a position to commit the crime and when, as was so apparent from the Boorns' contradictory statements, there was evidence that the accused had attempted to conceal a crime. On these issues, Sheldon claimed, "The evidence must be satisfactory to all reasonable intent, not beyond the *possibility* of doubt." Finally, Sheldon discussed the matter of confessions. He made no direct reference to Stephen's written confession, apparently fearing that he would weaken his case if he based it on a document that the jury had voted to exclude from the record. He contended that the prisoners' oral statements, Jesse's to Silas Merrill and Stephen's to William Farnsworth, were "sufficient" to establish guilt since they were corroborated by many other known facts. Merrill's story, he asserted, should not be judged unreliable simply because Merrill had told it while in jail, allegedly under a promise of reward.[28]

Leonard Sargeant, the youngest of the Boorns' attorneys, led off for the defense. The real issue, he maintained, was whether adequate proof of guilt had been offered. His answer was that it had not. The prosecution, he contended, had not even proved that Russell Colvin, who was known as "a roving man," was dead. To be sure, Thomas Johnson had witnessed a quarrel in progress, but the fact of a quarrel was not proof of Colvin's death. Lewis Colvin's testimony on the subject was so contradictory—"he never heard anything said in the family for two years; then one year; then a little more than a month"—as to be useless. The same, he argued, was true of the circumstantial evidence offered by the prosecution. The cellar hole where Colvin supposedly had been buried was too small to hold a body. The old knives and buttons found there were the sort of objects "often found about old houses," and Sally Colvin's identification of the items was not conclusive, since "knives and buttons are often alike." Testimony regarding threats made prior to Russell's disappearance in no way proved that Stephen murdered Russell. "Besides," Sargeant noted in a tart reference to Sally Colvin's reputation, "killing Colvin would not stop Sal's having children, such were her prostituted nature." In sum, Sargeant concluded, the prosecution's case "came to nothing."[29]

Sargeant's senior partner now rose to continue the defense team's summation. Skinner opened with a scathing critique of the town officials' carelessness relative to "the law about voluntary confession." He charged that both Stephen and Jesse had been badly used by officials who were less interested in determining the truth than in obtaining evidence against the prisoners. He was dismissive of the alleged revelations that followed from the pressure that the court officers had brought to bear on the Boorn brothers. However full of specifics Merrill's tale about Jesse's middle-of-the-night confession seem to be, he argued, it was in fact the handiwork of a known dissembler. "Who is Merrill?" Skinner asked. "All we know of him is he is a prisoner for the worst of crimes. Besides, since telling his story his case has been alleviated. He knew this would be the consequence."[30]

In Skinner's opinion, none of the remaining evidence offered positive proof either of Colvin's death or of his having died by Stephen's hand. Picking up on his young associate's assertion that the prosecution's case came to nothing, Skinner rapidly ticked off a list of allegedly incriminating facts that proved nothing. "The apple tree story," he said, "is nothing. The button and Jack knife story is nothing. The Toe nail story is nothing. The Bones story is nothing." Also, Skinner contended, even the "prisoners saying they knew Russell was dead is accounted for by its being their interest to have such a belief," since Stephen's comment that Russell was dead had been made to his sister Sally, whose illegitimate child would have to be supported by the Boorn family as long as the authorities believed her husband was alive.[31]

In his closing exhortation, Skinner urged the jury to draw a distinction between murder and manslaughter. He argued that even if, despite the defense counsels' best efforts, the jury concluded that a crime had taken place, the crime was manslaughter rather than murder. He reminded the jury that under Vermont law a murder conviction required

Judge Dudley Chase's trial notes: a page from the section summarizing Skinner's closing arguments.

evidence of what he called "the will to kill," and he asserted that the prosecution had failed to establish that in returning Russell's blow Stephen had acted with murderous intent.[32]

The prosecution and defense having finished their closing arguments, the two senior justices instructed the jury. According to Leonard Sargeant's account, Judge Doolittle gave the charge "in relation to the law of homicide, and Judge Chase in relation to the evidence." In his remarks, Chase cautioned the jury to determine whether any or all of the Boorns' confessions had been "incited by hope or fear," and to disregard any statements made under those conditions.[33] The jurors filed out. About an hour later they returned and announced that they were prepared to render a verdict. At Skinner's request the jurors were polled individually on how they had voted. Whatever other purpose this served, it added solemnity to the jury's report. One by one these twelve citizens of Bennington County stood and answered "guilty," first with regard to Stephen and then a second time with regard to Jesse. No distinction was drawn between the two brothers. Both were convicted of murder.

A recess followed, lasting about an hour. When the justices returned, Judge Chase, according to an eyewitness, "with the most tender and sympathetic emotion, which he was unable to suppress, pronounced the awful sentence" required by Vermont law. Stephen and Jesse were to be remanded to jail and held there until January 28, 1820, on which day, as Chase said, "between the hours of ten and two o'clock, they be hanged by the neck until each of them be dead; and may the Lord have mercy on their souls."[34]

The Reverend Lemuel Haynes, an observer sympathetic to the Boorns' plight, recalled that the prisoners asked through their attorneys to be permitted to speak. Their request was granted, whereupon, as Haynes put it, "In sighs and broken accents they asserted their innocence." After making his final plea, Stephen was so distraught that he was, according to Haynes, "unable to walk; but he was supported by others, and carried to prison."[35]

The jury's decision was decidedly popular. In the words of one eyewitness, the "verdict gave unqualified satisfaction to the crowds in attendance at the trial."[36] That fact, of course, sheds no light on the question of whether the trial was fair and the verdict justified. The key procedural issue undoubtedly involved the admissibility of the Boorns' confessions. As noted earlier, the defense attorneys did their best to keep these damaging statements from being admitted. Skinner challenged the correctness of allowing Merrill and Farnsworth to testify to what Jesse and Stephen had supposedly told them, arguing that improper pressure from court officers had influenced the prisoners' decisions to talk. The trial record indicates that the jury took Skinner's objections seriously and made a sincere effort to distinguish between what was admissible and what was not. It excluded Stephen's written confession because of the clear evidence of interference by court officers, but it voted to accept Merrill's and Farnsworth's testimony because there was no suggestion that either man had put Jesse or Stephen under pressure to confide in him. Perhaps the jury at times ruled unwisely, but unquestionably the jurors followed proper procedures according to the accepted practice of the time in Vermont, which held that the jury rather than the judge was to rule on both the admissibility of a confession and the truth of its content.

Even if it is granted that the trial was procedurally fair, there remains a question whether the Boorns were convicted on the evidence against them or because of the pressure of hostile public opinion. Richard Skinner felt that public prejudice had a lot to do with the verdict. He told a young friend that the trial was "an instance of those strange popular delusions, which sometimes sweep through the most intelligent and conscientious communities, subverting truth and reason and justice." But Skinner's was a minority opinion in the period immediately after the trial. The author of a letter that appeared in a Bennington, Vermont, newspaper in January 1820 was probably more representative of the views of most knowledgeable local observers at that time, which was that the verdict was convincing and that it was based on solid evidence rather than bias. The writer, who identified himself only as "A Citizen of Vermont," reported that he had been "wholly unacquainted with the Boorns when their trial commenced," denied that he was "swayed by prejudice in any of the proceedings," and declared that after attending the whole trial, he was convinced that the Boorns had received just what they deserved. "I am confident in stating," he wrote, "that twelve honest men could not be found in the civilized world, who with the same testimony and circumstances before them would not give the same verdict."[37]

Still, the verdict of murder and the sentence of death by hanging seem more severe than the evidence would have required. The only testimony that seemed to support the view that Stephen had a prior intention to injure Russell and thus struck his brother-in-law in a premeditated and deliberate way was William Wyman's report that Stephen had made vague threats against the Colvins before Russell disappeared. By contrast, quite a bit of evidence—Stephen's written confession, his statements to Farnsworth, and Lewis Colvin's testimony—had Russell striking the first blow, which might have served as the basis for a verdict of manslaughter rather than murder. In Jesse's case, there was little evidence to show that he was anything more than a bystander who, at worst, became an accessory after the fact by helping Stephen cover up the crime. To be sure, as an authority on Vermont law has observed, "by the common law then in force, the penalty was the same, whether the culprit was a principal in felony, or an accessory."[38] Nevertheless,

if a murder conviction and the death penalty seem harsh in
Stephen's case, they seem even more so in Jesse's, and one
cannot entirely dismiss the possibility that the harshness of
the verdict was the product of an anti-Boorn bias that had
led many Manchester residents and officials to declare Stephen and Jesse guilty long before the trial began.

Once the actual verdict was rendered, a small but significant shift began to take place in attitudes toward the
Boorns. The hard-liners' total victory gave some Manchester
residents cause to have second thoughts. Perhaps the stark
fact that the condemned men would soon be hanged was
enough to soften the hearts of a few. Others definitely felt
the sentences were excessive, especially in Jesse's case. Also,
some of the brothers' friends and relatives did not believe
that the Boorns were murderers, despite the jury's final judgment. The number of local citizens holding these views who
were willing to do something about them was very small,
but this minority now rallied in hopes of helping one or both
of the Boorns obtain a lighter sentence. To this end Leonard
Sargeant drew up and circulated a petition on the prisoners'
behalf. The petition's text noted that the trial had produced
testimony that tended "to alleviate their crime, and to di-
minish, if not entirely destroy, the presumption of malice."[39]
The closing lines appealed to the state legislature to pass a
law reducing the Boorns' sentences from death to life imprisonment.

Sargeant made it plain to prospective signers that they
could indicate support for both brothers or for either one
separately, and on this basis he collected a total of twenty-
six signatures. All who signed backed Jesse's appeal, but
only nine were ready to support Stephen's. In contrast to
Stephen, who had taken complete responsibility for killing
Colvin on himself, Jesse was viewed as being only an accessory to the crime. Of the nine men who signed on Stephen's behalf, three can be cited as representative of the
various sources of support for him. Gideon Barrett was a

relative through his marriage to Stephen's cousin Sarah, the daughter of Jared Boorn. Christopher Roberts was an old friend of the family, a wealthy resident of the north part of town whose ties with the Boorns dated back more than forty years to pioneer times when he and Stephen's grandfather Nathaniel Boorn had fought together for the patriot cause. Samuel Raymond was representative of those Manchester citizens who believed Stephen was guilty of murder but did not want to see him hang. As a town officer, Raymond had led the hard-liners who had promised to aid Stephen if he would confess, and he decided to honor his pledge even though Stephen had later retracted his written confession.

Seventeen men signed on Jesse's behalf and not on his brother's. Although they came from locations scattered all over town, a disproportionate percentage were Manchester Village residents, a pattern that was probably determined more by Sargeant's network of personal contacts than by the actual distribution of the Boorns' supporters in town. One subgroup among the signers was composed of town officers who had opposed the hard-line faction, notably John Pettibone, Truman Hill, and Joseph Burr, the town treasurer. Conspicuous by its absence was Josiah Burton's name. Burton, a hard-liner, had promised to aid the Boorns if they cooperated with the official investigation, but apparently he, unlike Samuel Raymond, did not feel either brother had met his conditions for assistance. One of Burton's nephews, Elijah Burton, Jr., did sign, however. Many of Jesse's supporters also had ties of one sort or another with the town's pioneer period and that era's relatively relaxed moral standards, and such ties in all likelihood led these men to be less harsh than some of their neighbors in judging the Boorns' behavior. Representatives of pioneer families who showed up on the list included John Pettibone, Eli Purdy, and Christopher Roberts's son Jonathan. Two tavern owners, Peter Black and

Jared Munson, signed. William Farnsworth, the heavy-drinking Dorset man whose testimony had been so damaging to Stephen's case, added his name to the list of Jesse's supporters, though he refused to aid Stephen.

Sargeant dated his petition November 6, 1819, which was a Saturday, and either on that day or early the following week he left Manchester for Vermont's capital, Montpelier, where the state legislature was in session. Sargeant's departure did not leave the Boorn brothers without friends and visitors, however, and among these none was more conscientious and sympathetic than the Reverend Lemuel Haynes, minister of the First Congregational Church. Haynes had begun to visit the Boorns during the summer of 1819, at first simply because he felt it was his duty to minister to the occupants of the jail just down the street from the meeting house. However, Haynes, who had faced a great deal of adversity and prejudice in his own life, eventually came to feel very sympathetic toward the Boorns, Stephen in particular, and to believe that the accused men were innocent.

From the Boorn brothers' viewpoint the Reverend Haynes was principally an invaluable ally, but from a broader perspective he was one of the most remarkable Americans of his time. Born in 1753, he was the illegitimate son of a black manservant and a white woman from a prominent Connecticut family. He was abandoned at the age of five months by his mother and placed out with a Granville, Massachusetts, couple who, fortunately for him, proved to be pious and warmhearted foster parents. When the American Revolution broke out, Haynes, who had just turned twenty-one, went off to fight for the patriot cause, participating in the siege of Boston and the Battle of Ticonderoga (1775). That his commitment to revolutionary principles extended well beyond the war's end is evidenced by a sermon entitled "The Nature and Importance of True Republicanism" that he preached on July 4, 1801, the twenty-fifth an-

*Lemuel Haynes
(1753–1833).*

niversary of the signing of the Declaration of Independence. In this address he condemned the enslavement of blacks as a form of despotism completely at odds with the ideals for which he and others had fought in the Revolution.

Once Haynes's military service was over, he decided that his religious and intellectual inclinations were such that he should seek a career in the ministry. While earning his living as a schoolteacher, he began to study Greek and Latin, and in 1780 he was granted a license to preach. He was then hired by the Congregational Church of Middle Granville, Massachusetts, thereby becoming the first black to preach on a regular basis to an all white congregation. It was the first of many firsts for Haynes and the beginning of an extraordinary career. In 1783 he married Elizabeth Babbitt, a white schoolteacher with whom he had ten children. He was ordained in 1785 and accepted a post at a church in Torrington, Connecticut. Encountering racial prejudice there, he moved to West Rutland, Vermont, where he served as the minister of the local Congregational Church for the next thirty years. The ways of West Rutland dismayed and challenged him. "I never knew infidelity more prevalent," he wrote soon after his arrival.⁴⁰ He immediately set out to combat the immorality, intoxication, and liberal religion that so often characterized Vermont frontier life. Theologically conservative, he was uncompromising in his affirmation of orthodox Calvinism. He won renown for a celebrated sermon, "Universal Salvation" (1805), in which he inveighed against the liberal doctrine of universal salvation espoused by Hosea Ballou, a Universalist clergyman. So well received was this sermon that a pamphlet version of it went through ten editions by 1821.

Haynes enjoyed growing respect from his white peers in the early 1800s. In 1804 Middlebury College awarded him the first honorary degree given a black by an American college, and in 1809 the Vermont Missionary Society made him its field secretary. During a triumphant tour of Connecticut in 1814, he preached to a packed meeting house in New Haven, speaking so eloquently that Yale's president reported that he was moved to tears. Moreover, Haynes not only was admired from a distance as an eloquent preacher but was a man his white associates liked to be around. One often-repeated story about Haynes's popularity with his fellow ministers concerned conferences at which conferees had to share beds, a common practice in an era when the scarcity of hotel accommodations frequently forced guests to bunk with strangers. When the time came to choose bedfellows at such meetings, the first cry to go up was usually "I will sleep with Mr. Haynes!" A black editor who reviewed Haynes's life in the 1830s also noted his ability to move comfortably and find acceptance in white circles. "He is," the editor wrote, "the only man of *known* African descent, who has ever succeeded in overpowering the system of American *caste*."⁴¹

Still, Haynes's career was not without its setbacks, one of which came in 1818 when, after thirty years of preaching to the West Rutland Congregationalists, he was forced to resign because of political prejudice against his loyalty to the Federalist Party, which he had continued to defend despite the overwhelming popularity of Jeffersonian Republicanism locally. He was sixty-five and not in search of another full-time post, but the Manchester Village church lacked a resident minister at the time and sought his assistance, first as a visiting preacher and then as a regular appointee. Haynes began to preach frequently at Manchester after the revival of 1816–17 had brought many new members into the church and just as the controversy over baptism was about to throw the congregation into turmoil. Although Haynes eventually sided with the orthodox majority, he was a man who had seen the baneful effects of political and theological disputes, and it clearly pained him to see the Manchester Village community divided over subjects on which he felt God alone should be the judge. Much more in Haynes's style as a unifier was his practice of stopping by to chat and joke with the people gathered at the door to Captain Black's Tavern just across the street from the meeting house.

As a result of his pastoral visits with Stephen Boorn during the summer and fall of 1819, the Reverend Haynes developed not only considerable sympathy for the prisoner's predicament but also great admiration for his spirit. Once, in response to Stephen's complaints that he was being persecuted for deeds he had not done, Haynes mentioned Christ as someone whose innocent suffering might deserve Stephen's emulation. Stephen exclaimed, "I am as innocent as Jesus Christ!" When Haynes chided him for his conceit, Stephen replied, "I don't mean that I am guiltless as he was; I know I am a great sinner; but I am as innocent of killing Colvin as he was."[42] Stephen's contrition for his sins and his anguished protest that he was innocent left Haynes deeply and favorably impressed. But there seemed little that he could do except pray with the prisoner.

Leonard Sargeant, the Boorns' other ally among the village elite, did have something that he could do, namely, present his petition to Vermont's General Assembly in hope of convincing the legislators to reduce the Boorns' sentences. (Until 1836 Vermont had a one-house legislature, the General Assembly, composed of one elected representative from each town; a Governor's Council of twelve members served as a review body.) Soon after his arrival in Montpelier he learned that several able members of the House, as the General Assembly was often called, were willing to support his project. The legislators, meanwhile, asked for and received Judge Chase's notes on the trial proceedings. Initially, Friday, November 12 was designated as the date discussion of the Boorns' petition would begin, but various delays led to a postponement until Saturday. On Saturday, however, no decisions were made, which left Sargeant on tenterhooks over the rest of the weekend. Finally, on Monday, November 15, the House devoted most of its afternoon session to an intense debate of the Boorn-Colvin case. The following morning the legislators voted, 104 to 33, to reduce Jesse's sentence to life in prison at hard labor. Stephen's appeal did not fare so well, however; a motion stating that it was "inexpedient to grant any relief" to him passed by better than a two-to-one margin, 97 to 43.[43] The favorable decision on Jesse's plea, which had the support of more than three-quarters of the representatives who voted, owed very little to members from his home county of Bennington, or from Rutland, the next county to the north. These near neighbors of the Boorns voted against Jesse's appeal by a thirteen-to-eight margin, while every other county's delegation showed a majority of at least two-to-one in favor of granting Jesse's request. Close to home, evidently, the Boorns' cause was still not popular.

Later on the day of the General Assembly's vote, the governor and council concurred with the decisions on the Boorns' petition. These were practically the last actions taken during the 1819 session. Knowing that a heavy snowfall, especially in the state's northern counties, might block Vermont's roads at any time from mid-November onward, the legislators were anxious to finish their business. After an early morning meeting on Wednesday, November 17, the governor and his council called it quits and headed for home. As it happened, Governor Jonas Galusha was from Shaftsbury, a Bennington County town not far south of Manchester. Since his route home took him through Manchester Village, the governor stopped at the jail to deliver personally the news of the General Assembly's and his council's actions on the petition. The prisoners' reactions were fairly predictable. According to the Reverend Haynes, "Jesse received the news with peculiar satisfaction; while Stephen was greatly depressed, being wholly left without hope."[44]

After Governor Galusha left, Leonard Sargeant visited Stephen and found him deeply despondent. Stephen wanted to know if there was really nothing else to be done. Sargeant replied that every available option had been exhausted. As Sargeant was about to leave, Stephen seemed to have a fresh thought. Why not, he asked, advertise in newspapers, asking for information regarding Russell Colvin's whereabouts? Sargeant, after drily observing that advertisements wouldn't do very much good if Colvin was dead, asked Stephen, "Did you murder Colvin as you confessed you did?"[45] Stephen protested vehemently that he had not, and Sargeant left after promising to do as Stephen wished.

Sargeant had never met Russell Colvin, so he went to his mentor Richard Skinner, who had dealt with Colvin and could provide a description of him. Skinner was skeptical of the whole enterprise. It was, he argued, "a foolish expedient." Given the "limited circulation of newspapers ... and the slow circulation of the mails," the advertisement was unlikely to reach any interested or knowledgeable parties in the barely two months left before Stephen was to be executed. Sargeant nevertheless pressed Stephen's cause, and Skinner prepared the following notice to be sent to the *Rutland Herald*.[46]

> **MURDER.**
> Printers of newspapers thro'. out the United States, are desired to publish, that Stephen Boorn, of Manchester, in Vermont, is sentenced to be executed for the murder of Russel Colvin, who has been absent about seven years. Any person who can give information of said Colvin, may save the life of the innocent by making immediate communication. Colvin is about five feet five inches high, light complexion, light coloured hair, blue eyes, about forty years of age.
> *Manchester, Vt, Nov. 25, 1819.*

Rutland Herald *advertisement for Russell Colvin.*

On November 29, four days after the advertisement was drafted, Sheriff Heman Robinson of Bennington County came to take Jesse from the Manchester jail to the Vermont state prison at Windsor, where he was to begin serving his life sentence. Stephen's spirits sank lower yet in the wake of his brother's departure. Events were moving all too rapidly toward his January 28th date with the hangman. Of this period his frequent visitor, the Reverend Haynes, later wrote, "I . . . endeavoured to turn his mind on the things of another world; telling him that, as all human means failed, he must look to God as the only way of deliverance." Haynes suggested that the condemned man might profitably read the Bible, and when Stephen pointed out that his windowless interior cell had no light by which to read, Haynes managed to get him a candle. The good reverend was pleased to see that the prisoner read scripture regularly, but was saddened to find Stephen's mood so changeable, "at times calm, and again impatient."[47]

Early in December, Haynes had another interview with Stephen that made such a marked impression on him that he recorded it at length in his account of the Boorn-Colvin case. He began by quoting Stephen's words, as follows:[48]

> "Mr. Haynes, I see no way but I must die; every thing works against me; but I am an innocent man; this you will know after I am dead." He burst into a flood of tears, and said, "What will become of my poor wife and children! they are in needy circumstances, and I love them better than life itself." I told him God would take care of them. He replied, "I don't want to die. I wish they would let me live even in this situation some longer; perhaps something will take place that may convince people that I am innocent." I was about to leave the prison when he said, "Will you pray with me?" He arose, with his heavy chains on his hands and legs, being also chained down to the floor, and stood on his feet during the prayer, with deep and bitter sighings.

The Dead Alive!

*To the utter astonishment of the whole community
...RUSSELL COLVIN YET LIVES!! and well may
it be exclaimed,* he was dead and is alive, he was lost
and is found!

—FROM A PAMPHLET ON THE BOORN CASE (1819)[1]

FRIENDS who visited Stephen Boorn in early December found the prisoner deeply despondent. It seemed almost certain that he would be executed. His only hope depended on the very slim chance that the advertisement his attorneys were circulating on his behalf would reach someone with information that Russell

---

The title of this chapter was originally a headline from the *New England Palladium and Commercial Advertiser* (Boston), December 14, 1819; Wilkie Collins used the phrase as the title of his short novel based on the Boorn-Colvin case, *The Dead Alive* (1874), discussed below, in chapter 5.

Colvin was still alive. But since most newspapers of the time were weeklies with small circulations, the advertisement was very slow in reaching the reading public. It first appeared on November 30, 1819, in the *Rutland Herald.* A week later it was reprinted in the *Vermont Journal* of Windsor, the town where Jesse Boorn's new home, the state prison, was located. After another ten days the notice was picked up and printed by the *Berkshire Star* of Stockbridge, Massachusetts, and five days after that, on December 21, it was published by the *National Standard* of Middlebury, Vermont. By then nearly a month had passed since Stephen's lawyers had drawn up the advertisement and only about five weeks remained until his scheduled execution. Appealing for news of Russell in this manner was clearly a dangerously slow process. Worse yet, several Vermont papers ignored the notice altogether, and even the *Rutland Herald,* which first printed it, appended a none-too-encouraging comment from the editors. They would be glad, they wrote, if someone responded positively, but it was their distinct impression that

Vermont State Prison at Windsor.

the trial had produced "clear and conclusive" proof of the Boorns' guilt.[2]

Jesse Boorn, meanwhile, was no longer in any danger of being hanged, but he did have to adjust to the unpleasant realities of life as an inmate at the new state prison at Windsor. Construction on this imposing three-story stone structure had begun in 1809. Its proponents were modernizers who, like their counterparts in other states, viewed imprisonment as an enlightened alternative to such traditional punishments as ear cropping, branding, and execution. But, as Jesse Boorn soon discovered, the new state prisons produced their own inhumanities. In Vermont, despite the fact that daytime temperatures often stayed below freezing for weeks at a time during mid-winter months, the prisoners' cells were unheated. One convict who served time at Windsor in the 1820s recalled that in winter he occasionally passed the hours by making "large [ice] balls by scraping the frost with my hand from the stone sides of my cell." Harsh punishments, including solitary confinement on a bread and water diet, were meted out for such infractions of the rules as smiling or speaking to a fellow inmate without permission, or even for being sick, since illness was almost always viewed as malingering. Prisoners were required to work, chiefly at weaving, and were paid a small wage for their efforts, but the working day could run as long as twelve to fifteen hours. Only the prisoners' uniforms, "party-colored clothes, half green and half scarlet," brightened the grim surroundings.[3]

As the Boorns languished in their respective prisons, an anonymous letter to the editors about the Boorn-Colvin case appeared in a New York paper, the *Albany Gazette and Daily Advertiser* (also known simply as the *Daily Advertiser*). Strangely enough, this letter, whose publication on November 25 preceded by five days the first appearance of the Boorns' attorneys' advertisement, would do the job that the advertisement had been intended to do. Identifying himself only as "a subscriber," the author of the *Daily Advertiser* letter wrote that he wanted to report "a most striking example of divine agency" that had been brought to his attention by "a gentleman of the first respectability." He proceeded to give a somewhat garbled account of the Boorn-Colvin case. Russell Colvin, he said, was "a man of respectable connections and character" who had "suddenly and mysteriously disappeared" from Manchester several years earlier. Colvin's fate might have remained unknown, the author asserted, had it not been "that we are watched over by a guardian providence." As proof of providential intervention, the author reported that "a person dreamt that [Colvin] appeared to him, and informed him that he had been murdered by two persons whom he named, and that he had been buried in such a place, a few rods distant from a sapling, bearing a particular mark, which he minutely described." Upon awakening, the dreamer gathered friends and searched for the sapling. They not only found the marked tree but they also discovered "the appearance of a grave." Upon digging, they unearthed "a human skeleton." Two men, identified in an editorial note as Stephen and Jesse Brown [*sic*], were arrested, and, "after a few days, confessed the deed."[4]

This story proved too sensational for many editors to resist, and reprints of the letter soon appeared, errors and all, in several major city papers, notably in the *New York Evening Post* on November 26. The next morning, James Whelpley, a New York City tavern owner and a former Manchester resident, happened to be one of a small group of men who were standing around in a public room of a New York City hotel. One of their number was entertaining the others by reading aloud from the previous day's *Evening Post*. When the reader began the *Daily Advertiser* item, Whelpley recognized it as the story of Stephen and Jesse Boorn. All the major actors in the Boorn-Colvin case were well known to Whelpley. His father and the Boorns' grandfather had settled in Manchester during the town's early pioneer period. The Boorns and the Whelpleys, including James and his wife, had attended the Baptist church in Manchester Center, and both families owned land in East Manchester. Moreover, Whelpley had until recently been the proprietor of a small store in Manchester Center that the Boorns had doubtless patronized. When the reading of the reprinted letter was completed, Whelpley immediately spoke up and regaled the small audience with stories about the Boorns, Russell Colvin, and the events in Vermont that led up to the Boorns' trial.

Also present in this group was a man named Taber Chadwick, a Methodist preacher from Shrewsbury, New Jersey, who was visiting the city. There is nothing to indicate that Chadwick spoke with Whelpley on the morning of November 27. The only extant sources make it sound as though Chadwick left the hotel without introducing himself to Whelpley and returned to Shrewsbury, where he spent more than a week mulling over everything he had heard on the 27th. Not until nine days later did he take action. On December 6, he composed a letter and mailed it to the editor of the *New York Evening Post.* He also sent a copy of the letter to the postmaster at Manchester, Vermont. Chadwick's startling news was that he believed Colvin was alive and well in New Jersey:[5]

SHREWSBURY, MONMOUTH, [N.J.] DEC. 6

To the Editor of the *New York Evening Post,*

Sir—

Having read in your paper of Nov. 26th last, of the conviction and sentence of Stephen and Jesse Brown, of Manchester, Vermont, charged with the murder of Russel Colvin, and from facts which have fallen within my own knowledge, and not knowing what facts may have been disclosed on their trial, and wishing to serve the cause of humanity, I would state as follows, which may be relied upon. Some years past, (I think between five and ten,) a stranger made his appearance in this county, and on being enquired of, said that his name was Russel Colvin, (which name he answers to at this time,) that he came from Manchester, Vermont—he appeared to be in a state of mental derangement, but at times gave considerable account of himself—his connections, acquaintances, &c.—he mentions the name of Clarissa, Rufus, &c.—among his relations he has mentioned the Browns above, Chase, as judge, (I think) &c. &c. He is a man rather small in statue, round favoured, speaks very fast, has two scars on his head, and appears to be between 30 and 40 years of age. There is no doubt but that he came from Vermont, from the mention he has made of a number of places and persons there, and probably is the person supposed to have been murdered. He is now living here, but so completely insane, as not to be able to give any satisfactory account of himself, but the connections of Russel Colvin, might know by seeing him. If you think proper to give this a place in your columns, it may possibly lead to a discovery that may save the lives of innocent men—if so, you will have the pleasure (as well as myself) of having served the cause of humanity. If you will give this an insertion in your paper, pray be so good as to request the different editors of news-papers in New-York and Vermont, to give it a place in theirs.

I am, sir, with sentiments of regard, your's &c.

TABER CHADWICK

Chadwick's letter appeared in *The New York Evening Post* on December 10. Its details, especially the references to Colvin's sister Clarissa and his son Rufus, strengthened the case that Colvin had been found. However, the phrase "Chase, as judge" is peculiar, since Colvin would have had no knowledge of the Boorn trial nor of its presiding judge. The *Rutland Herald*, the first Vermont paper to reprint Chadwick's letter, initially used the "Chase, as judge" phrase, but after learning from Manchester sources that Jesse Boorn's nickname was "judge," the *Herald*'s publishers assumed that the *Evening Post*'s version was a misprint, and they and many others subsequently rendered the line either "Jess, as judge" or "Jesse, as judge."[6] There is no doubt, however, that "Chase" was the name that originally appeared in the *Evening Post*.

As Whelpley later told the story, seeing Chadwick's letter galvanized him into action, and he set out as soon as possible for Shrewsbury, the small New Jersey shore town where Chadwick lived. Once Whelpley located the Methodist preacher, he learned that the man Chadwick believed to be Colvin was working for Chadwick's sister Mary and her husband, William Polhemus. The Polhemuses were owners of a farm and saw mill located in Dover Township, about twenty-five miles south of Shrewsbury. Repeating what he had written in his letter, Chadwick told Whelpley that a man calling himself Russell Colvin had showed up at the Polhemus place many years earlier. Through long service to the family as a laborer, this former transient had become a welcome member of the Polhemus household.

Whelpley next hired a man and a wagon and followed Chadwick's directions to Polhemus Mills, which was located between Kettle Creek and Mosquito Cove in what was then Monmouth County. (Today the area is called Silverton and is part of Ocean County, which split off from Monmouth in 1850.) He first spoke with William Polhemus, asking him for information about Colvin. According to Whelpley's account of his New Jersey sojourn, "Mr. Polhemus said there was such a man in his employ, that he had made known very little of his past history, that he at first gave his name as Colvin and afterwards changed it, that he was evidently deranged, but was a good, faithful man, and imagined he owned the farm of his employer." Since the said individual was then at work, Whelpley and Polhemus agreed to wait until he came home, at which time they would not mention Whelpley's name or the purpose of his visit. When the man returned, he noticed Whelpley and "he looked at him very sharply, but said nothing. After some time Whelpley spoke to him, calling him by name. He said Whelpley must be mistaken; Colvin was not his name; it had been once, but he was another man now." After another pause, Whelpley asked, "I see you have a scar on your forehead; how did you get that?" Colvin replied, "chopping on the mountain" for a certain Manchester man whom he named. Whelpley knew this to be true, and he casually began to mention the names of various "former friends and acquaintances." With a little prompting, Colvin gradually began to respond with stories about Manchester that removed any of Whelpley's remaining doubts and convinced him that the man before him was Russell Colvin.[7]

Satisfied that he had found Colvin, Whelpley had to figure out how to get him to Manchester. He suggested that Colvin join him in a visit to their former home, but Colvin was unwilling to go. Whelpley finally had to resort to a series of ruses to lure Colvin back to Vermont. For the first stage of their journey, the trip from Polhemus Mills to New York City, Whelpley enlisted the aid of "a young woman of Russell's acquaintance [who] agreed to accompany him, pretending that they only designed a visit to New-York."[8]

Whelpley reached New York City with Colvin in tow on Wednesday evening, December 15, a fact duly noted the next day by the *New York Evening Post* in an article entitled "The Vermont Murder." It reported that while in New York City, Colvin would be staying at Whelpley's inn on the corner of Cortland and Greenwich streets (where the World Trade Towers are located today). The *Evening Post*'s account erred in one particular, asserting that the Taber Chadwick letter that had led to Colvin's discovery was written in response to "an advertisement . . . published in behalf of the unhappy convicts." On other subjects the article offered a mix of old and new information, simply repeating Chadwick's remark that Colvin had been "in a partial state of derangement" at the time he arrived in New Jersey, but dating his arrival more precisely than previous accounts. He had, it said, first reached Polhemus Mills in March or April 1813, approximately ten or eleven months after he disappeared from Vermont.[9]

Whelpley's account of his travels with Colvin appears to embellish and even create incidents that emphasized his companion's mental deficiencies. For example, once the two men reached New York City, their female companion slipped away, and her departure made Colvin nervous. To prevent Colvin from wandering off, Whelpley fed him a story about "British men-of-war lying in the harbour," and told him that "unless he kept within doors, he would be kidnapped." The ruse worked, Whelpley implied, because Colvin was too out of touch with reality to realize that the War of 1812 had ended five years earlier. Similarly, according to one version of what happened when the two men left New York City, Whelpley got the unsuspecting Colvin to board a steamboat, saying that it would cross the Hudson River to New Jersey (where Colvin wanted to go), when in fact it was headed upstream for Albany. It now seems clear that this entire story was a tall tale of Whelpley's. Not only did an Albany newspaper report in 1819 that Colvin "arrived in the city on Tuesday evening in the New York stage . . . and on Wednesday proceeded in the Vermont stage to Manchester," but Whelpley himself, in a bill he submitted to the Vermont legislature in 1821, specifically listed a $24 item for "Stage fare to Albany for Colvin and myself."[10]

According to one early pamphlet on the Boorn mystery, Whelpley and Colvin spent the night of December 21 in Albany, where "the public flocked in multitudes, to behold (as was often remarked) 'the *murdered Colvin!*' " However, except for moments such as these when Colvin was the center of attention, the trip, especially in the hillier sections of the Albany–Vermont route, was, like most stage travel of the time, probably both boring and arduous. The stages and post coaches of the type Whelpley and Colvin took in 1819 were

Advertisement for a
stagecoach of the type
in which Colvin and
Whelpley rode on
their trip to Vermont
(December 1819).

only slightly more comfortable than the rough wagons from
which they had evolved. Passengers sat two or three abreast
on unpadded benches that had no backs. Only travelers on
the rear bench (or, in some newer coaches, the occupants of
a front bench that faced to the rear) had anything to lean
against. The coach was roofed, but its wide windows were
open to the elements unless the passengers agreed to draw
the thin leather curtains and sit in near darkness. Traveling
in mid-December, as Whelpley and Colvin did, passengers
had to endure bitter cold and a slow pace. Even under ideal
conditions, stages were lucky to make eight or nine miles
in an hour, and on winter roads progress was usually much
slower. The ride itself, one traveler recalled, was not unlike
"being tossed in a blanket, often throwing you to the top of
the coach, as to flatten your hat, if not your head."[11]

Whelpley and Colvin reached Bennington, Vermont,

around noon on December 22. Forewarned by newspaper reports and a letter from Whelpley, people had been anticipating Colvin's return without knowing the precise day it would occur. As the stage pulled up to James Hicks' Tavern in Bennington, word spread of Colvin's arrival. A short distance up the street the county court was in session; when the news reached it, proper courtroom decorum was destroyed altogether. According to one report, "the Court broke up in the greatest confusion, and Judges, Clerk, Sheriff, Lawyers and spectators jumped over benches and rushed through windows and doors to see the man who all had believed dead." For several hours people crowded around, vying with each other to make a positive identification of the returned wanderer. "Many who formerly knew him," an early source reports, "now saw that there could be no deception. Russell could call many of them by name." A messenger was dispatched by horseback to Manchester to spread the news, Paul Revere–like, that "Colvin has come!"[12]

The Bennington, Vermont, inn at which Colvin and Whelpley had lunch on December 22, 1819.

By passing the test of face-to-face encounters with old acquaintances at Bennington, Colvin took a crucial step toward being accepted for what he said he was when he reached Manchester later that same day. But Colvin's reception at Bennington was only the most recent in a series of events that smoothed the way for his return. These events had gradually, over a two-week period prior to his actual arrival in Manchester, begun to shift public opinion from extreme doubt that Colvin was alive to enthusiastic conviction.

As recently as the second week of December, when Taber Chadwick's letter to the postmaster at Manchester arrived, the news it bore was greeted with great skepticism. Even the postmaster, who was none other than the Boorns' young defense attorney Leonard Sargeant, apparently had little expectation that the letter's message would prove true. He showed the letter around, but, as he wrote many years later, since "every one scouted at the idea of Colvin's being alive, little notice was taken of it, and nothing done in regard to it." The Reverend Lemuel Haynes, writing about a month after the event, described what happened a bit differently. Although he agreed with Sargeant that "everyone was struck with consternation" and that the prevailing response was "it cannot be that Colvin is alive," Haynes reported that "a few partly believed."[13]

Haynes also went on to say that he soon visited Stephen Boorn, taking Chadwick's letter along to read to the prisoner. As Haynes described the ensuing scene, Stephen exclaimed that Chadwick's news was "so overwhelming" that "nature could scarcely sustain the shock." So flabbergasted was Stephen that he declared, "Had Colvin then made his appearance, it would have caused immediate death." Even the unconfirmed suggestion that Colvin might be alive created "a faintness . . . that was painful to endure." Despite Stephen's intense desire that Chadwick's information prove correct, the possibility that Chadwick was wrong, plus the skeptical response Chadwick's letter elicited from most Manchester residents, including some who said it was "an attempt to hoax," combined to keep Stephen from celebrating prematurely.[14]

Less than a week after Chadwick's letter reached Manchester, a letter from James Whelpley arrived saying that he was going to New Jersey to check Chadwick's story. Four or five days later, Whelpley wrote again to report that he had located Colvin and had brought him to New York City. A man named John Rempton, who claimed to know Colvin from the time when he had lived in Manchester, also wrote from New York, stating that "while writing Russell Colvin is before me." About the same time, probably December 18 or 20, the December 16 edition of the *New York Evening Post* arrived in Manchester. It contained the article entitled "The Vermont Murder," in which Whelpley's successful search for Colvin was described. At least five other papers that carried stories about Chadwick's letter or Whelpley's success (*The Columbian* and *National Advocate* of New York City, the *Rutland Herald* and *Windsor Journal* of Vermont, and the *New England Palladium and Commercial Advertiser* of Boston) might have reached Manchester before Colvin did, thus giving added weight to the case for believing that Colvin was who he said he was. Still, according to Reverend Haynes, acceptance of the notion that Colvin had been found was slow in coming. "Many," Haynes wrote, "gave no credit to the report," and such was the skepticism that "large bets were made" that Colvin was not alive.[15]

The complete success of Colvin's stop in Bennington dealt a significant blow to the doubters' case and eased the way for his triumphant return to Manchester. About sunset on the evening of December 22, the stage bearing Colvin and Whelpley clattered into Manchester Village, its approach heralded by a blast from the horn that early nineteenth-century stage drivers used to announce their arrival at a scheduled stop. However, in this instance no such signal was necessary, since Manchester Village was already "all bustle and confusion" with people running to meet the stage and to see the man they had believed was dead. "Several guns were discharged for joy," and the shout went up, "Colvin has come! Colvin has come!" as the stage pulled to a stop in front of Captain Black's Tavern.[16]

Colvin and Whelpley climbed out of the coach to find themselves surrounded by a crowd numbering in the hundreds. Lemuel Haynes, himself an enthusiastic observer, recalled that "people gathered around [Colvin] with such eagerness as to render it impossible to press through the crowd, or obtain a sight of him." Despite all the jostling and confusion, Haynes was somehow able to observe Colvin well enough to report that "almost all his old acquaintance he could recognize, and call them by name."[17]

A moment of high drama followed almost immediately. Someone ran to the jail, which was just across the street from Captain Black's, and brought Stephen Boorn from his cell. The prisoner's chains had been removed from his arms, but remained on his legs. Aware of Stephen's arrival on the scene, the crowd grew less raucous and pulled back to make a corridor by which Stephen could approach Colvin. Colvin stared at Stephen's chains for a while and then asked, "What is that for?" Stephen replied, "Because they say I murdered you." According to Lemuel Haynes, Colvin answered, "You never hurt me." Leonard Sargeant's account has him going on to say, "Jess struck me with a briar once, but it did not hurt me much." Neither on this nor later occasions did Colvin admit to any memory of a fight with Stephen or provide any details about when and why Jesse had hit him.[18]

Colvin did not say anything more of importance that evening. The explanation of this fact offered by the *Rutland Herald*'s editors less than a week after the incident was that "Colvin was too much confused to hold a regular conference with any one."[19] Local residents familiar with Colvin's past were quick to take his befuddled state as evidence of the mental derangement that he had often displayed before leaving town several years earlier. However, his confusion might equally well have been explained as the result of bewilderment at the swirl of activity that greeted him—people milling about, guns being discharged, shouts from all directions. Finally the Reverend Haynes managed to capture people's attention and to extract a moment's silence from the throng. He then led all in a prayer of thanksgiving for God's providential intervention on the Boorns' behalf in causing Colvin's discovery and return to Manchester. Having given the seal of his ministerial authority to the proceedings, Haynes stepped down and the revelry continued, although the level of activity steadily diminished as darkness set in.

The celebration resumed the next morning. Residents of Manchester and nearby towns flocked to Manchester Village to gather outside Captain Black's Tavern, where Colvin was staying, in hopes of glimpsing "the returned exile." The general mood was one of excitement and enthusiasm. Lemuel Haynes wrote, "I think I can say that I scarcely ever saw more exultation and tender sympathy on any occasion." Militiamen enhanced the festive mood by firing off as many as fifty salvos from the town's cannon. These demonstrations of "high satisfaction" continued for fully two days, December 23 and 24, even though some local citizens had lost sizable wagers by betting that Colvin was dead, and nearly everyone had, until Colvin returned, been calling for Stephen Boorn's execution. Perhaps a bit of guilt contributed to the sudden shift in the general attitude toward Stephen, or at least Leonard Sargeant seemed to think so. A bit tartly, he observed, "The most extravagant expressions of joy were indulged in by the people who, at last convinced of their error, were only too glad to make reparation."[20]

Colvin satisfied the citizens of Manchester not only by his physical appearance, but, more important, by his behavior. In an age before photographs, fingerprints, and dental records, the process of identification was highly subjective, dependent on a person's claims and on how successfully those claims were corroborated by the proofs that were offered. Colvin's absence of more than seven years made accurate identification even more problematical, since he could be expected to look a bit different and possibly to have changed in other ways as well. From the moment, therefore, that Colvin climbed out of the stagecoach in front of Captain Black's Tavern, every chance encounter, regardless of whether it was explicitly designed to do so, would be taken as a test of his identity.

Apparently, the Russell Colvin who returned on the evening of December 22 immediately behaved in ways that led to his acceptance as the genuine article. He displayed a combination of confusion and acuity that eventually convinced most doubters to become believers. Of Colvin's confused state Lemuel Haynes wrote, "It is observed by those who formerly knew him, that his mental derangement is much greater than it was when he left Manchester." Since peculiar statements and erratic actions were completely consistent with what people expected of a weak-minded man who had wandered off and stayed away more than seven years, Colvin's sometimes bizarre behavior was greeted with more laughter than frowns. For example, when he persisted in talking about the Polhemus farm as though he were its proud owner, his conceit of proprietorship simply amused those present. Yet he also often came up with detailed information about Manchester, displaying a more intimate knowledge of events and individuals than it seemed he could have had were he not Russell Colvin. As Haynes observed, "Many things that took place years ago he can recollect with accuracy." People were particularly impressed by his ability to recognize and name many former acquaintances. Sometimes, too, he impressed them even further by supplying people's titles, addressing them correctly as "Esquire, Captain, uncle," and so forth.[21]

There were a few awkward moments when Colvin said or did something that might have raised questions about his authenticity. For instance, his reaction to Sally, his wife, when she came to visit him struck some contemporaries as odd. He treated her coldly, muttering, "That is all over with," and refused to have anything more to do with her. How people explained this at the time is not known, but several modern writers have tried to provide explanations that might have struck Manchester residents as reasonable. One twentieth-century student of the case suggests that Russell possibly "had learned about the child born to Sally long after his departure." Colvin made another peculiar response when several of his children were brought to him. He displayed some fondness toward the youngsters, but seemed not to realize that these were his children. When told that they were, he expressed surprise and puzzlement. He did not understand, he said, how the children happened to be in Manchester, since he "had left them in New Jersey, and must take them back." In this case onlookers apparently agreed that his confusion was simply further proof that he was Russell Colvin.[22]

Manchester town officials were as caught up in the general excitement about Russell's return as the public at large. Less than twenty-four hours after the stage bearing Whelpley and Colvin had arrived, Squire Joel Pratt, the town clerk, sent a letter to Chief Justice Dudley Chase, who had presided over the Boorn trial. "Yesterday," Pratt wrote, "I had the inexpressible joy and surprise to see *Russell Colvin,* the very person who was believed to have been murdered by the Boorns, in full life; he is now in this place."[23]

The good news took more than a week to reach Chase. Pratt's letter was sent to Burlington, the seat of Chittenden County, where the Supreme Court justices were scheduled for a court session. As it happened, however, Pratt's letter and a similar communication to Chase from Richard Skinner, the Boorns' senior attorney, missed the chief justice, who was temporarily away visiting his family in the town of Randolph. Before forwarding the Pratt and Skinner missives, the associate justices, Doolittle and Brayton, took the liberty of opening them, explaining in a note to Chase that "public rumor" had alerted them to the probable contents. Having ascertained that the letters did, indeed, deal with the "extraordinary occurrence" of a murdered man's return, they wrote and asked Chase whether he had any idea what should be done regarding the Boorns if the news from Manchester proved true.[24]

The first step, legally, one that needed to be taken before the matter was submitted to the Supreme Court justices for review, required action by officials in Manchester. They believed, and rightly so, that it was their responsibility to subject the returned Russell to a formal examination that would establish his identity. To this end a court of inquiry was assembled in the courtroom on the upper floor of Captain Black's Tavern. Calvin Sheldon, the State's Attorney, was in charge of the proceedings. According to Leonard Sargeant, Colvin was "questioned most thoroughly." On this occasion he must have displayed more clarity than confusion, for Sargeant wrote that the returned wanderer "told so many little incidents that could not have been known to an imposter [*sic*], however well posted, that there could be no doubt in the mind of any rational person as to the identity of the man."[25]

Only one example survives of the sort of answers Colvin gave that so impressed his interrogators. He was asked who had built the tavern in which the courtroom was located. Colvin replied, "Captain Munson, and it is all of the best oak timber too." A member of the court, probably Calvin Sheldon, since he had not been a Manchester resident at the time the tavern was built, turned to old timers and asked whether they could confirm Colvin's statement. Yes, the answer came, Captain Thaddeus Munson had been the tavern's original proprietor, and the day that construction had begun on the tavern was a memorable occasion in Manchester history. As was customary in rural America, Munson had asked his friends and neighbors to help him raise the building's frame, heavy work that went best when undertaken as a community enterprise. To insure that many people would be available to pitch in, Munson chose as the date for his tavern-raising party March 4, 1801, a holiday that had been declared in honor of Thomas Jefferson's inauguration as president of the United States. The captain also let it be known that liquid refreshments would be abundantly available, and, according to one local historian, on the day the frame was raised "old New England rum flowed freely." Thanks partly to the captain's generous provisions, everything went swimmingly, and the "huge crowd had the job nearly done by dark." When completed, Munson's Tavern, "with its colonial front and elegant round pillars," was said to be "not only the showplace of Manchester, but the largest and finest inn for its time in Vermont." The inn's name was changed in 1816, the year that Peter Black purchased it from Munson's estate for $2,125.[26]

Captain Black's Tavern in Manchester. The county court-rooms were upstairs in 1819.

At the end of his session with the court of inquiry, Colvin apparently felt that he had completed his business in Manchester. He had convinced the town's officials and the general public that he was, indeed, Russell Colvin. Possibly some people who had known him in the past and who had met him upon his return still harbored doubts about his identity, but, if so, they did not voice them loudly at the time. In any event, less than a week after his triumphant return, Colvin began to make plans to leave town. He said he was restless in Vermont, which he no longer regarded as his home, and eager to return to the Polhemus farm in New Jersey, where he hoped to live out his days. Town officials agreed that he was free to leave, and on December 29, precisely one week after his arrival, Colvin, accompanied by Whelpley, took the stage for points south.

By the last week of December, the Boorn-Colvin case was attracting considerable attention in the national press, and the first pamphlet about it had already been rushed into print by William Fay and Charles Burt, the *Rutland Herald*'s enterprising publishers. The principal feature of these early accounts was sensationalism, as is illustrated by the wording of the *Rutland Herald*'s advertisement for its thirty-two page pamphlet, *Trial of Stephen and Jesse Boorn for the Murder of Russell Colvin:* "The trial of the Boorns, exhibits a curiosity, not to be conceived, and the discovery of Colvin renders it still more interesting."[27]

For all their attention to the more peculiar aspects of the Boorn-Colvin case, Vermont newspapers had nevertheless reported the Boorns' trial accurately. However, the same could not be said of some of the earliest out-of-state newspaper articles on the trial. During the first half of December, a period when solid factual information from Vermont sources had not yet been widely disseminated, some out-of-state newspapers published garbled accounts of the Boorn trial that highlighted bizarre background material, chiefly Amos Boorn's dreams of Colvin's ghost, and gave it a central role in the trial's result. Typical of this sort of treatment was the comment by a Boston editor that the Boorns "were convicted by the intervention of a dream." Other editors who had picked up on this story demanded to know how in an enlightened age and country two men could have been condemned to die based on what one newspaper characterized as "such incompetent testimony." Along the same lines, a few out-of-state editors assumed the worst about the Vermont criminal justice system (or at least about the jury that had convicted the Boorns) and suggested that Vermonters had a lot of explaining to do for having allowed such a gross miscarriage of justice. These barbed comments, though based on false impressions, stung nonetheless.[28]

An odd side effect of newspaper reports' focusing on the Boorns and the conduct of their trial was that Colvin, from the moment he left Manchester, attracted less and less news coverage. His final moment of celebrity seems to have come during a week-long stopover he and Whelpley made in Albany, New York, on their return trip. Several local newspapers carried advertisements dated December 31, 1819, to the effect that Colvin was "available at the Albany Museum" through Thursday morning, January 6, 1820. This institution, modeled after the Philadelphia Museum that the artist-naturalist Charles Willson Peale had founded in 1794, was a place where for a small admission fee the public could view both educational exhibits (art and natural history items) and displays of what a contemporary called "natural and artificial curiosities." An example of the latter offered at the Albany Museum in 1817 was an exhibit that permitted visitors to inhale gas and then, while exhaling, to apply a flame and set their breath on fire. For individuals more interested in natural history, the Museum in 1819 advertised that a full-grown live moose was on display. Russell Colvin, the man who returned to save the person convicted of his murder, was probably classified as one of these oddities.[29]

Back in Vermont, the fact that Colvin was alive left authorities with a number of legal issues to resolve, chief among these being how to reverse the judgments against the Boorns. Anticipating that something would be done, Manchester officials released Stephen from jail, but he was obliged to stay in town, living with his relatives in something of a suspended state while waiting for his sentence to be changed formally. Jesse, meanwhile, remained a resident of the state penitentiary at Windsor, his opinion of Vermont's prison system doubtless not improved by the chilling experience of confinement in an unheated stone building during December and January. Although he could look forward to eventual relief, the precise date that he would be freed was to be determined by the Vermont Supreme Court, whose justices seemed uncertain regarding what technical steps were needed to liberate the Boorns. Fortunately, the justices were scheduled to hold a court session at Bennington on January 18, 1820. Since their route to Bennington would take them through Manchester Village, they arranged to spend a night in town and agreed to work out a solution to the Boorns' situation at that time.

Many years later Leonard Sargeant remembered what had happened when he went to visit the three justices after they had settled into their room at the inn. All four men were soon engaged in a lively discussion of the Boorn-Colvin case. Finally, Sargeant recalled, Judge William Brayton turned to him and asked, "Well, Brother Sargeant, what are you going to do about it? I suppose you have some plan concocted." Sargeant acknowledged that he had a proposal, one based not on any legal precedent known to him but on simple common sense. He suggested that he "petition the Court for a new trial on the ground of newly discovered evidence." The justices debated the merits of Sargeant's plan among themselves, and although they expressed some reservations, they finally agreed that it was a logical solution, and in their Bennington session a few days later, they granted the Boorns a new trial. As State's Attorney, Calvin

Sheldon responded *nolle prosequi,* indicating that the state would not prosecute, and the tribunal declared the Boorns free men.[30]

As soon as he was able to do so, Stephen Boorn left Manchester for Windsor, his stated intention being to arrive at the state prison in time to greet his brother when Jesse was released. The only account of their meeting is a curious and possibly unreliable newspaper story that appeared in the *Vermont Republican & American Yeoman* of Windsor. According to this report, Jesse would not speak to Stephen at first. Asked to explain his sullen behavior, Jesse reportedly said, "He (Stephen) was a d——d rascal for confessing what he did, as it was the cause of all their trouble." Someone pointed out to Jesse that he had also confessed, to which he replied that "Stephen's confession made him *crazy,* or he should not have confessed at all."[31] If Jesse actually made these statements, they, like so many things the brothers had said, were at odds with the known facts. After all, in May 1819 Jesse had accused Stephen of killing Colvin, and in June Jesse allegedly told Silas Merrill that he was Stephen's partner in the crime, all of which took place long before Stephen's confession in August.

Once the Boorns were freed a few accounts literally remained to be settled, and various parties to the Boorn-Colvin case petitioned the State of Vermont for reimbursement of out-of-pocket expenses related to the incident. Of those making claims for assisting the Boorns, James Whelpley fared by far the best. In November 1821 he submitted a petition to the General Assembly asking that he be paid for his expenses in seeking Colvin in New Jersey and bringing him to Vermont. His total expenses had been $126.00, but since the muncipal government of New York City under Mayor DeWitt Clinton had already contributed $37.50, Whelpley asked for the balance of $88.50, which the Vermont legislature duly voted. By contrast, the General Assembly treated John Boorn, Stephen and Jesse's older brother, very poorly.

John wrote in October 1820 that since his "oppressed brothers" had been "wholly unable to furnish the means to defray the expenses" of their defense, he had paid to hire their attorneys, doing so out of a sense of "fraternal duty." Although he pointed out that if he had not paid Richard Skinner and the rest of the defense team the State of Vermont would have been forced to fund the Boorns' defense, the General Assembly responded so negatively that John withdrew his request.[32]

Jesse and Stephen Boorn also petitioned the General Assembly for financial relief in October 1820 and met with no more success than their older brother. Both of the younger Boorns placed particular emphasis on the harm they had suffered because of long stints in jail. Jesse claimed that his health was "greatly impaired," and Stephen stated that "his once vigorous constitution has become broken to that degree that since his liberation he has been unable to perform any hard or fatiguing labor on which himself and family wholly depended for their daily bread." Jesse added a complaint about the "unfounded charges" that had been brought against him. Stephen, declining to "cast any censure upon those persons by whose means the said prosecution against him was brought about," nevertheless stressed that his arrest had left "a wife and three children in destitute circumstances."[33]

Both the Boorns' petitions were supported by the signatures of friends and neighbors who claimed to be familiar with the brothers' troubles since being released. Once again, as in the earlier campaign to reduce the two men's sentences, Jesse's petition received more support than Stephen's, with forty-five signatures as compared to his brother's ten. Even now, after Colvin's return, more people were prepared to see Jesse than Stephen as an injured party.

It soon became plain that Vermont legislators were unwilling to treat either brother as deserving of restitution. Opposition to Stephen's petition was so strong that he withdrew it. In Jesse's case the General Assembly's Committee of Claims gave his petition a lukewarm endorsement, and the House as a whole voted to accept the report of its committee but refused to take any further action. In other words, Jesse's request did not have enough support in the House to reach the floor as a formal motion. The General Assembly's negative response to the Boorns' petitions was, in part, an expression of the same spirit of frugality that led the legislators to reduce to $18.50 Sheriff Heman Robinson's request of $24.50 for costs incurred in taking Jesse from Manchester to Windsor State Prison. However, some legislators seem to have blamed the Boorns for having caused a trial whose aftermath made Vermont a laughingstock all over the East Coast. Many members of the General Assembly also felt that the Boorns, through their confessions, had brought most of their troubles on themselves, and that Stephen and Jesse were owed nothing by Vermont's taxpayers. The brothers, it was said, were already the beneficiaries of more good fortune than they had any right to expect, and should be content to rejoice in the simple fact that they were once again free.

Mystery
Developed

*It is impossible to reconcile the singular and contradic-
tory circumstances which this affair has developed. The
various newspaper sketches, which we have seen, have
generally served . . . only to make the mystery more mysterious.*

—WOODSTOCK OBSERVER (VERMONT),
JANUARY 11, 1820

THE return of Russell Colvin to Manchester Village in December 1819 did not solve the
Boorn mystery. To be sure, Russell's return
seemed decisive proof that the Boorn brothers were not murderers, but it left unanswered the question of what had really
happened in May 1812. Moreover, it raised new issues, particularly the question of why the Boorns had confessed. Finally, Russell's return provoked the broadest question of all
about the Boorn mystery: What lessons were to be derived

from a case in which a murdered man returned to save his confessed killer from hanging?

Spurred by curiosity about questions such as these, a diverse group of writers—eyewitnesses, newspaper editors, legal scholars, and even a novelist—produced an impressive body of literature on the Boorn mystery before the end of the nineteenth century. Certain characteristics of this literature were apparent at an early date. For example, even in the pre–Civil War period, students of the Boorn-Colvin case did not limit their attention to its sensational and mysterious aspects. They also sought to explore the true meaning of the Boorn mystery from a variety of perspectives, religious, legal, psychological. Then, in the 1860s, more than forty years after Russell's return to Manchester and as many as three decades after his death in New Jersey, news of statements made by Jesse Boorn in 1860 added another and even more complex dimension to the mystery. The story of Jesse's revelations belongs chronologically in our sixth and final chapter, and it will suffice to say here that his statements reopened the subject of whether the returned Russell had been who he said he was. Even so, the question of whether the returned Russell was an impostor did not immediately assume a very large place in the literature on the Boorn-Colvin case after 1860. For most students of the case, the heart of the mystery still lay in the questions that were first formulated by writers in the period before the Civil War: What happened on May 10, 1812? What motivated Stephen and Jesse to confess? How could any court have convicted the Boorns? Was it divine providence, human intelligence, or pure luck that rescued the Boorn brothers from prison and the gallows? A brief history of how these questions emerged and were answered in the decades immediately after the trial provides additional interesting details about the leading figures in the case and reveals the currents of pre–Civil War thought that influenced early interpretations of the Boorn mystery.

One of the earliest commentaries on the case came from the Reverend Lemuel Haynes of Manchester's First Congregational Church. On January 9, 1820, less than two weeks after the returned Russell Colvin had left town, Haynes addressed himself to the mystery in a sermon entitled "The Prisoner Released." What Haynes said was based on intimate knowledge of the Boorns' situation, acquired through his close personal relationship with Stephen Boorn during the previous six months. Haynes was also aware that newspaper editors in New England and New York were already rushing into print with interpretations of the meaning of Colvin's return. To Haynes these newspaper accounts, as well as most of the talk about the topic among his neighbors and congregation in Manchester, had overlooked the most important lessons to be gleaned from the case. With ministerial zeal, he undertook to enlighten them.

Among Haynes's audience were many of the major figures in the recent murder investigation and trial. State's Attor-

Lemuel Haynes preaching, probably while on his Connecticut tour (1814).

ney Calvin Sheldon was a member of Haynes's church. The defense attorneys, Richard Skinner, Leonard Sargeant, and Daniel Wellman, were active in the Congregational Society, as were town officers such as Samuel Raymond, Josiah Burton, and Joel Pratt. One of Jesse and Stephen Boorn's sisters, Rachel Richardson, whose distress at hearing the jury's verdict against them was so great that she had fainted dead away, attended with her husband Elias, a church member, and joined the church herself later in 1820.

As Haynes rose to speak, however, the faces he must have been most pleased to see in the box pews before him were those of Stephen Boorn, the released prisoner, and his parents, Barney and Elizabeth Boorn, with whom Stephen was living while waiting for the Supreme Court decision that would free him. Stephen's presence in Haynes's congregation was one way of expressing gratitude for the good reverend's constant support and concern throughout his ordeal as a prisoner. Jesse Boorn may have felt somewhat the same, and he certainly would have been invited to attend had he not still been an inmate of the state prison, stuck there until the mills of justice ground out the decision that eventually liberated him.

Barney and Elizabeth Boorn's feelings toward Haynes are not known, but they certainly had reason to appreciate his kindness toward their sons, especially since his warm concern contrasted sharply with the hostile treatment the family had received from the local Baptists. It must have wounded the family's pride that members of the Baptist church the Boorns had traditionally attended had been so quick to sever ties with them in 1819. As mentioned earlier, Elizabeth, a long-standing member, had been summarily excommunicated in May 1819 by a vote taken after only a few minutes of discussion, and in January 1820 she was still outside the Baptist fellowship, a condition that remained unchanged at the time of Barney's death in January 1821. Another year passed before the Baptists "voted to restore

Sister Elizabeth Boorn to the fellowship of the Church" on February 2, 1822. Even that action did not end controversy over her case, since some members were upset because she had been reinstated without confessing to any wrongdoing, the price usually exacted before one was welcomed back to the fold. Finally, in April 1823, nearly three and a half years after Russell Colvin's return, Baptist church members reviewed the history of her case and agreed to insert a note in the records to the effect that she had been readmitted without a confession because "the Church had done wrong in excluding her."[1]

In January 1820 the Reverend Haynes, of course, could not foresee the specific ways that Russell Colvin's return would cause bickering of the sort that divided Baptists over Elizabeth Boorn's membership status. However, he was well aware of the acrimonious controversies that had flared up in Manchester prior to the Boorns' trial, and as a community leader of wide experience he was all too familiar with the human propensity to blame someone when things went wrong. One of Haynes's goals, therefore, in his nearly hourlong address (by no means an unusual duration for the sermons of the era) was to lead his flock—and their town—away from legalistic concerns and blaming behavior toward a joyful appreciation of how God had intervened to liberate Stephen Boorn from prison.

Haynes also labored to get across a second point (in some respects his central message), that all present would benefit spiritually if they saw in Stephen's release from prison an analogy to the Christians' hope that God would deliver them from "the prison of death and hell." Haynes took pains to describe both the similarities and differences between earthly justice and divine justice. Criminals condemned by civil courts, he said, were cut off from human society by being sent to prison, "a place of distress and trouble" from which the inmate "cannot extricate himself." Similarly, sinners were condemned by God to "the prison of eternal despair," where, separated from the saints, they lived in "pain all their days." For all the similarities between earthly criminal proceedings and God's judgment of sinners, however, Haynes stressed that there was a crucial difference between the two. Human courts and juries inevitably made mistakes, as had happened in Stephen Boorn's case, but God's judgments never erred.[2]

Haynes then went on to discuss the theme of deliverance, paying particular attention to the parallels between Stephen Boorn's liberation from jail and a sinner's deliverance from "the bondage of sin and condemnation." The element common to both cases, Haynes asserted, was that God's providential intervention was necessary. At the time Stephen was sentenced, Haynes noted, the evidence seemed decisive. The prisoner had confessed, the jury was unanimous in its verdict, and among the public there were "but few who did hesitate to bring in their verdict of GUILTY." As the date for Stephen's execution drew near, "not a gleam of hope" was evident until "from a far country" a man named Taber Chadwick had provided information that led to Colvin's discovery. Given the facts that Chadwick lived far from Manchester and that he ordinarily did not read the newspaper in which the story about the Boorn-Colvin case appeared, Haynes argued that these events were "directed by the invisible hand of Him who worketh all things after the counsel of his own will."[3]

What lessons were to be gleaned from the story of the Boorns' trial and release? In his closing section, Haynes addressed himself directly to Stephen and his parents, although one can see that in several instances Haynes was also laboring to convey a message about the virtues of humility and peacefulness to a congregation that had frequently been deeply divided in the past three years. First, Haynes said, "Look as favourably as possible on the side of innocence," since, as the Boorn-Colvin case illustrated, human error could lead to condemnation of innocent persons.

Second, "Be of a peaceable, forgiving temper," avoiding resentment and recriminations, even when wronged, and leaving revenge and retribution to God, the only trustworthy judge. Third, recognize that "there is a superintending providence that directs all events." Fourth, Haynes affirmed the Christian's responsibility to practice "strict attention to the truth" and asserted that Stephen, by failing in this regard, had been the cause of many of his recent difficulties. Fifth, he called his listeners to renewed faith and personal reform, urging them to realize that the deep happiness Manchester citizens had felt at Stephen's deliverance was nothing in comparison with the joy the saints would feel when they heard "the jubilee trumpet proclaiming salvation."[4]

The text of Haynes's sermon was published in early 1820, together with a brief presentation of his recollections of the Boorn-Colvin case, under the title "Mystery Developed." Many more accounts of the Boorn mystery were to follow from the pens of other authors, and scarcely a decade passed between the 1820s and the 1960s without the appearance of one or more new treatments of the story. Haynes's account, however, has a certain singularity. This was partly because he, unlike most of the other writers on the subject, had been on the scene at the time. What made his commentary truly unique was its religious emphasis, which was not retained as a principal theme by any of his successors. The fact that Haynes left Manchester Village in 1822 and moved to Granville, New York, where he died in 1833, may have contributed somewhat to the lack of influence his religious interpretation had on subsequent treatments of the Boorn mystery, but the more important reason was that the tide of fashion was against him. His didactic treatment, which stressed the moral and theological lessons to be derived from the Boorns' story, belonged to what was rapidly becoming an old-fashioned perspective. Prior to 1800, Haynes's approach would have been the dominant one, but by 1820, when he preached on "The Prisoner Released," the trend in newspaper accounts of murders was to present their horrible details with little or no moral commentary. As will be shown later in this chapter, the new sensationalistic style of reporting murders that was gaining popularity in the late 1810s became even more prevalent in the 1830s and after.

In addition to religious analysis, there were two other early approaches to the Boorn mystery, the legal-social commentary and the mystery narrative, and the latter two continued to be used well into the twentieth century. Over time both of these approaches to the case were modified in ways that mirrored broader changes in American intellectual tastes. For example, between 1819 and the Civil War mystery narratives of the Boorn-Colvin case gradually abandoned any discussion of serious issues and placed increased emphasis on the Boorn mystery's bizarre, amusing, and unsolved aspects. These accounts, essentially escapist literature, found a ready audience in the era's growing cities whose residents (like many of their country cousins) increasingly accepted the idea that one could read for entertainment rather than edification. By contrast, legal-social commentaries on the Boorns' story retained a serious focus, albeit one in which Haynes's concern for his audience's personal prospects for eternity was replaced by attention to secular issues such as how the proper administration of the young republic's criminal justice system could contribute to a stable social order.

One of the best commentaries on the legal and social implications of the Boorn-Colvin case was also one of the earliest. In April 1820, barely three months after Haynes's sermon on the Boorn mystery, the *North American Review,* then the preeminent American magazine of intellectual opinion, published an unsigned article on the subject. The author has since been identified as John Gallison, a Harvard-educated Boston lawyer whose promising career as a writer-editor on legal topics was cut short by his death in December 1820 at the age of thirty-two.

"The mysterious circumstances of this case," Gallison wrote, "have made it the subject of much public attention"— attention which, he feared, might have very harmful consequences.[5] What particularly worried him was the potential for a widespread reaction against the usefulness of circumstantial evidence and confessions, both of which had figured in the Boorn brothers' convictions and might thus be blamed for having jeopardized the lives of two men who were subsequently shown to be innocent. Gallison presented his analysis in hopes of preventing the Boorn-Colvin case from being interpreted in ways that might discredit the American criminal justice system and in so doing weaken the law as an agency of social order in the United States.

Turning first to the subject of circumstantial evidence, Gallison insisted that proofs based on such sources were as reliable as, if not more so than, direct testimony. He acknowledged that circumstantial evidence could mislead juries if the testimony were inaccurate or errors were made in interpreting the facts; but, he asserted, by applying time-tested methods—for instance, by comparing several sources to discover if they agreed—one could avoid potential pitfalls and reach a valid conclusion about the defendant's guilt or innocence. A problem with the Boorn murder trial, he contended, was that the court and jury had not followed the cautionary injunction of Sir Matthew Hale, the English jurist (1609–76), who said, "I would never convict any person of murder, or manslaughter, unless the fact were proved to be done, or at least the body found."[6] Since the jurors in the Boorn trial had neither a direct witness to Colvin's death nor his body as proof of his decease, they lacked the proper starting point for reasoning from circumstantial evidence regarding a murder charge.

In his discussion of the Boorns' confessions, Gallison asserted that too much weight had been given to admissions made outside the courtroom. Such "extrajudicial confessions," as he called them, were in his opinion often untrustworthy because they were too subject to influence by "fear, melancholy, disgust of life, or other causes, which disturb and delude the imagination." In fact, the record indicated that the Boorns' confessions had been prompted by a mix of fear of certain punishment and hope for at least partial alleviation of their sentences. Moreover, Gallison observed, the brothers' admissions were suspect in that they were so clearly contrived to achieve self-interested purposes, Jesse's to shift blame to either Stephen or his father, and Stephen's "to save them all from the punishment of death, and to substitute that of manslaughter." The point that Gallison hoped to drive home was that the error that led the jury in the Boorn trial to condemn innocent men arose, in part, because the jurors did not draw a careful distinction between extrajudicial confessions, which were unreliable, and formal confessions made before a magistrate, which were much more dependable.[7]

Gallison devoted the entire second half of his article to describing the injustices that result from trials such as the Boorns', in which verdicts were rendered based on false confessions. Some of his most shocking examples involved witchcraft cases, including the notorious Salem trials of 1692. "How absurd were confessions of sorcery in former times!" Gallison wrote. By implying that witchcraft trials were in some respects analogous to the Boorns' trial, Gallison was suggesting that Jesse and Stephen Boorn were convicted less because of solid evidence than because intense popular prejudice against them frightened them into making false confessions. Gallison concluded that the Boorns' trial in no way discredited "long established rules of evidence" regarding circumstantial evidence and admissions made outside the courtroom. Indeed, in his opinion, those time-tested rules were, in practice, the best defense against both the errors in law and biases in public opinion that contributed to the Boorn brothers' convictions in 1819.[8]

Gallison's belief that public opinion had negatively influenced the jury's decision was shared by the two leading members of the Boorns' defense team, Richard Skinner and Leonard Sargeant. Skinner's comment, dating from a few years after the trial, to the effect that a "torrent of passion and prejudice" had made the Boorns' convictions inevitable, was quoted earlier. Writing many decades after the trial, Leonard Sargeant, Skinner's protégé, agreed with his mentor. "Public feeling against the prisoners," Sargeant recalled, "was intense. Almost without exception they were believed to be guilty." Sargeant continued to maintain that the Boorns' confessions were invalid on the grounds that hard-liners among the town officials had pressured Jesse and Stephen into confessing. He also dismissed the evidence against the brothers as "entirely circumstantial and mostly unimportant." According to Sargeant, four factors—public pressure, the admission of the Boorns' confessions, dubious circumstantial evidence, and widespread acceptance of the assumption that Colvin was dead—combined to result in the conviction of two innocent men, a miscarriage of justice that he sardonically called an example of the "glorious uncertainty of the law."[9]

Leonard Sargeant in old age, about the time he wrote his pamphlet on the Boorn-Colvin case.

Given Sargeant's tart comment about the "uncertainty of the law" and his criticism of the way Manchester officials handled the Boorn-Colvin case, he might seem to have had serious grievances against both the criminal justice system and his contemporaries in the Manchester Village elite. However, although he was undoubtedly much more critical of the law's fairness to ordinary people than, for example, John Gallison, Sargeant was not so hostile to either the judicial system or his political contemporaries as to be significantly estranged from them. Both Leonard Sargeant and his mentor Richard Skinner enjoyed great political success in the years after the Boorn trial. Skinner was elected governor of Vermont in 1820 and returned for two additional terms in 1821 and 1822. Sargeant held a succession of important posts: State's Attorney for Bennington County (three years), county judge of probate (seven years), representative to the state legislature from Manchester (four years), and finally, in the mid-1840s, lieutenant governor of Vermont (two terms). Even more directly indicative of the two men's devotion to the social ideals of the Manchester Village elite was their support for the village's single most important institution, the First Congregational Church. In 1829, four years before his death from injuries sustained in a carriage accident, Skinner joined the church. Also in 1829, Skinner was, with Josiah Burton (a leading hard-liner in the Boorn-Colvin case), one of the largest contributors to a fund drive that raised money to pay for constructing a new meeting house in Manchester Village.

Although the meeting house project and the debate over the Boorn trial's legal implications might, at first glance, seem totally unrelated, a theme that ran through both was the contrast between a new and an old social order. John Gallison was distressed because the untoward influence of popular prejudices in the Boorn trial was all too reminiscent of the Salem witchcraft fiasco and other past miscarriages of justice that he felt should long since have ceased to occur.

In an analogous way, Manchester Village's physical condition in 1819—its major public buildings being a somewhat shabby meeting house, a county court house located on the second floor of a tavern, and an ancient log jail—seemed a remnant of the frontier era and its often disorderly social ethic. The contruction of a new brick meeting house in 1829–30 was only one of several physical improvements made in the town's central district between 1820 and 1840: the destruction of the old jail to erect a court house (1822), the opening of a handsome building to house the Burr Seminary* (1830), and the renovation and expansion of Captain Black's Tavern into the Vanderlip Hotel (1840). The new structures provided visible evidence that the town's pioneer period, of which the Boorn-Colvin case with its feud, ghost sightings, and trial was the last major event, was decisively over. A town that in the late eighteenth century had been, according to one resident, "an immoral place," Manchester Village achieved after 1820 the moral and physical tidiness that transformed it into "Manchester-in-the-Mountains," a popular summer spa from the 1850s onward.[10]

Not all commentators on the legal implications of the Boorn-Colvin case shared the social perspective of the respectables who blamed the erroneous convictions of the Boorn brothers on the public's prejudices and the jurors' supposedly inadequate understanding of legal principles. A forceful dissent from this elitist interpretation was penned by Leonard Deming of Middlebury, Vermont. He was the only contemporary writer on the Boorn trial who was not a member of the era's legal or professional elite. Deming was a blacksmith and proud of it. In his opinion, the problem in cases like the Boorns' was not that the general public abused

---

*The school was renamed Burr and Burton Seminary in 1855 in honor of its chief financial benefactors, Joseph Burr and Josiah Burton, both of whom had figured in the Boorn-Colvin affair. When it opened, Burr Seminary was a boy's school, but by 1849 girls were admitted and it became the first private coeducational academy above the elementary level in Vermont.

the law but that the law served the interests of lawyers and their rich clients rather than ordinary people. In a passage that would have sent chills up and down the spines of John Gallison and others of his persuasion, Deming wrote, "It is the prevailing opinion of people generally, who have not much experience in law affairs, that the law is founded on justice, and if compelled to resort to it, will have justice done to them; but many from actual experience have learned that such is not the fact."[11] Deming was speaking from first-hand knowledge; a lawsuit he believed unjust had recently forced him to abandon a retail egg business he tried to start.

Deming's interpretation of the Boorn-Colvin case was published in a volume entitled *A Collection of Useful, Interesting, and Remarkable Events* (1825). In the first part of the book he cited many examples of ordinary people, including the Boorn brothers, who had been wrongly accused and, though innocent, convicted and even executed for their alleged crimes. In the second section he told story after story of benign acts toward humans performed by both domestic and wild animals: the dog that saved a child's life, the lioness that helped a man who had been kind to her, and so forth. His point, in context, was quite clear: nature and nature's

Manchester Village's main street, showing some of the new buildings of the 1820–1840 period: the new Congregational meeting house at the far left and the new court house just to its right.

Clear the track, I am bound for the Law,
And not in want of any of your Jaw.

I have got the start, have been and got through,
And what is better I have gained my cause too.

Illustration from Leonard Deming's book, reflecting the anti-law, anti-lawyer bias of his presentation.

creatures were trustworthy and good. By contrast, the legal system and the courts were institutions created by the privileged classes to promote their special interests at the expense of the lives, liberties, and happiness of ordinary folk.

Deming's book was not written in support of any specific organized political or social reform campaign, but his diatribe against the legal system's injustices was in harmony with a democratizing spirit that flourished in the United States during the 1820s and 1830s. Vermont had been ahead of the times in granting universal suffrage to white males in its first constitution (1777). Many states did not abolish property and taxpaying qualifications for voting and office-holding until the period of 1816 to 1826. Then in the 1830s the Democratic and Whig parties emerged to organize the newly expanded electorate into two mass-participatory parties. The democratic impulse also led to popular attacks on many institutions of social and economic privilege, including the Masonic Lodge, the slave system, and the Bank of the United States. Public animosity toward the privileged position of the legal profession led to the passage of state laws that reduced the qualifications necessary to become a lawyer, with the result that many states no longer required any formal study of the law and a few asked only that a candidate for admission to the bar offer proof of good moral character and pay a small fee.

The legal elite did not passively endure these assaults on the status of the profession. Its leading defenders counter-attacked by proposing to strengthen graduate programs in legal studies and to establish journals that would educate practicing lawyers in correct legal principles. Two men who were instrumental in promoting efforts along these lines, Simon Greenleaf of Harvard Law School and P. W. Chandler, founder of *The Law Reporter,* also wrote commentaries on the Boorn-Colvin case. Not surprisingly, both men implicitly rejected Deming's interpretation.

Greenleaf, a former member of Maine's Supreme Court, joined the Harvard Law School faculty in 1833 and taught there until 1848. Harvard's law school, founded in 1817, was the first such graduate school organized under the auspices of a major American college. Greenleaf is credited, along with his colleague Joseph Story (an Associate Justice of the United States Supreme Court, 1811–1845), with firmly establishing the school's national reputation. Greenleaf's major work, an authoritative study entitled *Treatise on the Law of Evidence,* included a brief discussion of the Boorn-Colvin case. Like John Gallison twenty years earlier, Greenleaf emphasized that what had gone wrong in the Boorns' trial was not the result of flaws in the criminal justice system but a product of the improper application of legal procedures. The chief lesson to be learned, he asserted, was that "verbal admissions of guilt should be *received with great caution.*"[12]

P. W. Chandler, a student at Harvard Law School in the Story-Greenleaf era, was responsible for establishing in 1838 *The Law Reporter,* the first successful magazine devoted exclusively to legal subjects. In the journal's statement of purpose, Chandler declared that such a publication would serve the needs of "practicing lawyers" by educating them in high professional standards, the application of which would help dispel "the prejudices so rife in the community at large in regard to law." A staunch defender of "the dignity and consistency of the law," Chandler charged that critics of the American criminal justice system were guilty not only of focusing on what he called "imaginary evils" but of drawing incorrect conclusions about the system based on those supposed wrongs. Chandler used the trial of Stephen and Jesse Boorn as a case in point, reviewing it in *The Law Reporter*'s September 1842 issue. He did not deny that errors in law had contributed to the Boorns' wrongful convictions ("presumption," he wrote, "piled upon presumption to make out a case"), but he rejected the view advanced by Deming and others that the fault lay with the legal system's biases and insisted that the real problem was that long-established rules of law had not been correctly applied at the Boorn trial. He did not go on to give a detailed description of these rules or the way they had been misapplied in the Boorn case. His point was rather that the conviction of two innocent men had created a furor that reinforced popular prejudices against the law and that the public's confusion about the case was already, he believed, having deleterious effects on criminal proceedings. "In many trials," he complained, "the skeleton of the case . . . is raised, like the ghost of a murdered man, to scare the jury" and to create "a great cloud of 'reasonable doubts' " in order to save villains who otherwise would have been convicted. The cumulative, long-term effect of such actions, he feared, would do great harm to American society. In a passage that revealed his conservative political views, Chandler warned that if valid rules of evidence were abused and discredited, there was a danger that the rule of law would be replaced by mob violence, that is, vigilante justice and lynch law.[13]

By 1842, when Chandler's article on "The Case of the Boorns" appeared in *The Law Reporter,* the opposing positions in the debate over the case's legal implications were clearly defined: at one extreme was Leonard Deming's anti-institutional perspective that saw the Boorn trial as further proof that in America rich men's laws meant injustice for poorer citizens; at the other extreme was Chandler's defense of "the dignity and consistency of the law." Although it was not obvious in 1842, the future lay with Chandler and his allies rather than with men of Deming's persuasion. In the post–Civil War period, leaders of the bar campaigned successfully to reestablish stricter standards for admission to law practice, and, in a related development, formal training in law schools increasingly became the norm rather than the exception among American lawyers. In this intellectual milieu, the Chandler school of thought came to dominate discussions of the Boorn-Colvin case. Among evaluations of the case's legal aspects published after the Civil War—an anonymous piece in *Overland Monthly* (1870), Leonard Sargeant's account (1873), and L. E. Chittenden's analysis (1893)—none significantly challenged the Chandler line, although Sargeant pointed out that the law often produced injustices, and mentioned some of Deming's examples as illustrations. In the twentieth century the Boorn-Colvin case was cited repeatedly in major law texts: for example, John H. Wigmore, *The Principles of Judicial Proof* (2nd ed., 1931), John D. Lawson, *American State Trials* (1914–1936), and Edwin M. Borchard, *Convicting the Innocent: Sixty-Five Actual Errors of Criminal Justice* (1932). These sources included the Boorn episode in order to educate members of the legal profession to the dangers of "public superstition and excitability" (Borchard) and to "some of the unusual motives leading to false confessions" (Wigmore). Sherman Roberts Moulton's *The Boorn Mystery: An Episode from the Judicial Annals of Vermont,* published in 1937, remains the most thorough examination of the Boorn trial's legal significance to date. Moulton, who was then an associate justice of the Vermont Supreme Court and who later served as chief justice, used his close knowledge of Vermont law and history to argue convincingly that the Boorn trial jurors had been more scrupulous in fulfilling their legal responsibilities regarding the admission of confessions as evidence than their critics had been willing to concede. Beyond this point, however, the broad outlines of Moulton's discussion of the case did not deviate greatly from the interpretative line sketched out by Chandler and other members of the legal elite one hundred years earlier.[14]

Judge Moulton's book was practically the last study of the Boorn-Colvin case to analyze the legal significance of the trial. Only a small volume, *The Return of Russell Colvin*, published in 1945 and written by John Spargo, then director-curator of the Bennington Museum in Bennington, Vermont, devoted any further attention to the legal issues. Since 1945, commentaries have focused exclusively on the mysterious and unresolved aspects of the story. In so doing, however, modern authors have simply continued to pursue the form of writing about the Boorn case that had been the most popular approach from 1819 onward.

That so much of the writing about the Boorn-Colvin case should fall into the category of the mystery story is, of course, consistent with the incident itself. The disappearance of Russell Colvin was an enigma that inspired questions in Manchester from the time he was last seen in May 1812 through 1819, when the Boorn brothers were arrested, charged, and tried for his murder. Initially, however, these events attracted little attention outside of Manchester: only two articles on the case appeared in Vermont newspapers between the Boorns' arrest in May 1819 and their trial five months later. Press coverage of the case increased slightly in early November, after Stephen and Jesse were convicted and sentenced to hang. Between November 9 and 29, two weeklies, the *Rutland Herald* and the *Vermont Journal* of Windsor, regularly provided brief reports on the brothers' convictions, their petitions for clemency, and the state legislature's actions on those appeals. The tone of these articles was matter-of-fact, indicating that in early and mid-November editors did not yet see anything out of the ordinary about the case, and thus treated it as a straightforward story of two murderers and their trial, convictions, and appeals.

Toward the end of November, the first treatments of the Boorn-Colvin case as a mystery story began to appear in the press. The *Daily Advertiser* led the way on November 25 with the letter, discussed earlier, that called attention to several curious aspects of the case. Chief among these was the story of Amos Boorn's dream and of how it supposedly led to the discovery of a grave that contained "a human skeleton." This letter was reprinted verbatim by the *New York Evening Post* on November 26, as well as by the *Rutland Herald* four days later.[15]

The *Rutland Herald*'s November 30 issue also contained the advertisement, headed "MURDER," that Stephen Boorn had asked his attorneys to draw up and circulate. Although the *Herald*'s editors expressed some reservations about the notice, the very fact that a search was being made for the supposedly dead victim was sufficient to suggest that the Boorn-Colvin mystery might not have been resolved by the recent trial in Manchester. As the *Herald* observed: "From this notice an inference is readily drawn that Colvin absconded at the time it was supposed he was murdered seven years ago. We have heard intimations of the kind before but are incapable of forming an opinion as to the probability or improbability of the fact."[16]

The publication of Taber Chadwick's letter in the *New York Evening Post* on December 10, which led to the discovery that Colvin was alive and well in New Jersey, had the effect of transforming what previously had been a rather fragmented tale of odd events and minor unanswered questions into the dramatic mystery story that has engaged popular interest ever since. Coverage of Russell Colvin's return to Manchester, reports of which eventually appeared in newspapers from Vermont to Virginia, began as early as December 16, the day after James Whelpley returned to New York from New Jersey with Colvin. A *New York Evening Post* article, "The Vermont Murder," expressed concern that Jesse and Stephen Boorn had been convicted on the basis of the content of their uncle Amos's dream. If that proved to be true, the article stated, it would be a disgrace: "We can hardly believe," the editors wrote, "any twelve men, in this age of reason and intelligence, could be so superstitious as to condemn a fellow being to the gibbet" based on such evidence.[17]

The very next day a rival New York paper, the *National Advocate,* carried a story on the "Vermont Murder" that partly answered the *Evening Post*'s questions but raised many more of its own. Drawing on a New York informant (probably James Whelpley), who was identified only as "a gentleman" from the Boorns' "neighbourhood," the *National Advocate* traced the history of the Boorn-Colvin affair from its beginnings in 1812 to the recent discovery of Colvin in New Jersey. The article, which according to the practice of the day was soon reprinted verbatim by many other newspapers, contained a mix of true and erroneous information. It correctly reported that the Boorns' convictions had been based not on a dream's contents but on a combination of circumstantial evidence and the brothers' confessions, and that the dream had figured only in the discovery of the place where Colvin supposedly lay buried. However, the report of what was found at this location—a field owned by the "Browns" (as the Boorns were called throughout) in which "a large hole was usually kept open for preserving potatoes during the winter"—was not accurate. The hole was said to contain "a skeleton of a man, [and] a barlow penknife, bloody, and another knife, rusty, lay along side of him."[18]

Of course, no human skeleton had been found, nor was the penknife bloody, but these colorful details were repeated by the press as if true and became enshrined in popular lore.

Even in the 1940s, when John Spargo was doing research for his book on the Boorn mystery, he found Manchester residents who remembered old-timers who had been sure that "their fathers had seen the skeleton, one at least having helped to remove it from the cellar hole!" In 1819, of course, the *National Advocate,* having no reason to doubt the skeleton story, had to wrestle with the implications of Colvin's being alive even though a skeleton had been found where his ghost said it would be. The *National Advocate* concluded that the Boorns must be innocent of murdering Colvin, but since the family owned the field where the skeleton had been found, the brothers might know more about this skeleton, apparently another murder victim, than they had acknowledged. In a clever punch line, the editors suggested that "another dream may be more conclusive."[19]

Respectable Vermonters writhed with annoyance upon reading these stories about unidentified skeletons, strange dreams, message-bearing ghosts, and blundering juries. Clearly, East Coast newspapers were having a field day at Vermont's expense. Vermont editors rallied to defend their state's good name. In early January the *Woodstock Observer* asserted that critics were simply misinformed about the basis for the Boorn jury's decision. According to the *Observer,* Stephen and Jesse "were not convicted by the influence of dreams, visions, and omens, but by substantial testimony,— in short, by their own confessions." The *Vermont Journal* of Windsor agreed, but put the point in more emotional language. The Boorns' convictions were based on a combination of circumstantial evidence and the accuseds' confessions, and given those facts, the *Journal* said, it was time for critics "who have stigmatized judges and jury as convicting and condemning on the evidence of a dream, and deserving a *'ducking in a horse pond,'* if nothing worse, [to] retract some of their *wise sayings.*"[20]

As for the much-discussed stories of occult phenomena in the Boorn-Colvin case, Vermont's defenders were quick to claim the high ground of rationality. In his letter to the *Vermont Gazette,* quoted earlier, the anonymous "Citizen of Vermont" dismissed talk about "Ghosts, Hobgoblins, ominous Dreams, and Witches" as the product of overactive imaginations found among people with "weak brains," or as the work of "certain Editors" attempting to expand their paper's circulation. "We cannot," he concluded, "in this enlightened country apprehend any danger from [ghosts], tho' they become so numerous, as to run from the pen of every news-paper scribbler." In his account of the case, the Reverend Haynes treated Amos Boorn's dream respectfully but explained its origin in a rationalist manner. Haynes suggested that Amos had thought so long and hard in his waking hours about Colvin's disappearance that his "mind," as Haynes put it, "was prepared to receive similar impressions when asleep" and formulated them into an explanatory dream. The *Vermont Journal* also traced the dream to Amos Boorn's *"waking"* thoughts, but cynically suggested that he attributed his conclusions to a dream in order to avoid the "thirst for revenge to which he might have become the victim" by seeming to accuse his nephews of murder.[21]

Still, dreams and ghost stories, however mysterious, were peripheral, and one of the central unanswered questions— a real mystery—from the day of Russell's return onward was why the Boorn brothers had confessed. Editors of the *Rutland Herald* expressed their puzzlement very directly. "The idea," they wrote, "that a rational being should confess that he had committed a most wanton murder, and thereby expose himself to the awful doom which must consequently follow, and the whole be a fictitious story, is, to many, a mystery they are unable to unravel." One way to unravel it might have been to argue that the returned Russell was an impostor, but in the wake of Colvin's triumphant reception upon reaching Manchester, it no longer seemed reasonable to doubt his identity. Another solution was to assert, as the defense attorneys had done during the trial, that the brothers' confessions were false, having been extorted from them. But in a period when Vermont editors were closing ranks with their professional brothers to refute criticism of the state's judges and courts, the extorted-confession thesis was too embarrassing to be adopted openly. The best remaining answer seemed to be that because Russell disappeared after the fight in the field and did not return, Jesse and Stephen assumed that he had died, either from his wounds or some other cause. By confessing, the brothers tried both to satisfy their inquisitors and to construct their revelations in such a way that they might, as one paper put it, "escape the severity of the law, and in mercy receive a less rigorous punishment."[22]

The Boorn-Colvin case was, of course, not the only murder story being followed by East Coast newspapers in late 1819 and early 1820. Most newspapers of the period had folio formats, their four pages largely devoted to legal and commercial notices, advertisements, and texts of speeches by political leaders. The remaining space, perhaps two or three columns, contained the nonpolitical news, most of it of a nonlocal nature, such as the *New York Evening Post*'s piece on "The Vermont Murder." Scarcely any issue of an average newspaper was without a story about at least one violent crime. These stories were typically prefaced by such lurid headings as "Shocking Murder" (of a Virginia man felled by a musket shot that "literally tore [his abdomen] to pieces"), "Barbarity" (a traveler "murdered for his money"), and "Horrid Murder and Robbery" (perpetrated by a "ruffian" who was subsequently caught "skulking" in the woods nearby). Articles of this sort, embellished with such overwrought language as "cold-blooded depravity" and "atrocious deed," became increasingly common in American newspapers from 1810 onward. They were the harbingers of a phenomenon of the 1830s, the so-called penny papers exemplified by Benjamin H. Day's *New York Sun* and James Gordon Bennett's *New York Herald*. In pursuit of a mass readership, the penny papers fed their purchasers what one scholar has called "an increasingly spicy diet of horror, gore, and perversity." Moreover, the masters of mass-marketed human-interest stories gave the gory details without any moralistic gloss.[23]

In addition to newspaper accounts, contemporaries of the Boorns also used the so-called trial pamphlet as a vehicle for presenting the Boorn-Colvin case as a mystery story. Pamphlets on famous trials in 1819 and 1820 were commonly from twenty-four to forty-eight pages in length, and most, according to one student of the subject, were, like the Reverend Haynes's sermon on the Boorn trial, "filled with long warnings about God's anger against criminals and man's need to beg forgiveness in the face of divine wrath." However, just as newspaper treatments of crime and criminals underwent a transformation between the early 1800s and the 1830s, so too did the pious commentary in trial pamphlets gradually give way to an emphasis on the sensational aspects of crime stories. Not a great deal is known about how early trial pamphlets were distributed, but we do know that their circulation increased dramatically in the 1830s and 1840s and that they were "hawked in street bookstalls and railway depots." There were no railway depots in the 1819–20 period and, as we will see, the tone of most pamphlets on the Boorn-Colvin case reflected the more sober style of that time, but the early Boorn trial pamphlets nevertheless anticipated later developments both by their popularity and the sensational details they sometimes included. Curiosity about the Boorn mystery was so great that three different publishers put out pamphlets on the subject in 1819 and 1820, and one pamphlet sold so well that its publishers issued an expanded second edition.[24]

The race to be the first to have a pamphlet on the Boorn trial in print was won hands down by William Fay and Charles Burt, publishers of the *Rutland Herald.* In an introduction dated December 23, 1819 (only one day after Colvin and Whelpley reached Manchester), Fay and Burt gave

a public-spirited rationale for rushing into print. The discovery of Colvin alive, they wrote, had left public opinion in
an "agitated" state that had led to the expression of "opinions
unfavorable to the judicial tribunal" before which the Boorns
had been tried. They asserted that "it almost became the
indispensable duty of some one to endeavor to administer
something which may tend to pacify" the general public, and
their remedy was to apply a stiff dose of facts to offset the
rumors and false information that were swirling about.[25]
Since their firm was Vermont's official state printer for 1819,
they were well positioned politically to obtain a copy of Chief
Justice Dudley Chase's trial notes from the clerk of the General Assembly. Together with the grand jury's indictments,
these notes occupied the first twenty-seven pages of the pamphlet, which Fay and Burt entitled *Trial of Stephen and
Jesse Boorn for the Murder of Russell Colvin.* The pamphlet's
remaining five pages contained a brief narrative summary
of the events since the trial's end: the brothers' appeals for
clemency, the advertisement their attorneys had placed in
the *Rutland Herald,* and the story of James Whelpley's discovery of Colvin and his return with him to Manchester.

*Advertisement for the
Fay and Burt pamphlet
on the Boorn-Colvin
case.*

In early January 1820, Fay and Burt wrote Chief Justice Chase to ask whether he would assist them in preparing a second edition, there being still, as they put it, "a call for more of the work." They mentioned that they had also invited Richard Skinner, the Boorns' senior defense counsel, to contribute, but he had demurred. Chase seems not to have helped either, despite the publishers' none-too-subtle suggestion that in so doing he could allay what they called the "public anxiety" about the trial, thus presumably defusing some of the criticism being directed toward Chase and his fellow judges. With or without Chase's direct aid, an enlarged second edition was available by mid-January.[26]

The differences between the first and second editions are instructive and suggest that Fay and Burt, however much they might describe their motivation as disinterested public service, were also out to expand the pamphlet's sales by telling the most sensational mystery story they could. To be sure, they included a small amount of new material of a serious nature: a few sentences reminiscent of the Reverend Haynes's sermon ("The eye of an all-seeing Providence watched over the fate of these two unhappy mortals"), and some excellent biographical information on Russell Colvin. However, a large percentage of the new text seems to have been intended to titillate the popular imagination with lurid stories. Colvin's ghost was said to have "repeatedly called Mr. [Amos] Boorn from his slumbers at the 'hideous hour of midnight, when church yards yawn,' and screech-owls rend the air with horrid shrieks, and conducted him to the spot, where had been deposited his mangled flesh and broken bones." Colvin's apparition also reportedly pursued Stephen Boorn, who "had been tormented with most horrid dreams, and frightened at night by most frightful groans, . . . of some person in great distress [and] had frequently been awoke from his sleep at midnight, by the thundering of stones upon his house top, and the appearance of a spectre, (no doubt of Colvin,) which beckoned him to follow." Although valuable to present-day historians as examples of sensationalism in the era's popular literature, these stories, as noted earlier, outraged rationalists among Fay's and Burt's contemporaries.[27]

Less needs to be said about *Sketches of the Trial of Stephen and Jesse Boorn for the Murder of Russel [sic] Colvin,* a twenty-four-page pamphlet published anonymously in Boston in 1820. The bulk of the pamphlet consisted of three articles reprinted from newspapers, two of them on the Boorns and the third on an English case in which the real murderer of "Mr. B." was not discovered until after an innocent man had been executed for the crime. To these sources the editor of *Sketches* added a one-page introduction, two pages of concluding remarks, and a thirty-six-line poem entitled "The Dreamer." A lament by men who, like the Boorns, nearly lost their lives because of a dream, it begins:

> *Our fate is wretched hard indeed,*
> *The clamorous people say;*
> *'Some Impious wretch has dream'd a dream,*
> *And dream'd our lives away,'*
> *Can it be true in any land*
> *Where science sheds one ray,*
> *That idle dreams and prophecies*
> *Should take our lives away?*

The poet replies that even in "this enlightened day" a dream can lead "not only *simple ones,* but JURORS to astray." However, things take a turn for the better with a line that refers to Russell Colvin's return ("But lo, the MURDER'D MAN appears!"), and in the end the poor wretches are saved.[28]

Mystery Developed, the Reverend Haynes's pamphlet on the Boorn-Colvin case, included a reprint of his sermon on the topic, but supplemented this document with new material that had a very different thematic focus. In his sermon he had been principally concerned with weighty religious

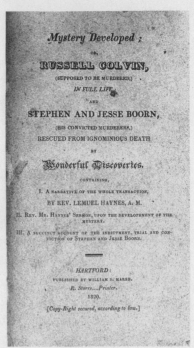

Mystery Developed;

OR,

RUSSELL COLVIN,

(SUPPOSED TO BE MURDERED,)

IN FULL LIFE

AND

STEPHEN AND JESSE BOORN,

(HIS CONVICTED MURDERERS,)

RESCUED FROM IGNOMINIOUS DEATH

BY

Wonderful Discoveries.

CONTAINING,

I. A NARRATIVE OF THE WHOLE TRANSACTION,

BY REV. LEMUEL HAYNES, A. M.

II. REV. MR. HAYNES' SERMON, UPON THE DEVELOPEMENT OF THE MYSTERY.

III. A SUCCINCT ACCOUNT OF THE INDICTMENT, TRIAL AND CONVICTION OF STEPHEN AND JESSE BOORN.

HARTFORD:

PUBLISHED BY WILLIAM S. MARSH.

R. Storrs....Printer.

1820.

[*Copy-Right secured, according to law.*]

Title page from Lemuel Haynes's pamphlet on the Boorn-Colvin case.

matters, the subject of salvation and the sinner's dependence on God's providential intervention. The new material in *Mystery Developed,* the most important of which was a nine-page narrative at the beginning of the pamphlet, had as its central focus the mystery story to which his title referred. The reasons Haynes gave for adding this information were secular and civic-minded, stemming from his desire to answer critics who, because the Boorn trial had nearly led to the hanging of an innocent man, were making, as he put it, "imputations of an unwarranted nature on the town of Manchester, and on the civil authority of Vermont." Like Fay and Burt, Haynes believed a clear presentation of the facts about what he called "this mysterious subject" would convince "judicious and candid" readers that criticism was unwarranted. Fair-minded readers, he argued, would see that such much-discussed incidents as Amos Boorn's dream and a dog's discovery of bones in a tree stump were not "miraculous" events but products of natural causes. Moreover, Haynes claimed that the supposedly significant revelations that came as a result of Amos's dream and the dog's digging had no influence on the Boorn trial, at which, he noted, "evidence not directly in point was not admitted." He insisted, therefore, that the Boorn brothers had been fairly treated. Even Stephen Boorn, he reported, had "repeatedly told me and others that he did not blame the authority for deciding against him, considering the evidence adduced."[29]

As we have seen, Haynes had come to believe, perhaps as much as six weeks before there was any proof of it, that Stephen was innocent. The author's sympathies explain both the strength and weakness of the pamphlet's contents. Its strength was that it provided more inside information on Stephen Boorn's moods and statements in the summer and fall of 1819 than any other source. But Haynes's sympathies also weakened his narrative, leading him to omit certain awkward topics, most notably all mention of Stephen's confessions. Caught between his twin purposes, defending Stephen and exonerating town and court officials, Haynes could produce no adequate explanation for the confessions that did not reflect some discredit on either Stephen or the court's officers or both.

Samuel Putnam Waldo, a Hartford lawyer and author of biographies of James Madison and Andrew Jackson that one critic described as containing "a pound of rhetoric to an ounce of fact," completed his pamphlet *A Brief Sketch of the Indictment, Trial, and Conviction of Stephen and Jesse Boorn* in early 1820. It was printed in Hartford and bound with copies of Lemuel Haynes's pamphlet and sermon. Perhaps because he was not a Vermonter, Waldo had no compunctions about criticizing nearly everyone and everything connected with the Boorn-Colvin case. He was particularly vehement in denouncing the frenzy of ghost sightings that followed news of Amos Boorn's dream and the impropriety of the pressures court officers brought to bear on the Boorn brothers to confess. Staking out his position as a man of reason, he described the ghost sightings as a "melancholy delusion." The responsibility for this outbreak of irrationality lay, he asserted, with "timid females, and *men* who think and act like timid females." According to Waldo, the "state of infatuation" that prevailed in Manchester scarcely had a parallel even in "the history of *witchcraft* itself." It was in this charged atmosphere that Stephen and Jesse Boorn, "humble" men with "naturally feeble" intellects, were arrested. Faced with "unconquerable prejudice" and "alarmed by denunciations, or allured by false hopes," the brothers confessed. This, in Waldo's opinion, explained the "mystery" of why two innocent men confessed to a crime they did not commit.[30]

In 1873, more than fifty years after Waldo's *Brief Sketch* appeared in print, a fifth trial pamphlet on the case was published. This was *The Trial, Confessions and Conviction of Jesse and Stephen Boorn for the Murder of Russell Colvin,* written by Leonard Sargeant, one of the Boorns' attorneys in 1819. As one of only two memoirs written by important participants in the events of 1819 and 1820 (Haynes's being the other), Sargeant's pamphlet contained significant new information on the Boorn-Colvin case. This was particularly welcome because for several decades writers who had treated the Boorn case as a mystery story had for the most part simply reworked old ground. Sargeant, however, provided fresh details on many aspects of the mystery, including the campaign to pardon the Boorns, James Whelpley's trip with Colvin to Vermont, the tests Colvin faced and passed upon reaching Manchester, and even an approximate date for Colvin's death, which Sargeant said took place in New Jersey "a few years subsequent" to Colvin's return there in 1820.[31]

Sargeant's trial pamphlet was followed less than a year later by the publication of a novel on the Boorn-Colvin case. Although the Boorns' story had long been treated as a mystery, before 1873 it had not attracted the attention of authors working in the new genre of fictionalized murder mystery, first developed by American writers around 1840. Edgar Allan Poe was the unquestioned genius among early American practitioners of the new genre, and his career provides a good illustration of the fact that, from the very beginning, writers of mystery fiction had been in the habit of mining popular accounts of crime for their material. Poe regularly scanned the popular press and trial pamphlets for actual murder cases he could incorporate into his stories. *The Mystery of Marie Roget* (1842), for example, was based on a sensational murder case, the murder of Mary Rogers in New York (August 1841). Wilkie Collins, an English pioneer of the mystery-detective fiction genre whose novels enjoyed great popularity in the mid-nineteenth century, also took an avid interest in headline-grabbing crime stories and based two of his best-known works, *The Woman in White* (1860) and *The Moonstone* (1868), on actual contemporary cases.

In September 1873 Wilkie Collins arrived in the United States for a reading tour that took him to a number of upstate New York cities, Albany, Troy, Syracuse, and Buffalo. Somewhere along the line he acquired a copy of Leonard Sargeant's pamphlet on the Boorn-Colvin case and immediately recognized it as adaptable to the type of mystery fiction of which he was a master. In early January 1874 *The Dead Alive,* Collins's version of the mystery, was published in Boston.

Collins followed the main outlines of the Boorn-Colvin case, taking liberties with details only. In fact, in a note at the end of the novel, he acknowledges his debt to Sargeant's pamphlet, and writes, "It may not be amiss to add, for the benefit of incredulous readers, that all the 'improbable events' in the story are matters of fact. . . . Any thing which 'looks like truth' is, in nine cases out of ten, the invention of the author." Collins eliminated the in-law relationship between the Colvin character, John Jago, and the brothers

Silas and Ambrose Meadowcroft who are accused of murdering him; instead he made Jago the man who manages the Meadowcroft farm for Ambrose and Silas's father. The brothers' jealousy at losing out to the dependable but slightly cracked Jago provides the motive for the murder. Collins also gave the story a love interest: Jago is hopelessly in love with Naomi Colebrook, a Meadowcroft cousin, but she has fallen in love with a visiting English lawyer, Philip Lefrank, who will later defend the Meadowcroft brothers at their trial. Most of the rest of the story is pure Boorn-Colvin. Jago disappears after having a quarrel with the Meadowcroft brothers. A local minister dreams that Jago is dead, and some bones, a knife, and two buttons are found at the site where Jago and the Meadowcrofts fought. The brothers are jailed and accused of murdering Jago. Ambrose confesses in hopes of being tried for manslaughter rather than murder, but he is sentenced to be hanged. An advertisement is placed requesting information on Jago's whereabouts, and he is spotted by chance in Jersey City, New Jersey. He returns, not because he is compelled to, but because he hopes that Naomi is in love with him. The Meadowcroft brothers are freed, but lose the family farm. Naomi and Philip marry, and learn that "John Jago had disappeared again, nobody knew where."[32]

Interest in the Boorn-Colvin case as a mystery story did not end with the publication of Collins's *The Dead Alive*. In the twentieth century, Edmund L. Pearson's classic *Studies in Murder* (1924) contained a chapter entitled "Uncle Amos Dreams a Dream." Other treatments followed, including Moulton's and Spargo's books, and articles in such popular journals as *Yankee, Vermont Life,* and *Rural Vermonter.*[33] Probably the main reason why so many authors and readers were attracted to the Boorn-Colvin case was fascination with the story of a murdered man who returned to save his condemned killer from hanging. However, the surprises connected with the case were not exhausted in 1819 when Russell Colvin came back to Manchester Village. Four decades later, in 1860, an incident occurred in Ohio that gave the Boorn-Colvin story a last twist, one that reopened and perhaps rendered unanswerable questions that had seemed closed for more than forty years.

A Counterfeit
Colvin?

*There can be no rational belief that the man who dra-
matically appeared in Manchester from Dover [Town-
ship], New Jersey, accompanied by James Whelpley, was
an impostor.*

—JOHN SPARGO,
THE RETURN OF RUSSELL COLVIN (1945)

AFTER the Vermont Supreme Court's decision in late January 1820 freed Stephen and
Jesse Boorn of all charges, the two brothers were
again able to go wherever they pleased. Neither displayed
any inclination to stay around Manchester. Stephen moved
his wife and children to Dorset, the town just north of Manchester where he had owned a farm in the mid-1810s. They
stayed in Dorset until the winter of 1822–23, and then returned to Denmark in upstate New York. After two or possibly three years in Denmark, they moved to the nearby

town of Champion. Finally, in the mid-1830s, Stephen took his wife, Polly, and their two sons and two daughters to Geauga County, Ohio, and settled near Burton, a small town approximately twenty-seven miles east of Cleveland.

Jesse Boorn eventually joined his brother in Ohio, but not before making a variety of intermediate moves himself. Immediately after his release from the state prison, Jesse found a new home "over the mountain" from Manchester (i.e., on the east side of the Green Mountain ridge line) in Londonderry, Vermont. Possibly because he was in poor health at the time Jesse hired a relative by marriage to move his wife, Keziah, and their young son, Sheldon, from Manchester to Londonderry. Cash poor, he agreed to pay the wagoner "one pig." Shortly thereafter, Jesse hired another man to drive the Boorn family cow over the mountain. In September 1821 Jesse went back to Manchester to sign over title to a small house that he had built on a friend's land. A brother-in-law, Elias Richardson, paid him one hundred dollars for the house, which had been standing empty ever since Jesse, his wife, and son had become residents of Londonderry.[1]

In the mid-1830s Jesse made one last attempt to earn his livelihood in Manchester. Late in 1834 he purchased a blacksmith shop and a parcel of land in town and moved there with his wife and two boys (a second son, Edgar, had been born sometime after 1820). He didn't last long, for he sold his property only a year after he bought it. Some time in the next nine years he decided to cut his ties with Vermont altogether. Keziah died in this period, and in 1844, during a brief sojourn in western New York State, he married Anna Bigelow. The following year, 1845, he bought a small parcel of land in Geauga County, Ohio, not far from where his brother Stephen had settled in 1833. Jesse and Anna subsequently had two daughters.

Ohio was the destination for thousands of migrating Americans in the early nineteenth century. The hope was that, by moving to new country where land was generally

less expensive than in the developed parts of the East, even
a poor farmer might acquire a farm or enlarge his holdings.
In reality, however, many obstacles stood in the way of making a major improvement in one's status. The cost of migrating west and the expense of establishing a new home
reduced the amount of capital pioneers had available for
purchasing western land. These factors would work most
strongly against men of modest means, such as Stephen and
Jesse Boorn, who arrived in Ohio after the best inexpensive
land had already been acquired by others. Moreover, the
Boorns were no longer young men with time on their side.
Stephen turned sixty in 1848 and Jesse in 1852. Not surprisingly, therefore, the brothers improved their economic
status only modestly by their move west. Curiously, the 1850
census shows Jesse and Anna Boorn as landless tenant farmers, although they owned at least one acre and possibly four
in the area west of the Cuyahoga River's west branch. Stephen owned a much larger farm about four miles southeast
of Jesse's place, but the land was not very good and the
assessed value of Stephen's real property holdings ranked
below that of nearly two-thirds of his neighbors in Burton
Township.

Stephen and Jesse did not escape their personal pasts
either. Although Burton was hundreds of miles from Manchester, many other Vermonters had migrated to Ohio, and
among the Boorns' new neighbors in Geauga County were
several families originally from Manchester or nearby Vermont towns. Apparently these former Vermonters kept their
ears open for news about the Boorns that could be included
in letters to relations back in Vermont. In the main, their
reports were favorable. Both brothers were said to have "sustained a good moral character" and to have done as well as
if not better economically than one might expect.[2]

Not all the stories that circulated about the Boorns were
flattering, however. Stephen was said to have gone "half-crazy" in old age. The evidence offered to support this con-

tention was that Stephen, who had let his hair grow long, "went around without a hat," which was eccentric behavior in an era when country men customarily wore hats as protection against the sun.[3] Without a hat to hold it in place, Stephen's hair flew about and gave him a wild look. Mounted on a jackass whose whitish pelt matched its rider's grey locks, he evidently struck people as a strange sight. He died sometime after 1852, when he sold his Burton property to his son George, and before 1860, when the census taker found Stephen's widow, Polly, living with their other son, Alfred, in the Portage County town of Brimfield, about twenty-five miles south of Burton. She died there in 1878.

Jesse Boorn was also the subject of gossip. It was said that he was an "unsociable" man who kept to himself. Indirect evidence indicates that he had no desire to have people connect him with his Vermont past. Although he settled in the same township as Stephen and some neighbors knew he was Stephen's brother, Jesse avoided drawing attention to his family ties and his Vermont background. In the 1850s he not only used an alias, going under the name Jesse Bowen, but described himself as being from Massachusetts. Nabby Hickox, a young woman whose brother lived next door to Jesse and his family, reflected the negative impression Jesse had made on many Burton residents when she wrote a friend in 1856 that there were some things one "would not tell old Jesse Bowen because," as she put it, "he was so wicked."[4]

However, neither Jesse's positive image as a respectable family man nor the stories that portrayed him as a friendless old reprobate were entirely accurate. The truth was that he worked closely with a number of associates, but their cooperative enterprise, the production of counterfeit coin, in no way qualified as a respectable business. By 1860 a few people outside the inner circle of the gang had begun to suspect that Jesse was not what he seemed to be. That summer Jesse was visited by a man who, according to an account published soon after this meeting occurred, was named

Hackett.* Hackett and Jesse went out to the orchard back of Boorn's house and had a long talk, or perhaps several long talks (a point on which the sources are not clear). Hackett told Jesse that he was a counterfeiter who had worked on his own for many years, that he had become tired of being a lone-wolf operator, and that he wanted to hook up with a gang. He wondered whether Jesse knew of a group of counterfeiters that he could join.

It was possible for the two men to exchange a good deal of information without Jesse actually admitting that he was in a position to help Hackett. Hackett had to win the old man's confidence by demonstrating an insider's knowledge of counterfeiting techniques, and Jesse could freely trade anecdotes about the long history of counterfeiting in northern Ohio without, in fact, implicating himself, for the subject had received widespread newspaper coverage. Perhaps the most famous counterfeiting ring was one led by Dan Brown, Jim Brown, and Colonel William Ashley (who happened to be a native of Vermont). Their operations had flourished in the mid-1830s. According to one nineteenth-century source, "Not only was silver coin counterfeited, but State bank notes, especially those of Indiana, were turned out by the bushel."[5] Although Jim Brown and Ashley were arrested and jailed in the late 1830s, Dan Brown escaped capture and remained at large until his death in 1851.

Throughout the 1850s, counterfeiting was still rife in northern Ohio, and federal officials labored long and hard to combat it. They made numerous arrests, but as of 1860 there was at least one major counterfeiting ring still oper-

*This account appeared in July 1860. The "Hackett" mentioned in this story seems to have been H. M. Hackett of Ravenna, Ohio. Another version of this story, published in 1866, identifies Jesse's visitor as Harry Newcomer. Since census and newspaper sources indicate that two men with these names were in about the right place at the right time, the most likely explanation for these seemingly overlapping claims is that there were two men, Hackett and Newcomer, both of whom talked with Jesse, either separately or together.

ating successfully in the Cleveland area. Newspaper accounts indicate that the distinctive feature of this ring was that its members lived "in small, out of the way places, where they outwardly maintain the utmost respectability, and in some instances even affect piety." The gang was divided into two groups, one that made the false coins and another that sold the coins to other criminals, who then passed the counterfeit currency. In this way, by not actually putting the coins into circulation themselves, the gang's members had avoided detection. It was this "well-organized and adroit" ring that Hackett told Jesse he wanted to join.[6]

Jesse eventually felt confident enough about Hackett's credentials as a crook to confide in him. Yes, Jesse said, he was a member of the gang that had given federal officials so much grief in recent years, and yes, he could introduce Hackett to other gang members. Hackett then asked Jesse to tell him the names of his future colleagues in crime. Jesse complied, telling him that Henry and Samuel Whitcomb and Josiah Dixon, all of Geauga County, would be Hackett's principal confederates.

Having shared secrets and agreed to become partners in crime, the two men relaxed and talked of other things. Hackett asked Jesse whether he had ever done anything in a criminal way besides counterfeiting. Yes, Jesse said, forty years earlier he and his brother had murdered their brother-in-law, and had been arrested, tried, and sentenced to hang. Jesse's account of what happened next was full of embellishment and made the story, and his role in it, even more dramatic than it had been. According to Hackett, Jesse told him that on the day he and Stephen were to hang, they had "ascended the scaffold, and the noose was placed around their necks, when the supposed dead man appeared in the crowd," and he and his brother were set free. The best part of the story, Jesse added, was that the man who came forward was an impostor, "a man from New Jersey, who bore a strik-

ing resemblance to the deceased," and who had agreed to
impersonate him, a ruse that completely fooled the people
of Manchester.[7]

When Jesse and Hackett parted, Jesse was under the
impression that he had acquired a new partner in crime.
Unfortunately for him, he had been deceived. Hackett was
a deputy U.S. marshal, working undercover. Hackett's true
identity became all too apparent on July 20, 1860, when he
and several assistants swept down on the Geauga County
gang and arrested Jesse and his confederates. Five days later
Jesse was indicted before the U.S. District Court in Cleveland and a trial date was set for August 1.

In the brief period between his arrest and his trial, Jesse
repeatedly denied that he had ever told Hackett or anyone
else that he had murdered Russell Colvin. Local newspapers
also reported that Jesse feigned "feebleness and palsy" in
hopes of winning the court's sympathy and a lighter sentence.[8] It was a vain hope. On August 1 he was tried, found
guilty, and sentenced to five years in jail, a much longer
term than the younger gang members received. The Whit-
combs were each given two-year terms, and Dixon was sentenced to serve one year.

On August 6, Jesse was incarcerated in the Ohio State
Penitentiary at Columbus. Prison admission records indicate that convict number 4913, Jesse M. Boorn, alias Jesse
Bowen, was a native of Vermont, that he gave his age as
seventy-five (he was, in fact, sixty-eight at the time), and
that he stood five feet five inches tall and had hazel eyes,
gray hair, and a dark complexion. In a column labeled "General Appearance," the admitting officer noted further details
that testify to the wear and tear of Jesse's hard life: "Has
oval face, medium forehead, eyes sunken; has small scar
near first joint thumb left hand; has two vaccination marks
on left arm. Has lost one lower front tooth. Has scar on left
leg below knee and small scar on knee."[9]

Jesse Boorn not only lost his freedom in 1860, but soon

thereafter he also lost his wife and farm. In January 1861 Anna Boorn petitioned the Geauga County Court of Common Pleas to grant her a divorce, custody of her two daughters, and "reasonable Alimony" from the couple's property. A sympathetic court approved Anna's requests in March 1861, and, because no other resources were available to support her and the Boorn children, she was given title to the couple's rather scanty estate: "one horse, one wagon, one cow, one yearling heifer, one calf," and an eight-acre homestead. Anna remarried in 1863, but her second husband, Jeremiah Mathews, died before the decade was over. In 1873 she was forced to sell her small homestead and entered the county home for paupers, where she died in December of 1883. As for Jesse, he was released from prison on November 23, 1864, at the age of seventy-two. His death date is not known, but he almost certainly died in the mid to late 1860s, since Leonard Sargeant stated unequivocally in 1873 that "Jesse Boorn died many years ago."[10]

When word of what Jesse had told Hackett in 1860 reached Vermont, it was greeted with aggressive disbelief. Present and former Manchester residents rose to insist that the Russell Colvin who returned to town in 1819 had not been an impostor. After a story about Jesse's revelations appeared in the *New York Tribune* late in July 1860, Edward C. Purdy, who had owned a Manchester newspaper in the early 1830s, wrote the *Cleveland Plain Dealer,* which had been quoted as the source of the *Tribune*'s story, to say that the idea that townspeople had been fooled in 1819 was "preposterous." In 1861, Henry E. Miner, the editor of the *Manchester Journal,* echoed Purdy's response in a brief history of Manchester published in the *Vermont Quarterly Gazetteer.* According to Miner, Jesse's statements were "worthy of no credence whatever. Colvin," he wrote, "was well known in town, and on his return was recognized on every side by those who had known him intimately, some of whom are still residents of Manchester." One such surviving eyewitness, Leonard Sargeant, endorsed the Purdy-Miner viewpoint in print with the comment that "some who were not personally acquainted" with the events of 1819 might be tempted to accept Jesse's story as true, but "no one who examined the proofs of the identity of Colvin believed it for a minute." Two other eyewitnesses who were still living near Manchester in 1860 whose reaction to the news from Ohio is, regrettably, unknown were Russell's widow Sally, now married to a man named Daniel Holmes and living in Shaftsbury, and her son Lewis Colvin, who was now a resident of Sunderland.[11]

The Purdy-Miner-Sargeant response to Jesse's revelations quickly became the standard interpretation, with the result that Jesse's assertion in 1860 that he and Stephen had murdered Russell Colvin merely added a bizarre footnote to the Boorn mystery without significantly influencing the way Vermont authors treated the case. The unchallenged hold that the Purdy-Miner-Sargeant interpretation had on Vermont authors into the mid-twentieth century is well illustrated by the treatment Jesse's statements received in Sherman Roberts Moulton's *The Boorn Mystery* (1937) and John Spargo's *The Return of Russell Colvin* (1945). Neither author attributed much importance to Jesse's revelations. Moulton devoted only a page and a half of seventy-seven pages of text to the incident, and Spargo gave it barely two pages out of eighty-four. Moulton even questioned whether Jesse Bowen, the counterfeiter who claimed to have gotten away with murder, was Jesse Boorn. He acknowledged that Leonard Sargeant and others had taken the two to be the same man, but Moulton's opinion was that "Jesse Bowen of evil fame was not the prosperous and law-abiding Jesse Boorn" described by former Manchester residents when writing home from Ohio. Spargo carried the same point one step further and declared flatly, "There is not a shred of evidence that Jesse Bowen, suspected of counterfeiting, was Jesse Boorn, formerly of Manchester." However, Spargo was wrong. Not only was Jesse Bowen identified as Jesse Boorn in contemporary Ohio newspapers that covered the breakup of the Burton counterfeiting ring, but other sources confirm that Bowen and Boorn were one and the same. Census records show that Jesse, his wife, and their daughter lived in a Burton household under the names Jesse, Anna, and C. M. E. Bowen, and, as noted earlier, Ohio prison records confirm that Jesse M. Bowen, formerly of Vermont, used "Bowen" as his alias. But even if Moulton and Spargo had realized that Jesse Bowen in fact was Jesse Boorn, they probably would not have changed their position, since for them, like their predecessors Purdy and Sargeant, the important point was that Manchester residents had accepted the returned Russell as authentic. As Moulton put it, "It seems so very improbable that an impostor could have passed the searching examination to which Colvin was subjected; or could have so completely impersonated him in appearance, manner and knowledge of local persons and affairs; or would have been recognized by so many of his former acquaintances."[12]

Could the people of Manchester have been duped in 1819? Since virtually every account of the Boorn-Colvin case that deals with this issue has been quick to dismiss Jesse's revelations as unbelievable, the opposite view remains, practically speaking, untested. What follows here, therefore, is a reexamination of the events of November and December 1819 in the light of Jesse's statement. Regardless of what can or cannot be proven in the process, the review itself will have the virtue of bringing to the fore aspects of the Boorn mystery that the traditional interpretation scarcely mentions, or overlooks altogether.

Before turning specifically to the events of November and December 1819, it may be useful to make two preliminary points. First, it was not as impossible to be deceived about the identity of a former neighbor as the worthy citizens of Manchester believed when they protested that they could not have been fooled by a Colvin look-alike. That such deception was possible is demonstrated by the well-known sixteenth-century case of an impostor named Arnaud du Tilh, who came to the French village of Artigat in 1556 and claimed to be Martin Guerre, a man who had left town eight years earlier. According to a modern account of the incident, du Tilh's initial success came, in part, because he "greeted everyone by name and reminded them accurately of things they had done together in precise circumstances many years before."[13] Almost three years passed before some incriminating evidence emerged that, when combined with growing tension between du Tilh and Guerre's uncle, led to a serious challenge to du Tilh's deception. Even then, witnesses at a hearing to determine whether he was truly Martin Guerre were divided fairly evenly, forty-five saying he was an impostor and thirty to forty asserting that he was not. Bear in mind that the witnesses who were still convinced that du Tilh was Martin Guerre had had nearly three years to learn otherwise, while Manchester residents did not have quite a full week to observe the returned Russell.

Second, it is important to remember that strong evidence corroborated Jesse's 1860 statement that Russell Colvin had been murdered in 1812. As we have seen, on May 10, 1812, Lewis Colvin ran from the field when he saw his father fall to the ground after being struck by Stephen. According to Sally Colvin, in 1815 Stephen told her that "Russell was dead and he knew it," and Jesse agreed with this statement. Moreover, in May 1819 Jesse told Truman Hill that he believed "Stephen had killed Colvin." Then, in his written confession of August 27, 1819, Stephen admitted that he had done the deed.[14]

If Colvin was dead, then by mid-November 1819 Stephen was definitely in a position to need to produce a Colvin look-alike, inasmuch as the legislature had turned down Stephen's plea for clemency and he was due to be hanged within two months. A conspiracy, if there was one, would have required several elements in order to succeed, including money to pay an impostor (and possibly other participants in the plot), and a group of individuals with the motivation to try to carry it off. Although the evidence for the existence of such a conspiracy is completely circumstantial, a logical explanation of how its necessary elements might have come together can be reconstructed from known facts.

When news of Jesse's 1860 revelations reached the East Coast, one objection that was immediately raised was that the Boorns could not have afforded to pay an impostor. Edward C. Purdy put the point succinctly. "The Boorns," he asserted, "were very poor, and of course had no friends who could assist them to purchase a substitute for Colvin."[15] Purdy was mistaken. His error lay in confusing the financial condition of Stephen and Jesse, both of whom were young, recently married men who had little or no surplus cash, with the Boorn family as a whole, which was certainly not impoverished. For generations most Manchester Boorns had ranked in the solid middle of local farm families, and, when necessary, the better established members of the family were perfectly capable of raising money to meet major expenses. The present generation was no exception. Jesse and Stephen's older brother John paid their father a very substantial sum of money—two thousand dollars—for a choice parcel of land in September 1819, and still had enough money left to pay Richard Skinner to defend his brothers at their trial only two months later. In an era when a hundred and twenty dollars was a solid year's income for a man employed as the New Jersey Colvin was, as a farm laborer, Stephen's father and older brother both clearly had the wherewithal to pay such a man to pass himself off as the murder victim.

There is no way of knowing when the idea of finding a look-alike to impersonate Colvin might have first occurred to Stephen, but such a plot would have to have been launched no later than mid-November, after Stephen got the bad news from the state legislature. If this was indeed done, a statement Stephen made to the Reverend Haynes early in December can be read in a different light. "I wish," Stephen said, "they would let me live even in this situation some longer; perhaps something will take place that may convince people that I am innocent."[16] In traditional treatments of the Boorn mystery this scene is taken to show Stephen grasping at straws and pursuing seemingly faint hopes just a short while before he was to receive positive news that exceeded his wildest expectations. That may be; certainly, plot or no plot, at this point in time Stephen did not know that he would soon be rescued. However, it is also possible that when he wistfully spoke of "perhaps something" taking place, he was fully aware that a few of his friends were doing their best to make that "something" happen.

The circle of conspirators need not have been large. At the Manchester end, Stephen's foremost ally would have been his father, Barney Boorn. Possibly Barney's oldest son John was also involved, although his participation was by no means essential. Outside of Manchester, James Whelpley, now a New Yorker, was the key figure. He was the primary link between the Boorns in Vermont and the New Jersey participants: Taber Chadwick, William Polhemus, and Polhemus's hired man, the Colvin look-alike. Barney Boorn's desire to save his son's life was an obvious enough reason for him to support the scheme, but what would have motivated the others to join in?

Nothing in the record directly answers the question why James Whelpley might have joined. However, if one reads between the lines, it appears that there was a longstanding friendship between the Whelpley and the Boorn families, and this may have had a lot to do with James Whelpley's readiness to help Stephen Boorn. As noted earlier, Whelpleys and Boorns had been early settlers and neighbors in the East Manchester and Manchester Center sections of town. James's father and Stephen's grandfather had been political associates in the pioneer period. Both families had taken active roles in founding the local Baptist church, and Stephen's parents and James Whelpley and his wife, Lydia, continued to attend Baptist services in the 1810s. A further indication of cordial relations between the two families, specifically between James's branch of the Whelpley clan and Barney Boorn, is found in a land transaction that took place in 1809. James Whelpley's uncle Joseph, as executor of the estate of James's deceased father, sold Barney Boorn a two-acre house lot on the main road from East Manchester to Manchester Center at what appears to be a friendship price.

James Whelpley and Stephen Boorn were almost the same age, James having been born in 1784 and Stephen in 1788. At one time James owned a store in Manchester Center that the Boorns, including Stephen, would certainly have patronized. Late in 1818, Whelpley and his wife left for New York City, where he became the proprietor of a tavern. His contacts with the many people who passed through his inn put him in a good position to find a passable substitute for Russell Colvin. Moreover, Whelpley was also a bit of a risk-taker. He had lost his Manchester Center store after over-extending himself financially and being taken to court by his creditors; and he had subsequently tried to recoup his fortunes in New York City, even then a highly competitive place. That he may again have overreached himself is implied by the fact that he abandoned his New York tavern business after only three years. Very likely he needed cash in 1819 and would have been glad to receive money from the Boorns in return for helping them. Possibly, too, Whelpley's unhappy experience with a legal system that had forced him out of business in Vermont would have made him more open to the idea of trying to outwit the law to save a former neighbor from the gallows.

If Whelpley the risk-taker was also Whelpley the trickster, then New York City was the ideal place from which to operate. During the first half of the nineteenth century a distinctive urban culture began to develop in the nation's largest cities, and in 1819, New York City, a bustling port with approximately 120,000 inhabitants, was America's most populous urban center. This emerging urban culture, characterized by commercial aggressiveness and intense dedication to material success, also had a shady underside. As one scholar has described it, "The proliferation of moveable wealth, especially commercial paper, in the early nineteenth century, and the growing confusion and anonymity of urban living, had made possible for the first time a wide variety of swindles, frauds, forgeries, counterfeiting activities, and other confidence games."[17] Although the magnitude and sophistication of such activities was not sufficient to pose a serious threat to public safety prior to 1830, it was nevertheless also true that New York City's rapid commercial expansion from the late 1810s onward had been accompanied by a gradual upswing in many crimes, including prostitution, counterfeiting, robbery, and schemes to defraud unwary country folk visiting the city. It was in this changing and sometimes unsavory urban environment that Whelpley the trickster would have set to work.

Whelpley would have needed the cooperation of the New Jersey conspirators, Taber Chadwick, William Polhemus, and the Colvin substitute. How might he have convinced them to aid him? Background information on the New Jersey participants is very limited, but one important fact does surface clearly. The three New Jerseyites were not strangers who had to be recruited individually. Ties of family and friendship made them a close-knit unit who came, as it were, as a package. Chadwick, the Methodist preacher, lived in northern Monmouth County. His sister Mary had married William Polhemus in 1797, and after Polhemus's father died, William and his brother John inherited half shares in a sawmill in Dover Township. Perhaps twelve years later, in 1813, a wandering man in his early thirties arrived at the home of William and Mary Polhemus. This man became a member of the Polhemus household and worked side by side with William at the family's farm and mill.

In addition to family connections, the New Jersey conspirators shared ties to Methodism. The Polhemus family had long played a leading role in a group of Methodists who first gathered in the 1790s at a Dover Township site that became known as the "Polhemus Preaching Place."[18] In 1809 Polhemus Chapel, a small log house of worship, was built on the property where the Polhemus sawmill was located. (Later, in 1830, William's widow, Mary, donated land for the construction of a larger chapel.) From the 1810s to the 1840s, Mary's brother, Taber Chadwick, served as a Methodist preacher in various towns farther north in Monmouth County.

Neither Chadwick's position as a Methodist preacher nor his brother-in-law's support for the Methodist church necessarily implied adherence to the kind of conventional respectability that would have precluded participation in a conspiracy of the sort under investigation here. In the first decades of the nineteenth century the social and educational status of Methodist preachers was generally far below that of ministers in rival denominations such as the Congregational, Episcopal, and Dutch Reformed churches. For instance, Methodist circuit riders, itinerant preachers who roamed the countryside in search of converts, received a maximum annual stipend of eighty dollars, at a time when Congregational ministers typically received five times as much. Even more settled Methodist preachers, such as Taber Chadwick, often had no church buildings in which to conduct services. As an old source reports, Chadwick for many years preached in "school-houses and private residences." The low pay and lack of church facilities were due not only to the fact that many Methodists of the time were poor people, but also to the influence of a widely held Methodist conviction that so-called social advantages—formal education, material comforts, and membership in the professions—were detrimental to true Christian piety. Egalitarian in spirit and practice, such early Methodists fostered what one scholar, Nathan O. Hatch, has called the "democratization of American Christianity." They took inspiration from such leading itinerants as Lorenzo Dow, who, as Hatch puts it, "sought the conversion of sinners at the same time that he railed at tyranny and priest-craft and the professions of law and medicine." Precisely how many of these social and political prejudices were shared by Taber Chadwick or William and Mary Polhemus cannot be ascertained, but if their Methodist affiliations did lead them to adopt egalitarian and antiestablishment sentiments, those sentiments might have made them willing to overlook legal niceties in order to aid the Boorns.[19]

In regard to Chadwick it is possible, of course, to suppose that Whelpley had some leverage that compelled the preacher to join the conspiracy, but it seems much more likely that humanitarian motives would have led Chadwick to help. For example, Whelpley might well have tried to arouse Chadwick's sympathy for Stephen by telling him that the Boorns had been convicted on testimony received from a ghost in a dream and unjustly condemned to hang for supposedly murdering a man whose body had not even been found. Chadwick, in fact, would find much the same story in the *New York Evening Post*'s reprint of the *Daily Advertiser* item. Moreover, Chadwick would have had an even stronger incentive to help Stephen if he believed that he was at the same time helping his sister's husband, William Polhemus. One of the few places that William's name shows up in the public record documents his severe indebtedness. Not long after William's death in the late 1820s, Chadwick, as coexecutor (with his sister) of William's estate, was forced by the courts to permit sheriff's sales of much of his brother-in-law's property to meet William's debts. Although these documents refer to events that took place years after the

Boorn-Colvin affair was resolved, they may represent the last stage of a history of financial problems stretching back as far as 1819. As for the New Jersey "Colvin," who lived with the Polhemus family and spoke of them with a fondness the sincerity of which there is no reason to doubt, taking part in the impersonation scheme would have been an opportunity to help his friends and himself. If he received (to take a generous figure) $250 for impersonating Colvin, it would represent more than two years' income for a hired man, and if Polhemus received a similar sum, it would be a tidy windfall for the Polhemus household. If Chadwick was reluctant to take money for doing good deeds, the sums paid Polhemus and "Colvin," plus a similar finder's fee to Whelpley, would come to $750, well within the means Barney Boorn had available to save his son's life.

Turning now to the well-known events connected with Russell Colvin's return to Manchester in 1819, the task is to watch for loose ends and odd details that might indicate that a fraud was being perpetrated—to see, in other words, whether the outline of an alternative to the traditional explanation of these events can be discerned. If a conspiracy was in progress, Stephen's request that his lawyers draw up an advertisement for Colvin can be seen as a first step toward providing the plotters with a way to explain the "discovery" of Colvin and why they had been looking for him in the first place. It is possible, moreover, that the anonymous letter about the Boorn trial that appeared in the *Daily Advertiser* even before Stephen's lawyers had placed their advertisement was another initiative taken by one of the conspirators. The fact that Chadwick's letter mentioned the *Daily Advertiser* item rather than the advertisement does not invalidate the theory about the role the advertisement was supposed to play in the plot. Whelpley, indeed, seems not to have distinguished between the letter and the advertisement, for he apparently told a reporter in mid-December that Chadwick's letter (in which Chadwick definitely gave the credit to the *Daily Advertiser* piece) had been written in response to the advertisement.

Since Whelpley is the sole source for virtually everything that is known about the Colvin story prior to Russell's return to Manchester, his statements require particularly close scrutiny. After the advertisement was placed, the next important episode in the traditional story was the scene at the hotel where Chadwick supposedly heard Whelpley expound on the Boorn-Colvin case. There is no way of knowing, assuming a conspiracy was in progress, whether this incident actually took place, but if it did, a few details about it seem peculiar. For example, Whelpley and Chadwick seem not to have spoken to each other on the morning of November 27, or at least neither man mentioned such a conversation. It seems odd that Chadwick would not have come forward immediately and told Whelpley that he knew of a man in New Jersey who might be Russell Colvin. Sargeant's explanation based on what he heard from Whelpley was that Chadwick reached home before it occurred to him that his brother-in-law's hired man was Colvin. Is it credible that Chadwick needed several days to remember that the man had called himself Colvin and claimed to be from Vermont (as Chadwick reported in his letter), or to figure out the implications of those facts? The reticence of both Chadwick and Whelpley on the matter of talking that morning might have another explanation. It could be that they talked but never mentioned it because they wanted to avoid the appearance of anything that might indicate collusion.

The timing of Chadwick's letter was itself very odd. Ten days passed between the twenty-seventh and December 6, the date of his letter to the *New York Evening Post* that announced the astonishing news that Colvin was apparently alive and well in New Jersey. Why the long delay in a matter that meant life or death to a condemned man? Perhaps it was because Chadwick needed the time to return to New

Jersey (possibly accompanied by Whelpley) to talk with William Polhemus's hired man to see if he would work out as a substitute Colvin. In other words, if there was a conspiracy in progress, that fact supplies a very good explanation for Chadwick's dilatoriness: no letter could be written until he knew for certain that the prospective impostor would join the conspiracy.

On the whole, the contents of Chadwick's letter to the *New York Evening Post* seemed to provide impressive documentation that the New Jersey Colvin was the genuine article. However, if read in the light of a possible conspiracy, two details of the letter leap out. First, Chadwick wrote that Colvin was living in New Jersey, "but so completely insane as not to be able to give a satisfactory account of himself." Such a phrase would give the substitute Colvin and his sponsors a ready-made excuse if he should fail to get the facts straight when examined by Vermont authorities. He would be excused, as indeed he was once he reached Manchester, because his mental deficiencies made it unreasonable to expect him to remember everything that a normal person should have. Second, Chadwick, in what appears to be a major slip-up, listed among the "connections, acquaintances, &c." of the New Jersey Colvin "Chase, as judge." The New Jersey Colvin would not have known Chief Justice Dudley Chase, the judge who presided at the Boorns' trial. A few Vermonters were quick to note this fact and, as mentioned earlier, upon learning that Jesse's nickname was "Judge," they assumed that "Chase" was simply a misprint and published revised versions of Chadwick's letter in which Jesse's name was substituted for Chase's. Although there is no evidence that contemporaries found the original version suspicious, its reference to Judge Chase seems to reveal Chadwick putting into Colvin's mouth words that could only have come from information provided by a co-conspirator, James Whelpley.[20]

An incident that Whelpley reported in relation to his first

meeting with the New Jersey Colvin at Polhemus Mills is similarly suggestive. According to the only available account, Whelpley spoke to Colvin, calling him by name, and the New Jersey man "said Whelpley must be mistaken, Colvin was not his name; it had been once, but he was another man now."[21] Unfortunately, the name the New Jersey Colvin was using at the time is not mentioned and therefore cannot be traced in New Jersey records. However, his use of this other name would serve to explain to neighbors in Dover Township why the man who had lived with the Polhemus family for the past six years had not been known to them as Colvin until December 1819. Of course, the fact that Polhemus's hired man apparently thought he had a double identity might well have been sufficient to convince those who knew him that he was every bit as mentally deranged as Colvin was supposed to be.

Whelpley and the New Jersey Colvin reached New York City on the evening of December 15. They stayed together at Whelpley's inn, where Whelpley kept Colvin closely confined to the premises. On the twenty-first, five days and six nights after they had arrived in New York, they began their trip to Vermont by boarding the morning stage to Albany. Why the long stay in New York, and why did Whelpley keep Colvin under wraps? The traditional interpretation of the Boorn-Colvin case offers no explanation for the delay, and adopts Whelpley's account as the answer to the second part of the question. As noted earlier, he said that Colvin was very anxious to return to New Jersey and was dissuaded from doing so only by a clever ruse: Whelpley told the befuddled Colvin that it was not safe to venture out because the War of 1812 was still in progress and British warships were lurking in the harbor in hopes of kidnapping unwary travelers. The more likely reason for the travel delay and Colvin's confinement to quarters was that the two men needed time together so that Whelpley could coach the substitute Colvin on the things he would need to know upon his arrival in Manchester.

As suggested earlier, the effect of Whelpley's stories about the fictitious British warships and about tricking Colvin into taking a ferryboat to Albany (when in fact they went by stagecoach) was to draw attention to Colvin's supposed mental deficiencies. Russell's behavior on the night he arrived in Manchester conveyed the same impression. One of the earliest accounts of this incident, quoted above, reported that Colvin "was too much confused to hold a regular conference with any one."[22] As we have seen, Manchester residents took his confusion as evidence that he was indeed the weak-minded fellow who had disappeared in 1812. However, within the context of a conspiracy, Colvin's confusion was an ideal disguise and one that contributed significantly to the success of the plotters' game of deception.

What about the proofs of his identity that the returned Russell offered and the good people of Manchester found so persuasive? If he was an impostor, how could he know so much about the history of the town and its people and also recognize so many former acquaintances? The first of these proofs, the memory of incidents, is easily explained within the conspiracy theory. With Whelpley's coaching over at least a week's time, the false Colvin was able to memorize information about Manchester history and to rattle it off at appropriate moments. Significantly, there were two subjects on which the returned Russell had almost nothing to say: one was the fight with Stephen, and the other the story of how he had gotten from Vermont to New Jersey. Referring specifically to his quarrel with the Boorns, an early source said that "Colvin appeared to be a stranger to the *transaction* generally."[23] Colvin's only statement that seemed to have any bearing on the fight was made just after he arrived in Manchester. As described earlier, during his dramatic encounter with the still-shackled Stephen, Colvin asserted that

Stephen had never hurt him, although Jesse had hit him once. This was a curious statement, inasmuch as every witness to the fight, including Stephen and Jesse, agreed that it was Stephen who had knocked Colvin to the ground. However, as part of a conspiracy this seemingly peculiar statement might well represent a calculated effort to exonerate Stephen from all possible charges, including felonious assault. Jesse's cause would suffer no ill effects, since listeners took Colvin's comment to refer to some previous altercation, and, in any case, the returned Russell made it clear that he had no complaint against either of the Boorns.

A false Colvin's capacity to recognize and name former neighbors is more difficult to explain, although the example of Arnaud du Tihl, the Frenchman who impersonated Martin Guerre, is again instructive. Du Tihl spent many months collecting information about the town of Artigat and its inhabitants before he actually announced his presence in the vicinity. He was able, as noted earlier, to identify many people whom the real Martin Guerre had known and to convince them that he was who he said he was by describing incidents in their lives and Guerre's. The returned Russell did not have nearly so long to prepare for his performance, but he had Whelpley as a very knowledgeable tutor and the disguise of Colvin's supposed derangement to retreat to, if necessary. The available descriptions of what happened when the returned Russell met people he had known are very sketchy. Leonard Sargeant said only that Colvin "recognized and called by name very many of his former acquaintances." Obviously, "very many" (another witness said "almost all") was somewhat short of "all."[24]

Clearly, however, even this was a very impressive achievement, and for a substitute Colvin to manage it, he would have needed a lot of help from Whelpley. Such coaching could have taken three forms. First, before their arrival in Manchester Whelpley would have described in detail people whose appearance was distinctive. Second, after the two conspirators had arrived in Manchester and were staying at Captain Black's Tavern, Whelpley could have pointed out individuals in the crowds that gathered outside in hopes of catching a glimpse of Colvin, who subsequently would have been able to recognize them. Third, Whelpley, who successfully presented himself as a civic-minded man on a mercy mission, was seemingly beyond suspicion, and as Colvin's escort, he was in a position to hover at the latter's elbow and prompt him. For instance, Russell's ability to state correctly the titles—Squire, Captain, Deacon, and so forth—of certain prominent citizens made many Manchester people accept him as the man who had disappeared in 1812. No specific instance of this is described in the sources, but it might well have taken the following form: Whelpley and Colvin find themselves face to face with Asa Loveland. An awkward pause occurs when Russell does not know what to say. Whelpley cues him by asking, "Do you remember Asa Loveland?" If Colvin then replied, "Yes, Deacon Loveland. You made the cherry coffin in which Edward Perkins was buried in 1804," any doubts created by Colvin's initial hesitation would be swept aside by the correct identification of Loveland as a deacon and as the carpenter who in fact had made Perkins's coffin.[25] Incidentally, du Tihl used much the same technique to convince people that he was indeed Martin Guerre.

There were other awkward moments that need to be examined in the light of a possible conspiracy. As we have seen, two such incidents involved Colvin's wife and children. For an impostor, any encounter with "his" wife was potentially very risky. Colvin finessed this by figuratively, and perhaps also literally, turning his back on Sally. According to one account, "Mrs. Colvin came to see her husband, but he took little notice of her, intimating that she did not belong to him." However, when he was momentarily unable to recognize his children, the returned Russell had to turn to other strategies. He quickly retreated to his favored disguise as a deranged man and babbled in a confused way about how the children had been left behind in New Jersey. Of course, in so doing he also redirected the audience's attention to his life in New Jersey, a safe topic and the one about which he talked most expansively while in Vermont.[26]

Colvin and Whelpley left Manchester Village by stage-coach on Wednesday, December 29, 1819, not quite a full week after they had arrived in town. According to the Reverend Haynes, Colvin had told people that "the family where he resided in New Jersey are fond of him and wish him to return and spend his days with them, of which he seems very desirous."[27] The traditional interpretation of the Boorn mystery accepts at face value Colvin's statement that he was eager to get back to New Jersey. However, his actions were not entirely consistent with his words. As we have seen, after their departure from Manchester Colvin and Whelpley went to Albany, arriving there on the evening of the twenty-ninth. They made arrangements for Colvin to appear at the Albany Museum and remained in town for that purpose through the morning of January 6, 1820. The striking thing here is that Colvin stayed only six days and seven nights in Manchester Village, but then, in spite of his expressed desire to get home to New Jersey, he spent an even longer period, seven days and eight nights, in Albany. His behavior was consistent with a plot to deceive. The sooner he could get out of Manchester, the sooner the possibility that his fraud might be exposed would end. Once safely out of Vermont, however, there was no need for haste, especially if he could parlay his new-found notoriety into a fee for a museum appearance.

News that the returned Russell had made a long stop in Albany appears not to have shaken the conviction of Manchester people that he was the genuine article any more than Jesse Boorn's revelations would do forty years later. Is it possible, however, that they were guilty of overconfidence? Suppose some were not truly in a position to judge the returned Russell's credentials, or that some people's hopes and fears regarding his identity distorted their perceptions of it? The Reverend Haynes, for example, had been convinced that Stephen Boorn was innocent for weeks before Russell's arrival, and then felt "joy and gladness" the night the missing man returned. Yet Haynes had never laid eyes on Colvin before that occasion and had no independent basis on which to evaluate the New Jersey man's claims. For somewhat different reasons, Stephen's lawyers—Skinner, Sargeant, and Wellman—may have been predisposed to give the returned Russell the benefit of the doubt, though not to the point of remaining silent if they were certain he was an impostor. But how would they have been sure? Skinner, at least, had met the original Colvin, but Sargeant, who later brusquely dismissed the import of Jesse's revelations, admitted to "not being personally acquainted with Colvin" in the past.[28]

As noted earlier, within Manchester's town limits there were a number of geographical subcommunities, each of which was to some degree isolated from the others. Members of the Manchester Village elite, the group from which the town officials responsible for verifying the returned Russell's claims were drawn, were the least likely to have known the man, or to have known him well. We have already seen that the Manchester Village leaders who testified at the trial—Josiah Burton, Truman Hill, Joel Pratt, Samuel Raymond, and Richard Skinner—displayed no firsthand knowledge of background events in the Boorn-Colvin case that had taken place in East Manchester prior to 1819. Moreover, of these witnesses, only Pratt and Skinner indicated that they had had dealings with Colvin prior to his disappearance in 1812. Calvin Sheldon, the prosecuting attorney at the trial and the chair of the court of inquiry before which the returned Russell appeared, was, like several other important figures in the Manchester Village elite, a relative newcomer in town, and he, in fact, was a more recent arrival than most. As such, he was perhaps particularly susceptible to being impressed when Colvin spoke confidently about events that had taken place before Sheldon moved to town and accurately described details about them that were new to the young prosecutor. On the other hand, the people who were most likely to have known Colvin previously, the residents of East Manchester and Manchester Center, where Russell had once lived, were also apt to be among Stephen Boorn's family and friends, and many of them might have been reluctant to be the first to challenge the returned Russell's credentials because to do so would be tantamount to signing Stephen's death warrant.

Defenders of the returned Russell's authenticity might well reply that a bogus Colvin and his mentor Whelpley would never have risked a trip to Vermont and a confrontation with Manchester officials because the chances of exposure were too great. According to this reasoning, if a fraud had been uncovered, Whelpley would have suffered, at the very least, deep embarrassment and serious damage to his good reputation, while Colvin, who doubtless was put under oath by the court of inquiry, might well have been charged with and convicted of perjury. Were such risks worth the possible reward?

Practically speaking, however, the danger of exposure was negligible. Suppose for a moment that Manchester officials rejected the returned Russell's claims. Rejecting his claims was a far cry from proving that he had intentionally tried to deceive town officials, unless, and this was highly improbable, one of the conspirators confessed. Moreover, Whelpley and Colvin arrived in Vermont well armed with excuses that probably would have protected them against legal action if their scheme had failed. Colvin's actions, of course, could be attributed to derangement. Town officials might be suspicious of the New Jersey man's behavior, but how could they prove that he was not sincerely convinced that he *was* Russell Colvin (as well as "another man," a fact he had readily admitted)? Whelpley, meanwhile, could protest that he had just been trying to do his civic duty and insure that justice was served in a life-or-death situation. Even if he later had to admit that he had been mistaken about the New Jersey man's identity, he could readily argue that it had been an innocent mistake and understandable too, given the man's resemblance to Russell Colvin and his somewhat incoherent account of himself. If pressed to explain how the returned Russell happened to know so much about Manchester and its inhabitants, Whelpley could even acknowledge that the man had gotten a lot of his information from their talks. This admission was not, by itself, incriminating, since Whelpley could claim that the process had been natural and well-intentioned.

Still, even if Whelpley and Colvin believed that they could pull off the Vermont trip, weren't there risks at the New Jersey end that would have dissuaded Chadwick and Polhemus from letting the scheme get off the ground in the first place? At the very least, wasn't there a danger that Polhemus's neighbors would suspect that something was not quite on the up and up when a "deranged" Russell Colvin was suddenly discovered in their midst? Moreover, even if Polhemus and Chadwick believed that legal action against them was very improbable because fraudulent intent was nearly impossible to prove, wouldn't the two men still have worried about the damage to their reputations that might result from Colvin's claims being rejected?

There can be no firm answers to these speculative questions, but certain aspects of the situation gave the New Jersey plotters considerable protection against exposure or embarrassment on their home turf. Chadwick, like Whelpley, could simply protest innocence and point out that his letter, for all that it strongly endorsed the likelihood that Colvin had been found, also included a number of qualifying phrases: the man was "probably" the murdered man; he was "so completely insane as not to be able to give a satisfactory account of himself"; perhaps people who had known Colvin in Vermont "might know" him if they saw him. In other words, the decision was up to the Vermonters; Chadwick had made no final claims. Similarly, Polhemus, if asked about his actions, could remind questioners that he had never disguised the fact that his hired man had used another name. He could also point out, as he in fact did, that in the six years the man had lived in the Polhemus household, "he had made known very little of his past history." Thus, about all one could say for sure of Polhemus was that he had been willing to let his employee accompany Whelpley to Vermont. There was no evidence anyone could cite that he had tried to influence the outcome of the trip.[29]

In New Jersey, as in Vermont, a crucial determinant in how people perceived Colvin's claims was his reputation for mental deficiency. Precisely what his contemporaries meant (or were describing) when they said he was "deranged," "confused," "insane," and "very simple" is impossible to know. One thing is certain, however; they did not view those terms as incompatible with the same person displaying normal behavior at other times. One witness at the Boorn trial described Colvin in successive sentences as "a weak man in mind" and "smart for business." The returned Russell's Vermont hosts observed both that he was more deranged than previously and that he was a man with "a placid and harmless disposition" who could remember many past events with "accuracy." This combination of confusion and clarity never seems to have struck Vermonters as improbable or suspicious, and New Jersey neighbors of the man called Colvin probably shared this view. All they knew about him was that he was a stranger who had wandered into town about six years earlier. He had not talked much about his past. (He may even have had something to hide.) Perhaps he had made vague references to Vermont as his former home. It could have been so, since as we have seen, the 1810s were a decade when many native Vermonters (including Stephen Boorn and James Whelpley) left the state in search of a better life elsewhere. Assuming that the New Jersey Colvin was from a part of Vermont or another state that was sufficiently far removed from Manchester to limit the possibility that he might run into former acquaintances, the danger of his past life coming to light and being used against him was slight in an era before fingerprints, mug shots, Social Security numbers, and a national police network.[30]

Regardless of what the New Jersey Colvin's neighbors had thought of him earlier, they probably would have found the fact that in 1819 he announced that he had two names and two life histories sufficient to confirm his reputation for confusion and derangement. All that is known for certain on this point is that New Jersey residents who met Polhemus's hired man after 1819 were sure that they had met Russell Colvin. This information was supplied in 1890 by a historian of Ocean County who had interviewed old-timers from the Dover Township area. "There are," he reported, "people in Ocean County, yet living, who remember Colvin." The testimony of these neighbors is significant in that it indicates that he was accepted as Russell Colvin in New Jersey as well as Vermont. Beyond that, however, this account of Colvin's New Jersey career does not tell us much. It says nothing about local perceptions of him prior to 1819, and in support of the contention that he was "partially insane," it mentions only that he "fancied" he owned the area where the Polhemus farm and mill were located. If that was all it took to strike one's neighbors as insane, it would not have been difficult for a false Colvin to maintain his reputation through the final years of his life.[31]

Could a scheme to deceive Manchester officials have been hatched so quickly, managed so smoothly in nearly every detail, and brought to a successful conclusion in such a short period of time? In retrospect, the supposed conspirators' good fortune in finding a Colvin look-alike who was willing and able to do the job seems no more improbable than certain aspects of the traditional version of what happened. One thinks, for instance, of the astonishing chain of coincidences that were involved. James Whelpley just happened to be at a New York hotel the day that another man was there reading aloud from a *New York Evening Post* article that just happened to be about the Boorn-Colvin case. Moreover, an out-of-town visitor, Taber Chadwick, happened to be present to hear Whelpley expound on the case, and Chadwick just happened to have a brother-in-law living in rural New Jersey on whose doorstep a stranger had turned up six years earlier, and that man just happened to be none other than Russell Colvin.

Where, then, does this extended reexamination of the Boorn-Colvin case lead? The most important result is to deepen the Boorn mystery by reintroducing the serious possibility that Russell Colvin was murdered in 1812 and that the man who showed up in Manchester in 1819 was an impostor. As we have seen, the traditional interpretation allowed no room for this second way of reading the record. The judgment of the witnesses who met the returned Russell was not questioned, and Jesse's claim in 1860 that the Boorns had gotten away with murder was dismissed as bragging meant to impress Hackett, whom Jesse thought was a partner in crime. Yet a close rereading of the record without these preconceptions suggests that the witnesses' perceptions may not have been as infallible as they believed, and that the case for the New Jersey Colvin being a look-alike does not depend on Jesse's statement alone but is supported by an impressive array of circumstantial evidence. To be sure, that Colvin was an impostor cannot be established for certain; but at the same time, one can no longer dismiss out of hand the possibility that, in what he said to the seeming outlaw Hackett, the counterfeiter Jesse was, for once in his life, telling the truth.

Notes

The Feud

Unless specifically stated otherwise, the source notes below contain references for quoted material only.

There are many editions of Chief Justice Dudley Chase's trial notes, which are the source of many quotations cited in the text. A manuscript copy is held by the Vermont Historical Society in Montpelier, Vermont. The edition printed in the *Journals of the General Assembly* of Vermont for 1819, cited in note 1, below, is the official printing of Chase's notes. It is also available on Readex cards in the *Early American Imprints* collection, item number 49982.

Notes

[1] Judge Chase's notes, *Journals of the General Assembly of the State of Vermont, at their Session begun and held at Montpelier, in the County of Washington, on Thursday, the Fourteenth of October, A.D. 1819* (Bennington, Vermont, n.d. [1819?]), p. 193. Source hereafter cited as Chase's Notes. The quoted words cited are found in a confession that Stephen Boorn later retracted, but they are used here because there is no reason to believe that Stephen falsified this part of his testimony.

[2] *Ibid.*, p. 194; *Trial of Stephen and Jesse Boorn for the Murder of Russel [sic] Colvin with the Subsequent Wonderful Discovery of Colvin Alive . . .* (2nd ed., Rutland, Vermont, 1820), p. 33; Leonard Deming, *A Collection of Useful, Interesting and Remarkable Events, Original and Selected from Ancient and Modern Authorities* (Middlebury, Vermont, 1825), p. 67; Leonard Sargeant, *The Trial, Confessions and Conviction of Jesse and Stephen Boorn, for the Murder of Russell Colvin, and the Return of the Man Supposed to have been Murdered* (Manchester, Vermont, 1873), p. 5.

[3] *Trial of Stephen and Jesse Boorn* (2nd ed.), p. 34.

[4] Chase's Notes, p. 189.

[5] *Ibid.*

[6] Lewis Cass Aldrich, *History of Bennington County, Vt.* (Syracuse, New York, 1889), p. 391; Lemuel Haynes, *Mystery Developed; or, Russell Colvin, (supposed to be murdered,) and Stephen and Jesse Boorn, (his convicted murderers,) Rescued from Ignominious Death by Wonderful Discoveries . . .* (Hartford, Connecticut, 1820), p. 5; Sargeant, *The Trial, Confessions and Conviction of Jesse and Stephen Boorn*, p. 5.

[7] Sargeant, *The Trial, Confessions and Conviction of Jesse and Stephen Boorn*, p. 5; Haynes, *Mystery Developed*, p. 31; Franklin B. Hough, *History of Lewis County, New York* (Syracuse, New York, 1883), p. 180.

[8] Nathan Perkins, *A Narrative of a Tour through the State of Vermont from April 27 to June 21, 1789* (Woodstock, Vermont, 1820), p. 14; The evangelist (Chester Wright of Montpelier) and John Clark of Clarendon are both quoted in David M. Ludlum, *Social Ferment in Vermont, 1791–1850* (New York, New York, 1939), pp. 20–21; Timothy Dwight, *Travels in New-England and New-York* (London, 1823), vol. 2, p. 390.

[9] Perkins, *A Narrative of a Tour*, p. 19; John A. Graham, *A De-*

scriptive Sketch of the Present State of Vermont (London, 1797), p. 53.

[10]John S. Pettibone, "The Early History of Manchester," *Proceedings of the Vermont Historical Society,* vol. 1 (1930), pp. 156–57; Loveland Munson, *The Early History of Manchester* (Manchester, Vermont, 1876), pp. 53–54.

[11]Lewis D. Stilwell, "Migration from Vermont (1776–1860)," *Proceedings of the Vermont Historical Society,* vol. 5 (June 1937), p. 87.

[12]Pettibone, "Early History of Manchester," p. 156.

[13]Robert Pierpont, as quoted in Ludlum, *Social Ferment in Vermont,* p. 73.

[14]Munson, *The Early History of Manchester,* p. 56.

[15]*Ibid.,* p. 57.

[16]Chase's Notes, pp. 188 and 190.

[17]*Ibid.,* pp. 188–89.

[18]*Ibid.,* p. 188.

[19]*Ibid.,* p. 190.

[20]*Ibid.*

[21]Entry for June 5, 1813, in "Records of the Baptist Church of Manchester, Vermont from June 22, 1781, to December 9, 1834" (ms., The First Baptist Church, Manchester Center, Vermont).

[22]*Ibid.*

[23]Land Records (Town Clerk's Office, Manchester, Vermont), vol. 8, p. 5.

[24]Chase's Notes, p. 189.

[25]*Ibid.*

[26]Stilwell, "Migration from Vermont," p. 101.

[27]Chase's Notes, pp. 188 and 194.

[28]*Ibid.,* p. 195.

[29]*Ibid.,* p. 192.

[30]*Ibid.,* p. 189.

[31]*Trial of Stephen and Jesse Boorn* (2nd ed.), p. 35.

[32]Chase's Notes, pp. 189–90.

[33]*Ibid.,* p. 188.

[34]*Ibid.*, p. 189; Zadock Thompson, *History of Vermont, Natural, Civil, and Statistical, In Three Parts* (Burlington, Vermont, 1842), Part 1, p. 45.

Colvin's Ghost

[1]Haynes, *Mystery Developed,* p. 6.

[2]Chase's Notes, p. 187.

[3]Samuel Putnam Waldo, *A Brief Sketch of the Indictment, Trial, and Conviction of Stephen and Jesse Boorn, for the Murder of Russel [sic] Colvin, at a term of the Supreme Court of the State of Vermont, Holden at Manchester, October 1819* (Hartford, Connecticut, 1820), pp. 42 and 40.

[4]Pettibone, "The Early History of Manchester," p. 58; Jack Larkin, *The Reshaping of Everyday Life, 1790–1840* (New York, 1988), pp. 79–80.

[5]Pettibone, "The Early History of Manchester," p. 58.

[6]John Putnam Demos, *Entertaining Satan: Witchcraft and the Culture of Early New England* (New York, 1982), p. 387.

[7]Daniel Pierce Thompson, *Locke Amsden; or, The Schoolmaster* (Boston, 1890), p. 100.

[8]Munson, *The Early History of Manchester,* p. 59.

[9]Chase's Notes, p. 186.

[10]*Ibid.*, p. 187.

[11]*Ibid.*, pp. 194 and 187.

[12]*Ibid.*, p. 195.

[13]*Ibid.*, p. 187; Waldo, *A Brief Sketch,* p. 43.

[14]Sargeant, *The Trial, Confessions and Conviction of Jesse and Stephen Boorn,* pp. 7–8.

[15]Haynes, *Mystery Developed,* p. 8; Chase's Notes, p. 193.

[16]Entry for May 16, 1819, "Records of the Baptist Church of Manchester, Vermont" (ms., Baptist Church, Manchester Center, Vermont).

[17]Sargeant, *The Trial, Confessions and Conviction of Jesse and Stephen Boorn,* p. 8.

[18]*New York Columbian,* January 1, 1820; Chase's Notes, p. 191.

Notes

[19]Chase's Notes, p. 191.

[20]*Ibid.*

[21]Winslow C. Watson, *The Life and Character of the Hon. Richard Skinner* (Albany, New York, 1863), p. 19; Sargeant, *The Trial, Confessions and Conviction of Jesse and Stephen Boorn,* pp. 6 and 8; Waldo, *A Brief Sketch,* p. 42; *Trial of Stephen and Jesse Boorn* (2nd ed.), p. iii.

[22]Chase's Notes, pp. 192 and 195.

[23]*Trial of Stephen and Jesse Boorn* (2nd ed.), p. 35; Waldo, *A Brief Sketch,* p. 41.

[24]Waldo, *A Brief Sketch,* pp. 40 and 42; Haynes, *Mystery Developed,* p. 5; Sargeant, *The Trial, Confessions and Conviction of Jesse and Stephen Boorn,* p. 6.

[25]Entry for February 23, 1824, "Church Records, A: Clerk's Records, 1804–1828" (ms., Manchester First Congregational Church).

[26]Ludlum, *Social Ferment in Vermont.* The Asa Burton quotation is found on p. 52.

[27]Perkins, *A Narrative of a Tour,* p. 19.

[28]Entry for April 29, 1818, "Church Records, A: Clerk's Records, 1804–1828" (ms., Manchester First Congregational Church).

[29]*Ibid.,* entries for September 12, 1813, and February 18, 1819.

[30]*Ibid.,* entry for April 28, 1819.

[31]Chase's Notes, p. 193.

[32]*Ibid.,* p. 192.

[33]*Ibid.,* p. 193.

[34]*Ibid.,* pp. 193–94.

[35]Sargeant, *The Trial, Confessions and Convictions of Jesse and Stephen Boorn,* p. 28.

The Trial

[1]George Rich et al., to Dudley Chase, December 29, 1819, "Boorn Trial Records: Judge Dudley Chase's Files" (ms. 26, no. 49; Vermont Historical Society). Hereafter: "Boorn Trial Records."

[2]Haynes, *Mystery Developed,* p. 9.

[3]Sherman Roberts Moulton, *The Boorn Mystery: An Episode from the Judicial Annals of Vermont* (Montpelier, Vermont, 1937), p. 31.

[4]Watson, *The Life and Character of the Hon. Richard Skinner,* p. 12.

[5]Haynes, *Mystery Developed,* p. 9; and Sargeant, *The Trial, Confessions and Conviction of Jesse and Stephen Boorn,* p. 9.

[6]Sargeant, *The Trial, Confessions and Conviction of Jesse and Stephen Boorn,* pp. 27–28; and Moulton, *The Boorn Mystery,* p. 30.

[7]Chase's Notes, p. 187.

[8]*Ibid.*

[9]*Ibid.*

[10]*Ibid.,* p. 188.

[11]*Ibid.,* p. 189.

[12]*Ibid.*

[13]Moulton, *The Boorn Mystery,* p. 38.

[14]Chase's Notes, p. 190.

[15]*Ibid.*

[16]*Ibid.,* p. 191.

[17]*The Laws of the State of Vermont* (Randolph, Vermont, 1808), vol. 1, p. 334.

[18] Moulton, *The Boorn Mystery,* p. 62.

[19]Chase's Notes, p. 192.

[20]*Ibid.*

[21]*Ibid.*

[22]*Ibid.*

[23]*Ibid.,* pp. 193–94.

[24]*Ibid.,* p. 194.

[25]*Ibid.*

[26]*Ibid.*

[27]*Ibid.,* pp. 187 and 195.

[28]Dudley Chase, notes on arguments of counsel, in "Boorn Trial Records."

[29]*Ibid.*

[30]*Ibid.*

[31]*Ibid.*

[32]*Ibid.*

[33]Sargeant, *The Trial, Confessions and Conviction of Jesse and Stephen Boorn,* p. 10.

[34]Haynes, *Mystery Developed,* p. 9.

[35]*Ibid.*

[36]Sargeant, *The Trial, Confessions and Conviction of Jesse and Stephen Boorn,* p. 10.

[37]Watson, *The Life and Character of the Hon. Richard Skinner,* p. 19; *Vermont Gazette* (Bennington, Vermont), January 11, 1820.

[38]Moulton, *The Boorn Mystery,* p. 65.

[39]*Trial of Stephen and Jesse Boorn,* 2nd ed., p. 28.

[40]Timothy Mather Cooley, *Sketches of the Life and Character of the Rev. Lemuel Haynes* (New York, 1837), p. 83.

[41]*Ibid.,* p. 214; *The Colored American* (New York), March 11, 1837.

[42]Haynes, *Mystery Developed,* p. 8.

[43]*Journals of the General Assembly of the State of Vermont . . . 1819,* p. 207. The vote totals given in the text are from these journals. Other contemporary sources give slightly different figures.

[44]Haynes, *Mystery Developed,* p. 10.

[45]Sargeant, *The Trial, Confessions and Conviction of Jesse and Stephen Boorn,* p. 11.

[46]*Ibid.* (but note that Sargeant incorrectly dates the draft November 26, 1819).

[47]Haynes, *Mystery Developed,* p. 10.

[48]*Ibid.*

The Dead Alive!

[1]*Trial of Stephen and Jesse Boorn, for the Murder of Russell Colvin, Before an Adjourned Term of the Supreme Court, begun and holden at Manchester, in the County of Bennington, Oct. 26,*

Notes

A.D. *1819* (Rutland, Vermont, 1819), p. 30. Hereafter: *Trial of Stephen and Jesse Boorn* (1819 edition).

[2]*Rutland Herald,* November 30, 1819.

[3]John Reynolds, *Recollections of Windsor Prison: Containing Sketches of Its History and Discipline* (Boston, 1834), pp. 11 and 15.

[4]*Albany Gazette and Daily Advertiser,* November 25, 1819; the item was reprinted in the *New York Evening Post* on November 26.

[5]*New York Evening Post,* December 10, 1819.

[6]See *Rutland Herald,* December 21, 1819, for the "Chase, as judge," version, and the *Herald*'s pamphlet, *Trial of Stephen and Jesse Boorn* (1819 edition), p. 29, for the earliest use of "Jess, as judge."

[7]Sargeant, *The Trial, Confessions and Conviction of Jesse and Stephen Boorn,* p. 13.

[8]Haynes, *Mystery Developed,* p. 13.

[9]*New York Evening Post,* December 16, 1819.

[10]Haynes, *Mystery Developed,* p. 13; an unidentified Albany newspaper from 1819 quoted in Joel Munsell, *The Annals of Albany* (Albany, New York, 1856), vol. 7, p. 142; "Petition of James Whelpley praying for reimbursement of expenses incurred . . . ," October 24, 1821 (ms., Office of the Secretary of State, Montpelier, Vermont).

[11]Larkin, *The Reshaping of Everyday Life,* p. 225.

[12]Sargeant, *The Trial, Confessions and Conviction of Jesse and Stephen Boorn,* p. 14; Haynes, *Mystery Developed,* p. 11.

[13]Sargeant, *The Trial, Confessions and Conviction of Jesse and Stephen Boorn,* p. 13; Haynes, *Mystery Developed,* p. 11.

[14]Haynes, *Mystery Developed,* p. 11; *Trial of Stephen and Jesse Boorn* (2nd ed.), p. 31.

[15]Haynes, *Mystery Developed,* p. 11.

[16]*Ibid.,* pp. 11–12.

[17]*Ibid.*

[18]*Ibid.,* p. 12; Sargeant, *The Trial, Confessions and Conviction of Jesse and Stephen Boorn,* p. 14.

[19]*Trial of Stephen and Jesse Boorn* (1819 edition), p. 31.

Notes

[20]Haynes, *Mystery Developed*, p. 12; Sargeant, *The Trial, Confessions and Conviction of Jesse and Stephen Boorn*, p. 14.

[21]Haynes, *Mystery Developed*, p. 12; Deming, *A Collection of Useful, Interesting, and Remarkable Events*, p. 76.

[22]Sargeant, *The Trial, Confessions and Conviction of Jesse and Stephen Boorn*, p. 14; John Spargo, *The Return of Russell Colvin* (Bennington, Vermont, 1945), p. 60; Haynes, *Mystery Developed*, p. 12.

[23]Joel Pratt to the Honorable Dudley Chase, December 23, 1819, "Boorn Trial Records."

[24]*Ibid.* (see note, dated December 28, 1819, appended at end by one of the associate justices).

[25]Sargeant, *The Trial, Confessions and Conviction of Jesse and Stephen Boorn*, p. 15.

[26]*Ibid.*, p. 15; Edwin L. Bigelow and Nancy H. Otis, *Manchester, Vermont, A Pleasant Land Among the Mountains* (Manchester, Vermont, 1961), p. 203.

[27]*Rutland Herald,* December 28, 1819.

[28]*Columbian Centinel* (Boston), December 15, 1819; *New York Evening Post,* December 16, 1819. See also: *The Columbian* (New York), December 11, 1819.

[29]*Albany Argus,* January 4, 1820; Munsell, *The Annals of Albany,* vol. 7, p. 160.

[30]Sargeant, *The Trial, Confessions and Conviction of Jesse and Stephen Boorn*, p. 15.

[31]*Vermont Republican & American Yeoman,* January 31, 1820.

[32]"Petition of John Boorn praying remuneration of expenses incurred . . . ," October 1, 1820 (ms., Office of the Secretary of State, Montpelier, Vermont).

[33]Petitions: (a) Jesse Boorn, dated October 1, 1820; (b) Stephen Boorn, same date (mss., Office of the Secretary of State, Montpelier, Vermont).

Mystery Developed

[1]Entries for February 2, 1822, and April 7, 1823, "Records of the Baptist Church of Manchester" (ms., Baptist Church, Manchester Center, Vermont).

[2]Haynes, *Mystery Developed,* pp. 18–20 and 22.

[3]*Ibid.,* pp. 24, 25, and 27.

[4]*Ibid.,* pp. 27, 29–30, 32, and 35.

[5]John Gallison, "The Admission of Confessions in Evidence," *North American Review,* vol. 10 (April 1820), p. 418.

[6]*Ibid.,* p. 421.

[7]*Ibid.,* pp. 422–23.

[8]*Ibid.,* pp. 424 and 429.

[9]Watson, *The Life and Character of the Hon. Richard Skinner,* p. 19; Sargeant, *The Trial, Confessions and Conviction of Jesse and Stephen Boorn,* pp. 8–9 and 22.

[10]Pettibone, "Early History of Manchester," p. 156; Bigelow and Otis, *Manchester, Vermont,* p. 198.

[11]Deming, *A Collection of Useful, Interesting, and Remarkable Events,* p. viii.

[12]Simon Greenleaf, *A Treatise on the Law of Evidence,* 2nd ed. (Boston, 1846), vol. 1, p. 256.

[13]"Preface," *The Law Reporter,* vol. 1 (April 1, 1839), pp. iii–iv; "The Case of the Boorns," *The Law Reporter,* vol. 5 (September 1842), pp. 195 and 199.

[14]"Preface," *The Law Reporter,* vol. 1 (1839), p. iv; Edwin M. Borchard, *Convicting the Innocent: Sixty-Five Actual Errors of Criminal Justice* (Garden City, New York, 1932), p. 20; John Henry Wigmore, *The Principles of Judicial Proof,* 2nd ed. (Boston, 1931), p. 500.

[15]*Albany Gazette and Daily Advertiser,* November 25, 1819.

[16]*Rutland Herald,* November 30, 1819.

[17]*New York Evening Post,* December 16, 1819.

[18]*National Advocate,* December 17, 1819.

[19]John Spargo, *The Return of Russell Colvin,* p. 81; *National Advocate,* December 17, 1819.

[20]*Woodstock Observer,* January 11, 1820; *Vermont Journal,* January 3, 1820.

[21]*Vermont Gazette,* January 11, 1820; *Vermont Journal,* December 27, 1819.

[22]*Rutland Herald,* January 11, 1820; *Sketches of the Trial of*

Notes

Stephen and Jesse Boorn for the Murder of Russel [sic] Colvin (Boston, 1820), p. 23.

23David S. Reynolds, *Beneath the American Renaissance: The Subversive Imagination in the Age of Emerson and Melville* (New York, 1988), p. 171; *National Advocate,* January 4, 1820; *Rutland Herald,* December 21, 1819; *Vermont Gazette,* December 7, 1819; *The Columbian,* November 27, 1819.

24Reynolds, *Beneath the American Renaissance,* pp. 175–76.

25*Trial of Stephen and Jesse Boorn* (1819 edition), p. 3.

26William Fay and Charles Burt to Dudley Chase, January 4, 1820, "Boorn Trial Records."

27*Trial of Stephen and Jesse Boorn* (2nd ed.), pp. iii, 33, and 35.

28*Sketches of the Trial of Stephen and Jesse Boorn,* pp. 15 and 24.

29Haynes, *Mystery Developed,* pp. 5, 13, and 27–28.

30"Samuel Putnam Waldo," *Dictionary of American Biography* (New York, 1943), vol. 19, p. 335; Waldo, *A Brief Sketch,* pp. 40 and 42–43.

31Sargeant, *Trial, Confessions and Conviction of Jesse and Stephen Boorn,* p. 15.

32Wilkie Collins, *The Dead Alive* (Boston, 1874), pp. 19 and 156–57.

33A list of publications on the Boorn-Colvin case, arranged in chronological order, may be found in section 2 of the Bibliography.

A Counterfeit Colvin?

1"Petition of Jesse Boorn," October 1, 1820; "The Richardson Account Book" (ms. in typescript version; V.H.S.), p. 62 (the corresponding page in the original is 159).

2As quoted in Moulton, *The Boorn Mystery,* p. 56.

3Hough, *History of Lewis County, New York,* p. 180; Historical Society of Geauga County, *Pioneer and General History of Geauga County* (n.p., 1880), p. 467.

4As quoted in Moulton, *The Boorn Mystery,* p. 56; Nabby L. Hickox to Daniel and Catherin Dayton, December 1, 1856, in

Notes

Frances H. Held, comp., *Letters by Nabby L. Hickox, Burton, Ohio, 1854–1868* (Hudson, Ohio, 1983), p. 39.

⁵William H. Perrin, *History of Summit County, Ohio* (Chicago, 1881), p. 538.

⁶*Cleveland Plain Dealer,* July 27, 1860.

⁷*Ibid.*

⁸*The Jeffersonian Democrat* (Chardon, Ohio), August 10, 1860.

⁹Entry for Jesse M. Boorn, Convict no. 4913, "Prisoner's Register, 1829–1939, Ohio State Penitentiary, Columbus, Ohio" (ms., Ohio Historical Society Archives).

¹⁰"Anna Boorn versus Jesse Boorn," Geauga County Court of Common Pleas (ms., Geauga County Courthouse, Chardon, Ohio), vol. 36, pp. 404–6; Sargeant, *The Trial, Confessions and Conviction of Jesse and Stephen Boorn,* p. 16.

¹¹*Cleveland Plain Dealer,* August 2, 1860; Henry E. Miner, "Manchester," in Abby Maria Hemenway, ed., *The Vermont Historical Gazetteer* (Burlington, Vermont, 1868), vol. 1, p. 206 (the essay first appeared in the *Vermont Quarterly Gazetteer* for October 1861); Sargeant, *The Trial, Confessions and Conviction of Jesse and Stephen Boorn,* p. 16.

¹²Moulton, *The Boorn Mystery,* p. 57; Spargo, *The Return of Russell Colvin,* p. 83.

¹³Natalie Zemon Davis, *The Return of Martin Guerre* (Cambridge, Massachusetts, 1983), p. 67.

¹⁴Chase's Notes, pp. 187 and 189.

¹⁵*Cleveland Plain Dealer,* August 2, 1860.

¹⁶Haynes, *Mystery Developed,* p. 10.

¹⁷Karen Halttunen, *Confidence Men and Painted Women: A Study of Middle-Class Culture in America, 1830–1870* (New Haven, 1982), p. 7. More specifically on New York City, James F. Richardson writes, "From the mid-1820s on, crime and disorder increased rapidly. . . . The social controls of a stable society had broken down in many areas of the city by 1830" (Richardson, *The New York Police: Colonial Times to 1901* [New York, 1970], pp. 15–16).

¹⁸Vivian Zinkin, *A Study of the Place-Names of Ocean County, New Jersey, 1609–1849* (Ann Arbor, Michigan, 1973), pp. 348–49.

¹⁹Franklin Ellis, *History of Monmouth County, New Jersey* (Phil-

220

Notes

adelphia, 1885), p. 798; Nathan O. Hatch, *The Democratization of American Christianity* (New Haven, 1989), p. 36.

[20]*New York Evening Post,* December 10, 1819.

[21]*Ibid.;* Sargeant, *The Trial, Confessions and Conviction of Jesse and Stephen Boorn,* p. 13.

[22]Haynes, *Mystery Developed,* p. 12; *Trial of Stephen and Jesse Boorn* (1819 edition), p. 31.

[23]*Ibid.*

[24]Sargeant, *The Trial, Confessions and Conviction of Jesse and Stephen Boorn,* p. 15.

[25]"Asa Loveland's Account Book" (ms. in typescript version; V.H.S.). (The record of the coffin made for Perkins is on page 41 of the typescript.)

[26]Sargeant, *The Trial, Confessions and Conviction of Jesse and Stephen Boorn,* p. 14; and Haynes, *Mystery Developed,* p. 12.

[27]Haynes, *Mystery Developed,* p. 12.

[28]*Ibid.;* Sargeant, *The Trial, Confessions and Conviction of Jesse and Stephen Boorn,* p. 11.

[29]*New York Evening Post,* December 10, 1819; Sargeant, *The Trial, Confessions and Conviction of Jesse and Stephen Boorn,* p. 13.

[30]Chase's Notes, p. 194; Haynes, *Mystery Developed,* p. 12.

[31]Edwin Salter, *A History of Monmouth and Ocean Counties* (Bayonne, New Jersey, 1890), p. 424.

Selected Bibliography

1. *Primary Sources*

a. MANUSCRIPTS

"Asa Loveland's Account Book" (Vermont Historical Society).
Baptist Church Records (Baptist Church of Manchester):
"Records of the Baptist Church of Manchester, Vermont, from June 22, 1781 to December 9, 1834."
"Record of the Baptist Society, 1784–1909."
"Record of the Baptist Church in East Dorset, 1802–1812."
"Boorn Murder File" (Manchester Historical Society, Manchester, Vermont).

Selected Bibliography

"Boorn Trial Records: Judge Dudley Chase's Files" (ms. 26, no. 49; Vermont Historical Society).

Congregational Church Records (Manchester First Congregational Church, Manchester, Vermont):

"Catalogue of Members, 1784–1908."

"Church Records, A: Clerk's Records, 1804–1828."

"Society Records, A: 1818–1831."

"Second Meeting House."

Joseph D. Wickham, "History of the Congregational Ministers in the Church of Manchester from the Settlement of the Town."

Manchester Town Records (Town Clerk's Office, Manchester, Vermont):

Cemetery Records, Dellwood and Factory Point cemeteries.

Land Records, vols. 3–12.

Proprietor's Records, books A and B.

Tax Lists: 1801, 1802, 1803, 1811, 1820, 1821.

Vital Statistics files.

New Jersey Records (Monmouth County Hall of Records, Freehold, New Jersey):

Deed Records: books Q, E3, G3, I3, and K3.

Ohio Records: Geauga County (Chardon, Ohio):

"Anna Boorn vs. Jesse Boorn," Geauga County Court of Common Pleas Record; vol. 36, pp. 404–406.

Deed Record, Geauga County Recorder's Office; vols. 18, 36–38, 41–46, 51, 57, 60, and 74.

Tax Duplicates, Geauga County Treasurer, 1843–1858 (microfilm copy; Geauga County Public Library).

Ohio Records; State Records:

"Prisoner's Register, 1829–1939," Ohio State Penitentiary, Columbus, Ohio (Ohio Historical Society, Columbus, Ohio).

"The Richardson Account Book," (Vermont Historical Society).

Vermont, Original State Papers (Office of the Secretary of State, Montpelier, Vermont): vol. 54, pp. 99–101 and vol. 55, pp. 156 and 247.

Selected Bibliography

b. PUBLISHED DOCUMENTS (INCLUDING TYPESCRIPTS)

New Jersey:

George and Florence Gibson, comp., *Marriages of Monmouth County, New Jersey, 1795–1843* (Baltimore, Maryland, 1981).

Ronald Vern Jackson, comp., *New Jersey Tax Lists, 1772–1822* (Salt Lake City, Utah, 1981).

Silverton Cemetery Records, Dover Township (Ocean County Historical Society, Toms River, New Jersey).

Ohio Records, Geauga County:

Frances H. Held, comp., *Letters by Nabby L. Hickox; Burton, Ohio, 1854–1868* (Hudson, Ohio, 1983).

Marriage Records from Geauga County, Ohio, 1806–1860 (typescript; Western Reserve Historical Society, Cleveland, Ohio).

Violet Warren and Jeannette Grosvenor, *A Monumental Work: Inscriptions and Interments in Geauga County, Ohio Through 1983* (Evansville, Indiana, 1985).

Ohio Records, Portage County:

Combination Atlas Map of Portage County, Ohio (Chicago, 1874).

Vital Records of Portage County: Cemetery Inscriptions (typescript; Western Reserve Historical Society, Cleveland, Ohio).

Vermont:

State of Vermont, General Assembly, *Journals of the General Assembly of the State of Vermont, at their Session begun and held at Montpelier, in the County of Washington, on Thursday, the Fourteenth of October, A.D. 1819* (Bennington, Vermont, n.d. [1819?]).

State of Vermont, General Assembly, *Journals of the General Assembly of the State of Vermont, at their Session begun and held at Montpelier, in the County of Washington, on Thursday, 12th of October, A.D. 1820* (Bennington, Vermont, n.d. [1820?]).

E. P. Walton, ed., *Records of the Governor and Council of the State of Vermont* (Montpelier, Vermont, 1878), vol. 6.

c. NEWSPAPERS *(unless otherwise noted, the dates consulted were 1819 and 1820)*

Selected Bibliography

Connecticut:
  American Mercury
  Connecticut Gazette
Massachusetts:
  Berkshire Star
  Columbian Centinel
  Independent Chronicle and Boston Patriot
  New England Palladium and Commercial Advertiser
New Jersey:
  Newark Centinel
  Palladium of Liberty
  Trenton Federalist
  Washington Whig
New York:
  Albany Argus
  Albany Gazette and Daily Advertiser
  The Columbian
  National Advocate
  New York Evening Post
  New York Tribune (1860)
Ohio:
  The Jeffersonian Democrat (1860–61)
  Cleveland Leader (1860)
  Cleveland Plain-Dealer (1860)
Vermont:
  National Standard
  Rutland Herald
  Vermont Gazette
  Vermont Journal
  Vermont Republican & American Yeoman
  Woodstock Observer

2. *Writings about the Boorn-Colvin Case Listed in Chronological Order by Date of Publication.*

Selected Bibliography

1819. *Trial of Stephen and Jesse Boorn for the Murder of Russell Colvin, before an adjourned term of the Supreme Court of Vermont, begun and holden at Manchester, in the County of Bennington, Oct. 26, A.D. 1819. To which is subjoined, the particulars of the Wonderful Discovery thereafter, of the Said Colvin's being alive, and his return to Manchester, where it was alleged the murder was committed; with some other interesting particulars, relating to this mysterious affair disconnected with the trial* (Rutland, Vermont, 1819).

1820. *Sketches of the Trial of Stephen and Jesse Boorn for the Murder of Russel* [sic] *Colvin, before the Supreme Court of Vermont: Held at Manchester, October 26, 1819. To which is added the particulars of said Colvin's discovery and return to Manchester. After the conviction and sentence of the Boorns, for his alledged* [sic] *murder and the rejoicings on that occasion* (Boston, Massachusetts, 1820).

1820. *Trial of Stephen and Jesse Boorn for the Murder of Russel* [sic] *Colvin and the Subsequent Wonderful Discovery of Colvin Alive, and an account of his return to Manchester, where the murder was alleged to have been committed; with other interesting particulars, relating to this Mysterious Affair in addition to the Trial* (2nd ed.; Rutland, Vermont, 1820).

1820. Lemuel Haynes, *Mystery Developed; or, Russell Colvin, (supposed to be murdered,) and Stephen and Jesse Boorn, (his convicted murderers,) Rescued from Ignominious Death by Wonderful Discoveries, containing, I. A Narrative of the Whole Transaction. II. Rev. Mr. Haynes' Sermon, upon the development of the Mystery* (Hartford, Connecticut, 1820).

1820. Samuel Putnam Waldo, *A Brief Sketch of the Indictment, Trial and Conviction of Stephen and Jesse Boorn, for the Murder of Russel* [sic] *Colvin, at a term of the Supreme Court of the State of Vermont, Holden at Manchester, October, 1819, together with remarks upon that extraordinary proceeding* (Hartford, Connecticut, 1820).

1820. [John Gallison], "The Admission of Confessions in Evidence," *North American Review*, vol. 10 (April 1820), pp. 418–29.

1825. Leonard Deming, "State of Vermont vs. Stephen Boorn and Jesse Boorn, for the Murder of Russell Colvin," in *A Collection of Useful, Interesting, and Remarkable Events, Original and Se-*

lected from Ancient and Modern Authorities (Middlebury, Vermont, 1825), pp. 67–77.

1842. "The Case of the Boorns," *The Law Reporter,* vol. 5 (September 1842), pp. 193–200.

1846. Simon Greenleaf, *A Treatise on the Law of Evidence* (2nd ed., Boston, 1846), vol. 1, p. 257.

1856. Lucius Manlius Sargeant, *Dealings with the Dead* (Boston, 1856), pp. 301–33.

1861. Henry E. Miner, "Manchester," in Abby Maria Hemenway, ed., *The Vermont Historical Gazetteer* (Burlington, Vermont, 1868), vol. 1, pp. 198–206 (a reprint of the essay that originally appeared in *Vermont Quarterly Gazetteer,* October 1861).

1870. "Confession of Crime—Its Values," *Overland Monthly,* vol. 5 (September 1870), pp. 251–56.

1873. Leonard Sargeant, *The Trial, Confessions and Conviction of Jesse and Stephen Boorn, for the Murder of Russell Colvin, and the Return of the Man Supposed to have been Murdered* (Manchester, Vermont, 1873).

1874. Wilkie Collins, *The Dead Alive* (Boston, 1874).

1889. "The Colvin Murder Case," in Lewis Cass Aldrich, *History of Bennington County, Vermont* (Syracuse, New York, 1889), pp. 365–66.

1893. "The Boorn Case," in L. E. Chittenden, *Personal Reminiscences, 1840–1890* (New York, 1893), pp. 328–39.

1899. "The Trial of Stephen and Jesse Boorn for the Alleged Murder of Russell Colvin," in LaFayette Wilbur, *Early History of Vermont* (Jericho, Vermont, 1899), vol. 1, pp. 281–306.

1924. "Uncle Amos Dreams A Dream," in Edmund Lester Pearson, *Studies in Murder* (Garden City, New York, 1924), pp. 265–85.

1931. "The Case of the Boorns," in John Henry Wigmore, *The Principles of Judicial Proof, or The Process of Proof* (2nd ed., Boston, 1931), pp. 501–5.

1932. "A Corpse Answers an Advertisement," in Edwin M. Borchard, *Convicting the Innocent: Sixty-five Actual Errors of Criminal Justice* (Garden City, New York, 1932), pp. 14–21.

1937. Sherman Roberts Moulton, *The Boorn Mystery: An Episode from the Judicial Annals of Vermont* (Montpelier, Vermont, 1937).

Selected Bibliography

1942. "They Put Him Where Potatoes Would Not Freeze," in Richard Dempewolff, *Famous Old New England Murders and Some That Are Infamous* (Brattleboro, Vermont, 1942), pp. 113–47.

1945. John Spargo, *The Return of Russell Colvin* (Bennington, Vermont, 1945).

1959. W. A. Swanberg, "The Corpus was Not Delicti," *Yankee*, vol. 23 (May 1959), pp. 60–63.

1959. Richard Sanders Allen, "The Boorn Murder Mystery," *Vermont Life Magazine*, vol. 14 (autumn 1959), pp. 20–25; 1971 (reprint). Richard Sanders Allen, "The Boorn Mystery," in Walter R. Hard, Jr., and Janet C. Greene, *Mischief in the Mountains* (Montpelier, Vermont, 1971), pp. 103–13.

1961. Richard Sanders Allen, "Return of Jesse Boorn," *Vermont Life Magazine*, vol. 15 (summer 1961), p. 60.

1965. Bernard Lamere, "The Boorn Enigma," *Rural Vermonter*, vol. 4 (December 1965), pp. 39–41.

3. Background Readings

a. SOURCES ON MANCHESTER, VERMONT

Lewis Cass Aldrich, *History of Bennington County, Vermont* (Syracuse, New York, 1889).

Edwin L. Bigelow and Nancy H. Otis, *Manchester, Vermont, A Pleasant Land Among the Mountains* (Manchester, Vermont, 1961).

Joseph S. Brown, *Historical Sketch of the First Baptist Church in Manchester, Vt.* (Chester, Vermont, 1916).

Henry E. Miner, "Manchester," in Abby Maria Hemenway, ed., *The Vermont Historical Gazetteer* (Burlington, Vermont, 1868), vol. 1, pp. 198–206.

Loveland Munson, *The Early History of Manchester* (Manchester, Vermont, 1876).

John S. Pettibone, "The Early History of Manchester," *Proceedings of the Vermont Historical Society,* vol. 1 (1930), pp. 147–66.

Mary Utley Robbins, "Manchester-in-the-Mts.," *Manchester Journal,* August 6–December 6, 1923.

Selected Bibliography

Robert J. Wilson and Phebe Ann Lewis, *The First Congregational Church, Manchester, Vermont, 1784–1984* (Manchester, Vermont, 1984).

b. SELECTED ADDITIONAL SOURCES, ARRANGED BY CHAPTER

The Feud

Four excellent sources on the social and religious history of Vermont prior to 1820 are as follows: Abby Maria Hemenway, ed., *The Vermont Historical Gazetteer*, 5 vols. (Burlington, Vermont, 1868); David M. Ludlum, *Social Ferment in Vermont, 1791–1850* (New York, 1939); Randolph A. Roth, *The Democratic Dilemma: Religion, Reform, and the Social Order in the Connecticut River Valley of Vermont, 1791–1850* (Cambridge, England, 1987); and Lewis D. Stilwell, "Migration from Vermont (1776–1860)," *Proceedings of the Vermont Historical Society*, vol. 5 (June 1937), pp. 63–246.

Colvin's Ghost

Two especially useful sources for this chapter were Jack Larkin, *The Reshaping of Everyday Life, 1790–1840* (New York, 1988) for information on the everyday lives of ordinary Americans, and John Putnam Demos, *Entertaining Satan: Witchcraft and the Culture of Early New England* (New York, 1982) on witchcraft.

The Trial

For further information on Richard Skinner, see Winslow C. Watson, *The Life and Character of the Hon. Richard Skinner; Discourse Read before and at the Request of the Vermont Historical Society, At Montpelier, October 20, 1863* (Albany, New York, 1863). The best sources on the Reverend Lemuel Haynes are as follows: Timothy Mather Cooley, *Sketches of the Life and Character of the Rev. Lemuel Haynes, A.M., for Many Years Pastor of a Church in Rutland, Vermont, and Later in Granville, New York* (New York, 1837), which contains reprints of Haynes's account of and sermon on the Boorn-Colvin case (pp. 214–52), and Sidney Kaplan, *The Black Presence in the Era of the American Revolution, 1770–1800* (New York, 1973), pp. 102–8.

Selected Bibliography

The Dead Alive!

The memoirs of a man who was an inmate at Vermont's state prison about the same time as Jesse Boorn are found in John Reynolds, *Recollections of Windsor Prison, Containing Sketches of its History and Discipline, Strictures, and Moral and Religious Reflections* (Boston, 1834). A book that puts the early-nineteenth-century prison reform movement in perspective and supplies some good information on Vermont's situation is Orlando F. Lewis, *The Development of American Prisons and Prison Customs, 1776–1845* (Patterson Smith edition; Montclair, New Jersey, 1967). On the history of stagecoaches in the United States, see Oliver W. Holmes and Peter T. Rohrbach, *Stagecoach East: Stagecoach Days in the East from the Colonial Period to the Civil War* (Washington, D.C., 1983).

Mystery Developed

Helpful background readings on this chapter would include the following five sources, their topics readily apparent from their titles: Robert Ashley, "Wilkie Collins and a Vermont Murder Trial," *New England Quarterly,* vol. 21 (September 1948), pp. 368–73; Burton J. Bledstein, *The Culture of Professionalism* (New York, 1976); Frank Luther Mott, *American Journalism* (3rd ed., New York, 1962); A. E. Murch, *The Development of the Detective Novel* (New York, 1958); and David S. Reynolds, *Beneath the American Renaissance: The Subversive Imagination in the Age of Emerson and Melville* (New York: 1988).

A Counterfeit Colvin?

An essential starting point for any discussion of historical impostors is Natalie Zemon Davis, *The Return of Martin Guerre* (Cambridge, Massachusetts, 1983). The faint trails left by the principals after they left Vermont—Russell Colvin in New Jersey, Stephen Boorn in New York and Ohio, and Jesse Boorn in Ohio—may be glimpsed in the following: Edwin Salter, *A History of Monmouth and Ocean Counties* (Bayonne, New Jersey, 1890); Franklin B. Hough, *History of Lewis County, New York* (Syracuse, New York, 1883); and Historical Society of Geauga County, *Pioneer and General History of Geauga County* (n.p., 1880).

Index

Index

Barrett, Gideon, 109–10
benevolence, doctrine of, 73–74
Bennett, James Gordon, 167
Bennington, Vt., 128, 129, 130, 131
Black, Peter, 110, 137
bones, discovery of, 58–60
Boorn, Amos, 14–15, 55; Colvin's ghost, visits from, 48, 49, 51, 69, 70; court of inquiry, 56, 59; economic-social successes, 49–50; homestead of, *50;* suspicions of nephews regarding Colvin's death, 51; trial testimony, 88–89
Boorn, Anna Bigelow, 179, 180, 185
Boorn, Barney, 15, 16, 65, 147; arrest, 63; Colvin's murder, possible role in, 65, 66; defense of sons, 47; grandchilden, care for, 37–38; homestead of, *16;* impostor conspiracy, possible role in, 189, 190, 195; land sale to Johnson, 40–41; marriage, 16
Boorn, Elizabeth Lewis, 16, 33, 147; defense of sons, 47; excommunication, 62–63, 147–48; grandchildren, care for, 37–38
Boorn, Freelove, 12, 13
Boorn, Jared, 14, 15
Boorn, Jesse, 16; arrest, 55; at beating of Colvin, 4, 65–66, 132; Colvin's son, handling of, 33–34;

confessions, 58, 62, 65–66, 95, 96–97, 102, 104, 107, 153; confessions, third-party speculation on, 166–67, 174; counterfeiting operation, 181–83, 184; court of inquiry, 56, 57, 58, 63–66, 80–81; death, 185; death of Colvin, private acknowledgment of, 39–40, 58; farm purchase, 44; guilty verdict against, 106–7; "impostor" revelation, 145, 183–84; indictments against, 80–81; Johnson, relationship with, 43; legacy, concern about, 41; Londonderry, move to, 179; Merrill, confidences to, 64–66, 80–81, 101; Ohio, move to, 179, 180; "out of town" alibi, 47; people's attitude toward, 12; petition on behalf of, 109–11, 114–16; in prison for counterfeiting, 184–85; in prison for murder, 117, 121, 140; queries about Colvin, response to, 32, 33, 44–45; reduction of sentence, 115–16, 117; reimbursement petition, 142–43; reversal of judgments against, 140–41; trial, 85, 93, 106–7; "wild and reckless" nature, 17, 25
Boorn, John, 16, 17, 33, 40–41, 91, 141–42, 189, 190
Boorn, Keziah, 179

Index

Boorn, Nathaniel, 12–14
Boorn, Nathaniel, Jr., 14, 15, 51, 89
Boorn, Polly, 181
Boorn, Stephen, 16; accusers, attitude toward, 173; advertisement for Colvin, 116; alibis, development of, 46–48; arrest, 61–62; barn fire and, 42; beating of Colvin, 4–5, 65–66, 79, 98–99; Colvin's return, 130, 132; Colvin's son, handling of, 33–34; confessions, 58, 78–80, 94–96, 97–99, 102, 104, 107, 153; confessions, third-party speculation on, 166–67, 174; confession text, 98–99; court of inquiry, 62, 63–64, 66, 68, 78–81; death of Colvin, private acknowledgment of, 39–40; Dorset, move to, 44–45; execution, waiting for, 116–18, 119–20; final years, 180–81; grievance against Colvin, 35–36; guilty verdict against, 106–7; Haynes, gratitude toward, 147; impostor conspiracy, possible role in, 189–90, 195; indictments against, 80–81; innocence, posttrial insistence on, 114, 116; Johnson, relationship with, 43; legacy, concern about, 41; New York, move to, 45–46; Ohio,
move to, 178–79, 180; people's attitude toward, 12; petition on behalf of, 109–11, 114–16; queries about Colvin, response to, 32, 33, 44–45; reimbursement petition, 142–43; reversal of judgments against, 140–41; on Sally Colvin, 11; threats against Colvin, 34–35; trial, 85, 93, 106–7; "wild and reckless" nature, 17, 25
Boorn, William, 34–35, 47, 58
Boorn family, *13*
The Boorn Mystery (Moulton), 186
Borchard, Edwin M., 161
Bowen, Jesse (alias of Jesse Boorn), 181, 184, 186, 187
Brayton, William, 83, 136, 140
brides, pregnancy among, 9
A Brief Sketch of the Indictment, Trial, and Conviction of Stephen and Jesse Boorn (pamphlet), 173–74
Brown, Dan and Jim, 182
Burgoyne, Gen. John, 20
Burr, Joseph, 110, 156n
Burr Seminary, 156
Burt, Charles, 138, 168–70
Burton, Ohio, 179, 181
Burton, Asa, 73
Burton, Elijah, Jr., 110
Burton, Hulda Powel, 53–54
Burton, Capt. Isaac, 53

Index

Day, Benjamin H., 167
The Dead Alive (Collins),
175–76
Deming, Benjamin, 47
Deming, Leonard, 156–58
democratizing movement of
1820s and 1830s, 158–59
Denmark, N.Y., 45, 178
deodands, 87
Dixon, Josiah, 183, 184
Doolittle, Joel, 80, 83, 106,
136, 140
Dorset, Vt., 30, 41, 44, 45, 46,
178
Dover Township, N.J., 192,
193, 198
Dow, Lorenzo, 194
drinking by Vermonters, 21–
22, 24
Du Tilh, Arnaud, 188, 200, 201
Dwight, Timothy, 21–22

excommunication, 36–37, 62–
63, 147–48

Farley, Abel, 72
Farnsworth, William, 71, 78,
97–98, 111
Fay, William, 138, 168–70
Ferguson, Clarissa Colvin, 7,
42–43, 100
flogging, 27

Gallison, John, 151–53, 155
Galusha, Jonas, 116
Graham, John A., 22
Greenleaf, Simon, 159
Guerre, Martin, 188, 200, 201

Hackett (deputy U.S. mar-
shal), 181–82, 183, 184,
208; H. M. Hackett, 182n

Hale, Sir Matthew, 152
Hatch, Nathan O., 194
hat discovery, 42–43
Haynes, Elizabeth Babbitt,
112
Haynes, Lemuel, *112,* 116,
146; background, 111–
14; baptism controversy,
76; Colvin impostor the-
ory and, 202, 203; Col-
vin's return, 130, 131,
132, 133, 134; commen-
tary on Boorn-Colvin
case, 146–51, 166; pam-
phlet on Boorn-Colvin
case, 171–73; support for
Stephen Boorn, 117–18;
trial of Boorn brothers,
83, 85, 106
Hickox, Nabby, 181
Hill, Truman, 110, 203; arrest of Stephen Boorn,
61, 62; Congregational
Church controversy, 70,
74–75, 77; court of in-
quiry, 55, 58, 64, 66, 78;
trial testimony, 90, 96
Hitchcock (lawyer), 39, 92
Holmes, Daniel, 186
horse racing and breeding,
22–23, *23*
housing standards, 41

impostor conspiracy. *See* Colvin impostor theory

Johnson, Michael, 43
Johnson, Thomas, 34; apple
tree disappearance, 43;
Boorn brothers, relation-
ship with, 43; Colvin's
hat, discovery of, 42;

About the Author

Gerald McFarland is a native Californian now living
in Leverett, Massachusetts. He is a professor of history
at the University of Massachusetts in Amherst, and the
author of two previous books, *Mugwumps, Morals and
Politics, 1884–1920* (1975) and *A Scattered People: An
American Family Moves West* (1985).